THE
PLUNDERED
SEAS

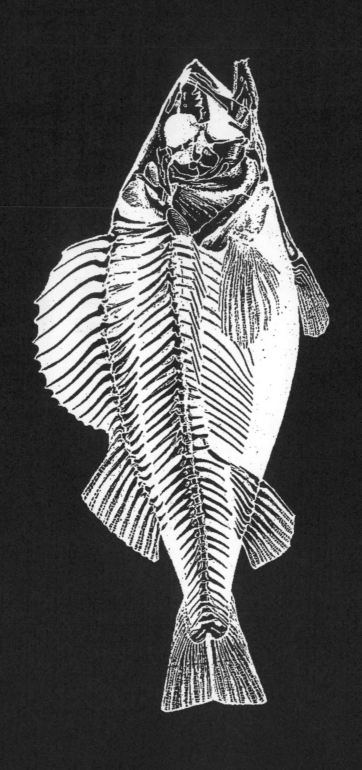

THE
PLUNDERED
SEAS

Can the WORLD'S FISH Be Saved?

MICHAEL BERRILL

Foreword by David Suzuki

Sierra Club Books
SAN FRANCISCO

Originally published by Greystone Books, a division of Douglas & McIntyre Ltd., 1615 Venables Street, Vancouver, British Columbia.

LIBRARY OF CONGRESS CATALOGUING IN PUBLICATION DATA

Berrill, Michael.
    The plundered seas: can the world's fish be saved? / Michael Berrill.
        p.   cm.
    Includes bibliographical references and index.
    ISBN 0-87166-945-0 (alk. paper)
        1. Fishery conservation.   2. Fishery management, International.
        3. Fishery law and legislation.   I. Title.
    SH327.7.B47 1997
    333.95'618—DC21   97-8192
                                        CIP

Editing by Nancy Flight
Cover design by Tom Brown
Maps and graphs by Rob Loney
Illustrations by Angela Kingsley
Text design and typesetting by Val Speidel
Printed and bound in Canada by Friesens
Printed on 100% acid-free paper ∞

10 9 8 7 6 5 4 3 2 1

CONTENTS

FOREWORD

Biological warfare is going on all over the planet, but unlike the carnage of conventional wars, the devastating effects of this conflict are not obvious. The battles are being fought over the world's forests, topsoil, wetlands, rivers and lakes, as animals and plants are being exploited and their habitats destroyed beyond their regenerative capacity. Nowhere is the combat more explosive than in the oceans of the Earth. Each of us can feel the effect directly in the price of fish—once one of the cheapest of animal meats, fish is now the most expensive, a direct reflection of its increasing scarcity.

We are an air-breathing, terrestrial animal, a fact that imposes restrictions on our behaviour and on our perspective. As land dwellers, we are confined to a fraction of the 29 per cent of the Earth that is above water. Beneath the surface of the vast ocean that encircles the globe are unimaginably diverse habitats, from great flowing currents to estuaries, coral reefs, deep canyons and undersea pinnacles. Our windows into this complex world are minuscule, offering only brief glimpses from the surface or through inspection of the contents of nets and traps and observations made with scuba and underwater vehicles.

This mysterious and alien world nourishes us spiritually as well as physically. Hundreds of millions of people build their lives and cultures around the capture and preparation of fish, which provide as much animal nutrition as all of the world's chickens and cows combined. But that relationship is changing with explosive speed.

When I was in high school in the early fifties, one of my teachers informed us that the oceans were "a vast reservoir of limitless food." Our impressions of the oceans were of Atlantic cod in unbelievable abundance, huge bluefin tuna so plentiful they were used as cheap pet food and limitless Pacific salmon in runs all along the B.C. coast. People believed that there was no end to the ocean's productivity. In my lifetime, this belief in the nearly limitless bounty of the oceans has been completely transformed into an awareness that the oceans are in crisis. The shutdown of the northern cod fishery in Newfoundland in 1992 was a belated admission that the warnings of fishers and scientists of disastrous declines in cod were true, and now in British Columbia the reality of a salmon crisis is hitting home.

What has happened? At the heart of the global eco-crisis of which the ocean fisheries are a part is a profound change in the way we perceive the world. In the exuberance of the postwar economic and technological boom, it was easy to believe that we could manage our surroundings and use all of nature for human benefit. Parts of nature became "commodities" or "resources" that could be exploited to the maximum. Modern technology—radar, satellite navigation, huge nylon nets, factory ships—increased efficiency and productivity. Scientism, a faith in the power of scientists to provide knowledge and control, underlay political programs, while modernity, the notion that what is new is best and that old ideas and practices are often superstitious, irrational and incorrect, has become widely embraced. These shifts in attitude have made us a demanding species capable of altering the biophysical features of the planet.

In this century, the dramatic shift of human populations from rural, village communities to large cities has weakened our personal experience of nature. The vagaries of weather, seasons and climate impinge on our lives with far less immediacy. So the destruction of vast tracts of forests, wetlands, topsoil, deep aquifers or underwater habitat and the consequent extinction of large numbers of species are not readily apparent. Coupled with a global economy based on maximizing profits, constantly expanding markets and the consumer demands of a rapidly growing population, these fundamental attitudes and values have led us, as a species, to wreak havoc on an unprecedented scale.

The speed of change has been breathtaking. When I returned to live in Vancouver in 1963, I would go fishing for herring in Squamish harbour and fill a bucket in minutes. And each summer, sportfishers would compete in a salmon derby, intercepting the huge chinook bound to spawn in the Squamish River. Today those herring and salmon are gone, and those who have no experience of them neither miss them nor mourn their passing.

That's what makes *The Plundered Seas* such a powerful document. It provides the historical, social, economic and political context for what is happening all around us. Michael Berrill's document tells a compelling story that balances the depressing litany of greed and destruction with many examples of ideas and programs that contain the seeds of a way out, that will allow us to find a sustainable balance with the productive generosity of nature. We can no longer afford not to face up to the reality of what has happened. The good news is that there are solutions and that most scientists believe there is still time to save much of the rich marine bounty on which humanity has long depended.

David Suzuki
Vancouver, British Columbia

PREFACE

The newspapers are filled with a continuing litany of disaster stories about our fisheries. Sometimes the problems of a particular fishery capture international attention, such as the collapse of the Atlantic cod or the dolphin kill associated with catching Pacific tuna. For the most part, however, we read about the problems closest to us and hear but rumours of what occurs elsewhere on the planet.

This book looks at the state of the world's fisheries. How bad is the situation? How did we get into such a predicament? What are we doing—or not doing—to try to protect fisheries so that we will have a continuing supply of fish protein to help feed the global population, which continues to grow far too quickly? I have chosen major fisheries from the Atlantic and Pacific Oceans as examples to explore what appear to be the more critical issues. The world has shrunk so much that the issues are everywhere much the same.

I have tried to write from the point of view of the fish, for without the fish there are neither fishers nor fisheries left to be concerned about. I am not writing on behalf of fishers or in defence of managers, and I am not writing a lament for the decline of fishing communities, no matter how sad that decline may be. It is critical that the fish populations survive to continue to help feed us, and it is obvious that we cannot persist in the attitudes that got us where we are. There are reasons to be hopeful that it is not too late to change and that with new laws and new attitudes both fish and fishers will continue to exist.

A lot has been written about the world's fisheries. Apart from the many articles that have appeared in the newspapers, a few good books focus on the fisheries of a particular region, some detailed technical books and innumerable technical reports have been written by specialists for other specialists, the Food and Agriculture Organization of the United Nations has published a series of reports that are detailed and fascinating but hard to obtain, environmental organizations have made a variety of pronouncements, and journalists have explored the fisheries and the issues in many magazine articles. The brief bibliography that I have included can only barely acknowledge my debt to the many biologists, policy makers, analysts and journalists whose work informs this book.

I wish to thank Rob Loney, who produced the maps and graphs, and Angela Kingsley, who drew the fish. I am grateful to Shirley Taylor and Rob Stephenson for their helpful and detailed criticisms of the text, and to Nancy Flight at Greystone Books for her thoughtful questions and comments as well as her encouragement. I also wish to thank Peter Adams, Member of Parliament from my part of Ontario, for continuing to prod the Canadian government to finally ratify the Law of the Sea.

CHAPTER I

BOOM AND BUST: HOW NOT TO DO IT

"O Oysters," said the Carpenter,
"You've had a pleasant run!
Shall we be trotting home again?"
But answer came there none—
And this was scarcely odd, because
They'd eaten every one.

Lewis Carroll

THROUGH THE LOOKING GLASS

People in coastal communities have always eaten fish. Until a couple of hundred years ago the fish must have seemed infinitely abundant. Easy to catch in inshore waters with simple hooks, nets, traps and weirs, fish provided the communities with much of the protein they needed. By the beginning of the twentieth century, when the exploding human population reached about 1.5 billion, fishers still caught only about 5 million tonnes of fish each year, compared with 80 million tonnes today. Although fish stocks in a few places had already declined by then, no one really thought that there was any limit to the abundance of fish the sea could and would provide. There would always be plenty of fish in the sea.

Now as we approach the end of the century, we see how ignorant we were. There will soon be six billion of us, pushing hard on the earth's capacity to feed us all. We are going to need all the fish we can catch, and every year we are going to need more. In Africa and in East and Southeast Asia, people still obtain 20 to 30 per cent of their protein from fish. North American and European markets for fish continue to expand. Fish are caught not just for direct human consumption but also to feed our poultry and pigs and even to feed more valuable fish species that are now farmed.

To meet the increasing demand after the end of World War II, for twenty years the total global catch of fish grew at an astounding 6 per cent per year, several times faster than the human population was growing (Figure 1). When the fishery for Peruvian anchovies crashed from 12 million tonnes per year to almost nothing in the early 1970s, the global catch began to grow more slowly, at 2.3 per cent per year, but it still grew. In 1989 it peaked at 82 million tonnes of fish. Since then it has dropped back to about 80 million tonnes per year. We are obviously close to, and probably exceeding, the maximum global catch that is possible to sustain. Fish stocks are now in decline along every coastline, yet we have ever more humans to feed.

The picture is grim everywhere you look. Canada has closed down the cod fishery on the Grand Banks and much of the salmon fishery in southern British Columbia, and the United States has closed most of the groundfishing on Georges Bank and has declared the salmon-fishing region of Washington and Oregon a disaster area. Larger, more valuable species such as cod and halibut have become increasingly rare, while smaller, more abundant but less valuable species of the herring family replace them on the most-hunted lists. Paradoxically, even though the world catch of all species has stopped growing, the size and the number of fleets searching for fish have continued to expand.

≈≈≈≈≈≈≈≈≈≈≈≈≈≈≈≈≈≈≈≈≈≈≈≈≈≈≈≈≈≈≈≈

We are obviously close to, and probably exceeding,
the maximum global catch that is possible to sustain.

≈≈≈≈≈≈≈≈≈≈≈≈≈≈≈≈≈≈≈≈≈≈≈≈≈≈≈≈≈≈≈≈

Throughout the world, a million boats fish the seas, far more than is necessary to catch the available fish. The Food and Agriculture Organization (FAO) of the United Nations has estimated that over $90 billion (U.S.) is spent each year to catch $70 billion worth of fish. The huge difference is made up by government loans and subsidies, an economic situation that is both impossible and unwise to sustain. The FAO also reports that fully two-thirds of the world's fish stocks are now either overexploited and are in dangerous decline or are fished to capacity, unable to withstand any increase in fishing pressure without also declining.

Fishing communities from Indonesia and China to West Africa, Western Europe and North America are dying as fish stocks collapse and as high-tech commercial boats make small-scale fishing operations unprofitable. Around

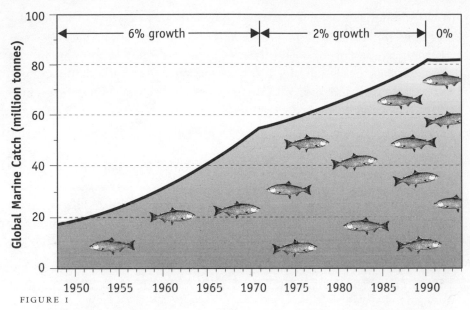

FIGURE I

The Global Catch. From 1950 to 1971, the total catch of fish (and shrimp and other shellfish) grew at about 6 per cent per year. After that, it continued to grow, but at a slower rate, until 1990. The total catch has not grown since 1990, even though more vessels are searching for the fish. Source: FAO.

the world, 200 million people depend on fishing to make a living, and for many that living is at risk. An infamous example is Newfoundland, where 50 000 people who had depended on the cod fishery until 1992 have little other work to turn to now that the fishery has closed. There, as elsewhere, fishers are losing their boats, their jobs, their way of life. When a fishery dies, people have to leave their communities for work in other sectors that they have no training for, usually in cities they don't want to live in. As an ex–fish plant manager from a Newfoundland outport has said, quoted in the *Toronto Star*, "The only thing that will be left in town is elderly people, and nobody left to bury them."

This scenario occurs wherever there is unregulated, open access to a fish stock. Where the stock has been large—for example, the schools of herring and cod on the banks off the northeast coast of North America—it may take a couple of centuries of heavy fishing to deplete the stock. Often two or three decades have been enough to cause a stock to crash. And sometimes just several years of heavy fishing will do the job. But wherever there is open access to fish, the fishery inevitably declines and will probably crash. When a fishery crashes, the stock that remains is too small to be worth hunting and is considered commercially extinct.

Just as inevitably, before the stock crashes, controls and regulations proliferate and enforcement becomes necessary. These measures rarely work, though they extend the life of the fishery. Repeated over and over during the past several centuries—and depressingly often over the past decades as both the global population and the demand for fish have escalated—the cycle of discovery, exploitation, depletion and collapse describes the history of fisheries. The cycle of boom and bust.

THE CYCLE

The cycle of boom and bust has occurred so often that its major stages are easy to recognize. The first stage is the discovery of a new stock, usually in some place that has not been previously fished. Word spreads quickly, and the second stage of rapid growth and exploitation begins. The catch is good, fishers

≈≈≈≈≈≈≈≈≈≈≈≈≈≈≈≈≈≈≈≈≈≈≈≈≈≈≈≈≈≈≈≈≈

Discovery, exploitation, depletion and collapse: this is the pattern of events in an open-access fishery, a pattern that has been repeated again and again.

≈≈≈≈≈≈≈≈≈≈≈≈≈≈≈≈≈≈≈≈≈≈≈≈≈≈≈≈≈≈≈≈≈

make a lot of money, employment mushrooms. Individuals expand their own operations, with more or bigger boats or equipment, and new fishers are attracted into the fishery. Then, as the race for fish intensifies, boat skippers find they have to increase their fishing effort even further in order to meet their boat payments and pay their crew, and the time of the easy money is over.

The third stage is the stage of decline or depletion. The size of the fish stock decreases, the catch per boat declines even though the fishers put in longer hours and more days, and still more fishers try to squeeze into the ever tighter competition. There comes a point when the cost of fishing equals the value of the harvest, and the less successful fishers start to lose money. The stock is further depleted, yet the fishers still have their boat mortgages to pay and payrolls to meet. By then they may have invested in far larger boats, stronger engines, bigger nets and better fish-finding equipment, worth far more than the fish they catch could ever pay for. The result is an overextended, overcapitalized fishery, and then everyone starts to lose money. At that point, some governments agree to step in and subsidize the fishers, whereas others are more reluctant to intervene. In either case, the fishery has had it.

The final stage is the collapse of the fishery. Fishers lose their jobs, to be supported by welfare if welfare exists and other jobs are unavailable. Their boats lie idle. If the fishery supported a community, the community dies: The fishery is often closed in the hope that it will somehow recover.

In the towns of Newport, Pacific City and Astoria along the coast of Oregon, where the coho salmon fishery has closed and salmon fishing has virtually collapsed, fishers try to choose among what they see as unattractive options. Some struggle on as fishers, working nonstop in other fisheries and probably commuting to Alaska, attempting to sustain at all costs the way of life they so prefer. Others find the cost in time and separation from family to be intolerable and tie up their boats, perhaps forever, to search for alternatives on shore. Some have converted their boats to whale-watching vessels, pleased to still be afloat, fishing for tourists rather than salmon. Many are seeking relief funds that should have come to them as a result of the region's designation as a federal disaster area. Some have become involved in a new subsidized program to rehabilitate damaged river habitats in hopes of reestablishing salmon runs. All remember the good days of past fishing, however, when unemployment and poverty were unthinkable and they ran their own lives on their own schedules.

Discovery, exploitation, depletion and collapse: this is the pattern of events in an open-access fishery, a pattern that has been repeated again and again. We are not stupid. We know, usually, when we are fishing a declining population, and we know that continuing to fish under those circumstances will mean even fewer to fish in the near future. Yet we continue to fish. Not unrealistically, all fishers realize that the stock is going to decline whether they fish or not and so they had better get what they can before there is nothing left. Better for them to catch the last fish than for another fisher to catch it. They will do whatever is required. They will hunt longer hours; they will use better gear, faster and bigger boats; they will pay their crews less or change to gear that needs less crew. If necessary, and especially if everyone else is doing it, they will cheat. They have a boat to pay off, a crew to sustain, a family in need, and probably there is no other work for them in the region.

The world is full of excellent examples of boom-and-bust fisheries. The stories of the California sardine and the Peruvian anchoveta are as good as any.

THE CALIFORNIA SARDINE

California once had remarkably rich waters. By the 1880s, the salmon, the near coast whales, the various seals and the sea otter, and most of the valuable inshore invertebrates such as abalones and oysters had all declined quite drastically. Most of the coastal rivers had suffered major contamination from the gold rush, which began in 1849, contributing to the decline of the salmon, in particular. The state government recognized that overfishing and habitat destruction, rather than natural causes, had been responsible for the decline of all these species. Regulations were introduced to protect the fisheries, and the fishers responded by cheating.

Jack London, author of *The Call of the Wild* and *The Sea Wolf*, spent a year as a fisheries patrol deputy in San Francisco Bay in 1892, when he was sixteen years old. He had already spent a few seasons as an oyster poacher, and he knew how to get around the emerging regulations. He wrote about his adventures in *Tales of the Fish Patrol*, and lawless times they were. Always under sail power in a small sloop, he helped chase down and capture fishers who fished with illegal gear or at illegal times or places. He described the men he caught, or tried to catch, as "rough men, gathered together in isolated communities and fighting with the elements for a livelihood. They lived far away from the law and its workings, did not understand it, and thought it tyranny. Especially did the fish laws seem tyrannical. And because of this, they looked upon the men of the fish patrol as their natural enemies." Fisheries officers like London were few and overworked, and the fishers got away with most of what they tried to do, including, occasionally, murder. Those were early days of conservation and, even allowing for the embellishments of a good storyteller like London, the conflicts between fishers and enforcers were often ferocious.

Around this time, with the potential for management in place, the sardine fishery began. By 1910, larger, seagoing vessels had arrived and started fishing offshore for salmon, tuna, pilchards and sardines. The sardines were canned or, with the oil and water squeezed out of them, reduced to fish meal and used as fertilizer and poultry food. During World War I, fishing in the North Sea between the United Kingdom and Western Europe ceased because it was too risky, and California sardines replaced North Sea herring in world markets. The California fishery rapidly expanded. The forced closure of the North Sea's fisheries during the war, however, had allowed many of the stocks to recover to new, more exploitable levels by the time the war ended, and North Sea herring soon dominated the markets once again. The California sardine fishery struggled along, unable to compete. Then, in 1925, new diesel purse seiners, which were able to fish far more efficiently than the older sardine fleet, were introduced on the Californian coast. At the same time, sardine oil began to be used in soap, linoleum, shortening and paint, and the remains of the fish continued to be valued as fertilizer. There was more pressure than ever on the sardine stock.

Sardines, like all species of the herring family, live in schools. Schools of the California sardines were immense, up to 8 kilometres (5 miles) in diameter, a few hundred million fish per school. As the sardine stock declined under the increased fishing, the fish formed fewer schools, not smaller ones, and continued to be all too easy to hunt. As fishers hunted primarily older, larger fish,

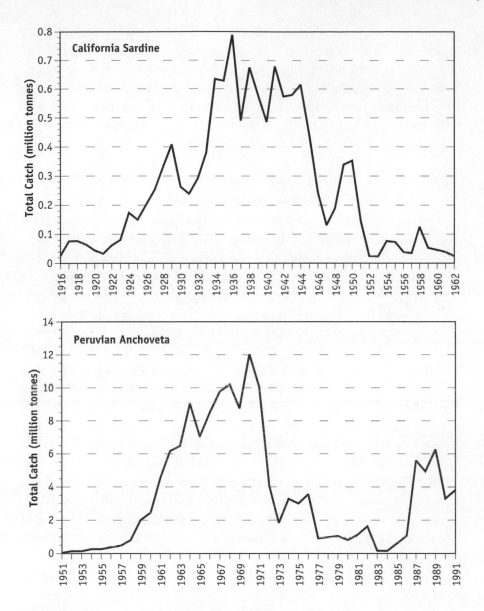

FIGURE 2

The Cycle of Boom and Bust. The California sardine and the Peruvian anchoveta illustrate the cycle all too well. The exploitation of the Peruvian anchoveta followed the collapse of the California sardine and for a decade supported the largest fishery the world has known before it in turn collapsed.

these fish disappeared from the schools. In the peak harvest year of 1936–37, 40 per cent of remaining adults of all sizes were caught in the seine nets, a rate of exploitation far beyond sustainability (Figure 2).

Cannery Row, in Monterey, California, was one of many canning sites along the coast where the sardine fishers brought their catch. Although he didn't actually write about the fishery, John Steinbeck made Cannery Row famous in his book *Cannery Row*, which takes place in the late 1930s, when the catch reached its highest levels, and in *Sweet Thursday*, which takes place about a decade later, after the fishery had crashed. In the following passage from *Cannery Row*, Steinbeck graphically describes the abundance of the fish brought in each day:

> In the morning when the sardine fleet has made a catch, the purse-seiners waddle heavily into the bay blowing their whistles. The deep-laden boats pull in against the coast where the canneries dip their tails into the bay. . . . Then cannery whistles scream and all over town men and women scramble into their clothes and come running down to the Row to go to work. . . . They come running to clean and cut and pack and cook and can the fish. The whole street rumbles and groans and screams and rattles while the silver rivers of fish pour in out of the boats and the boats ride higher and higher in the water until they are empty.

The stock collapsed after World War II. In 1944–45, an astounding 75 per cent of the adults were caught, and the ships began to seine for still younger fish. Prices rose quickly, and fishing continued. Then, in 1949–50, the remaining stock failed to spawn, and the fishery died. As Steinbeck wrote in *Sweet Thursday*, "the canneries themselves fought the war by getting the limit taken off of fish and catching them all. It was done for patriotic reasons, but that didn't bring the fish back. . . . The pearl-grey canneries of corrugated iron were silent and a pacing watchman was their only life. The street that once roared with trucks was quiet and empty." All the canneries along the coast failed, along with the fishery, pushing countless people on to other jobs and other places. Only Cannery Row, because of Steinbeck's books, eventually reemerged, metamorphosed into a strip of T-shirt boutiques to satisfy the tourist trade.

THE PERUVIAN ANCHOVETA

A change of scene. Another species, the Peruvian anchoveta, schools in the sea off the coast of Peru, nourished by the upwelling nutrients in the northward-moving Humboldt Current. Until the 1950s, seabirds had relatively exclusive access to the anchovetas, but with the crash of the California sardines, the situation quickly changed. Recognizing an opportunity at a time when fish meal was becoming increasingly valuable, Peru bought the California seiners and sardine canneries and went into the anchoveta business with a vengeance. At first Peru provided fish meal for just the California poultry and pig farmers. Eventually it provided much of the fish meal for North America and Europe. The fishery grew to such a size that by the mid-1960s, Peruvian anchovetas made up a quarter of the total world catch of 60 million tonnes (Figure 2).

The Peruvian fleet had also overcapitalized by the mid-1960s. In 1966 managers closed the fishery for a season to protect the remaining fish. The fishery soon reopened and the fishing firms built bigger boats, caught more fish faster and doubled their catch by 1970. Once again, such harvest rates could not be sustained. This time, however, a major environmental catastrophe intruded to destroy the weakened fish stocks. In March 1972, the severest of El Niño events began, raising water temperatures a crucial 2 degrees Celsius (3½ degrees Fahrenheit) along the west coast of South America, making the water too warm for the anchovetas to reproduce.

Fisheries biologists in Peru knew quite well what was about to happen with the arrival of the El Niño and advised that the fishery be kept closed in 1972. But closing a fishery is an unpopular act, and the government delayed, hoping for a more attractive alternative. The remaining fish moved inshore in search of cooler water, and the huge, overcapitalized fleet met them there and fished them out. Another decline became a total collapse. The human toll this time was particularly great, for much of the Peruvian economy had come to depend on the anchoveta fishery. Thousands of fishers and fish processors lost their livelihoods, and the country lost its major export.

The story doesn't stop there. The collapse of the Peruvian anchoveta left a large hole in the world market for fish meal. Farmers began to grow soybeans as a substitute, and Californian fishers began to hunt the California anchovy as another substitute. In 1978, the state established a minimum stock size for the anchovy, prohibiting harvesting if the stock dropped below that minimum. Unfortunately, the stock extended into Mexican waters, where fishing persisted and U.S. regulations could not reach, and it collapsed anyway.

This is a hundred-year saga. Some recovery of both the sardine and the anchoveta has occurred, and perhaps this time they will be managed by a rational scheme that acknowledges how vulnerable fish stocks are to the pressures of overfishing and the stresses of unpredictable environmental changes.

Perhaps. Our memory for environmental catastrophe is short, however, and overfishing can often be difficult to recognize. A standard way to determine whether a fishery is in decline has been to measure how much is caught in a given period of time, a measure known as catch per unit effort, or CPUE in the business. But if fishing technology is improving, if the actual size of the area being fished is increasing, if the number of fishers fishing is increasing, then increasing harvests from a declining stock are likely. When the decline due to overfishing is finally acknowledged, it may be too late.

THE CONTINUING COLLAPSE

In the mid-seventies, when most coastal countries extended their jurisdiction over fish stocks to 200 miles (320 kilometres)* offshore and in many cases evicted most of the foreign vessels fishing in their new-found waters, fisheries managers and politicians thought that derby-style scramble competition for fish would cease. They expected fish stocks to be safe from overfishing. They could not have been more wrong, as the collapse of the fisheries on the Grand Banks and Georges Bank off the coasts of New England and the Atlantic Provinces bears discouraging witness.

≈≈≈≈≈≈≈≈≈≈≈≈≈≈≈≈≈≈≈≈≈≈≈≈≈≈≈≈≈≈≈

*O*pen access as a management approach is terminal,
eventually, for every fishery.

≈≈≈≈≈≈≈≈≈≈≈≈≈≈≈≈≈≈≈≈≈≈≈≈≈≈≈≈≈≈≈

New Bedford, just south of Boston, serves as an example of the economic collapse associated with depletion of the fish populations, but many other ports in New England, Oregon and Newfoundland would do as well. So would other ports scattered around the world. But New Bedford is perhaps special because of its extraordinary history. It has been a fishing port since its days as a British colony well before the American Revolution and was involved in the cod trade as early as 1630. It became the home of the world's largest whaling fleet in the 1850s, immortalized in the opening chapters of *Moby Dick*, where Ishmael meets up with Queequeg. A couple of decades ago, it became the most valuable fishing port in the United States, its fleet largely manned by its experienced community of fishers of Portuguese descent. Now its fleet sits mostly idle; the fishers watch their boats deteriorate; the jobless rate for the city has soared to 15 per cent, one of the highest in the nation; the fishing grounds have been closed or access to them has been radically reduced; and recovery is a remote hope at best. As journalist Timothy Egan reported in the *New York Times Magazine*, "Boats weighed down with overdue bank notes stand idle. Taverns fill at mid-morning. And with too many vessels and not enough

---

* Because jurisdictional distances at sea are usually given in miles, this book also uses miles for such measures, generally without the metric equivalent.

fish, the Federal Government has been asked to buy out all the deeply indebted fishermen that it helped bring into the industry in the first place." And of course the fishers again hate to let go of what they had. A boat captain lamented to Egan, "I don't want to sell my boat. I just want to fish. How come I can't just fish? . . . I just want to fish."

This certainly isn't what anyone planned. When the 200-mile limit came into force in 1976, the U.S. fleet expanded to replace the departing foreign distant-water fleets. Steel-hulled trawlers, 16 metres (50 feet) long or more, were built, and over the years their owners have provided them with sophisticated navigational equipment, upgraded sonar and access to COMSAT satellite images. Fish schools became easier to find and easier to catch. The number of boats rapidly increased. The regional council that set the harvest limit set it high, at a level we now know could never be sustained. By the end of the 1980s, far more boats trawled for fish than were needed for the job. By 1989, the catch had dropped to a quarter of what it had been in 1969, before the foreign fleet left. An unregulated free-for-all, open access for everyone, had occurred. Again.

Now the fishing grounds are mostly closed. Dockside companies, restaurants, hotels are closed. The Portuguese radio station is dominated by discouraging news about plans to restrict the fishing even further. The talk is about a permanent change in life and lifestyle, the end of an era, fishers going the way of the cowboys, seeking jobs elsewhere or shifting into the business of eco-tourism, catering to the yuppie world most fishers have shunned until now.

Must it always be this way? What alternatives exist to the way we operate? What is going on around the world to cause pessimism or hope? And why is it so difficult to manage fish stocks, considering how much effort and research have gone into fisheries management for so many years? Open access as a management approach is terminal, eventually, for every fishery. Limiting access is essential. But how can that be done equitably? It can't. There will always be winners and losers, whether they are fishers themselves, or fishing communities, or fishing nations.

There is some reason to hope, however, even as the stocks continue to crash. The new United Nations Law of the Sea is an evolving document with the potential to guide countries to agreements unimaginable a few decades ago. At the same time, two diametrically opposed ways of managing fisheries, one involving strict rules of efficient economics, the other involving community participation at all levels of decision making, are under way around the world. There are alternatives to the kind of management that has invariably led to the collapse of fisheries. Recovery is possible. The seas need not become empty. The race for fish can be controlled. We have no choice.

CHAPTER 2

WHO FISHES FOR WHAT

First fisherman: *"Master, I marvel how the fishes
            live in the sea."*
Second fisherman: *"Why, as men do a-land; the great
            ones eat up the little ones."*

Shakespeare, PERICLES

*To test its freshness make sure that its eyes are bulging and its gills are
reddish, that the scales are adhering firmly to the skin, and that the flesh, when
you press it, is firm to the touch.*

Irma Rombauer &
Marion Rombauer Becker
THE JOY OF COOKING

Fish have in the past been so abundant along the coasts of the world, eaten by everyone, that they became a symbol of abundance and in some cultures a symbol of good luck, fertility, creativity or power. They have also been incorporated into the myths of old and into the religions of the present. The Japanese believed that the world rested on an immense fish. In ancient Rome and Greece, both the goddesses Venus and Aphrodite were changed into fish, and on Fridays, their holy day, people ate fish to share in their fecundity and fertility. In Babylon, fish was the sacred food of the priests, and in Judaism, fish has been considered the food of the blessed and eaten at the Sabbath meal. Among Native societies on the west coast of North America, fish have been sacred totemic figures, symbolic of the power of the clan. Fish have even become the symbol of a saviour. When the Hindu god Vishnu was transformed into a fish by Brahma, he recovered the Vedas from the great flood and saved humankind. Christ as well has been symbolized as a fish, and intertwined fish came to represent Christian baptism.

Despite the rich symbolic nature of fish in human affairs over the past millennia, humans have for the most part just eaten them. We hunt fish because we are omnivores with a taste for eating the muscle tissue of other animals to satisfy our need for protein. Despite the great number of potentially edible marine species, there really aren't that many that support large-scale commercial fisheries—perhaps only a hundred or so. To be worth catching, they must be numerous and easily caught or so valuable that the greater effort needed to catch them is worthwhile.

THE FISH

The fish that we fish for are mostly bony fish, such as tuna, herring, cod and salmon. Although cartilaginous fish, such as sharks and rays, do support some limited and local fisheries, in the global scheme they are of less commercial interest. They don't form large, catchable schools; some of them, especially the larger sharks, can be difficult to handle; and so far we have not developed much of a taste for them. Many bony fish, however, do form large schools, or aggregate seasonally in large numbers, and have become the target of fisheries around the world.

There are more than 13 000 marine species of bony fish, and another 7000 species live in fresh water. They really are one of the greatest success stories in the evolution of life over the past half-billion years. Fish first evolved more than 400 million years ago, and bony fish turn up in the fossil record from more than 200 million years ago. Although they evolved further into several distinct lines or orders over the next 100 million years, they still remained relatively rare. Only after the great extinction event of 65 million years ago, when the earth was apparently hit by a large and devastating asteroid, did their rate of evolution suddenly change. Just as on land birds and mammals diversified explosively into most of the major families of species we know and love or mourn today, so also did the bony fish radiate into an amazing array of species. They rapidly came to dominate the world's shallow water systems, where light penetrates, plants and algae grow, herbivores graze, and fish can feed on the herbivores, on the smaller predators or on the plants and algae themselves. From anchovy to swordfish, sea horse to moray eel, bony fish have exploited an extraordinary diversity of niches.

Bony fish have remarkable adaptations that help explain their success. Those that swim off the bottom are streamlined for rapid swimming. All of them can move with great precision, coordinated by the interaction of their pectoral, pelvic, tail and dorsal fins. Their vision is excellent, and their brains are dominated by the parts responsible for the analysis of visual input. Because they live in water, where sound travels much more rapidly than in air because of the far greater density of water, their hearing is also excellent. But like all fish, they also have the ability to detect slight water turbulence, giving them a kind of distant touch sense. A series of small sense organ receptors, called neuromasts, are embedded in grooves, or lateral lines, running along each side of their bodies. Water cannot be compressed, so a fish pushes a bow wave ahead of itself as it swims, no matter how streamlined it may be. As the wave rebounds off nearby obstacles, other fish in the school or potential prey, the sensitive receptors of the lateral lines detect the changes in turbulence and provide the fish brain with information to be interpreted.

The other great innovation of bony fish, in an evolutionary sense, is their jaws. These extraordinary jaws, which are detached from the skull, have allowed the evolution of an immense diversity of feeding abilities. Again, because water cannot be compressed, when a fish opens its mouth quickly water rushes in, carrying food as well as oxygenated water. The food is swallowed, while the water is pushed out over the gills in the gill chamber. Many fish feed this way, approaching zooplankton or smaller fish, opening their mouths and sucking them in.

FISH LIFE HISTORIES

Fishers identify fish as either pelagic or groundfish. Pelagic fish, such as herring, anchovies, mackerel and tuna, swim around off the bottom, often near the surface of the sea. They feed on zooplankton and on the smaller fish that eat the plankton. Purse seines, gillnets and driftnets catch the surface schools, while longline fishing reaches the larger, deeper fish such as the larger tuna and billfish. In contrast, groundfish live on or near the bottom and are mostly caught with trawls and longlines. Groundfish vary more than pelagic fish, for they include species such as cod and haddock, as well as those very odd flatfish such as sole and flounder. Groundfish feed on bottom-dwelling animals, including many invertebrates, as well as juveniles of their own species; a main food of large cod has probably always been smaller cod.

Although there are exceptions, such as salmon, most pelagic and groundfish typically shed their eggs and sperm into the water above them, where fertilization takes place. Fish school for a variety of reasons—for example, to feed, avoid predators or migrate—but they also school for successful spawning. If a sexually mature individual, male or female, spawns at the wrong time or the wrong place—for instance, away from the school—it spawns alone, and the heavy hand of natural selection discards its contribution to the next generation. In fish that spawn while schooling—as do most of the species hunted on the high seas and in coastal waters—there is powerful pressure to remain in the school.

Unlike birds and most mammals, fish just keep on growing when they reach sexual maturity, although the rate at which they grow is likely to slow down. One of the most important considerations in the management of any fishery is to understand this growth rate, and for two quite distinct reasons. A large fish is generally more valuable than a small fish. And as a female grows larger, she produces increasing numbers of eggs. A female cod that is a metre long may spawn a million eggs. Fecundity increases, often exponentially, with the age of a female.

Two fish of a particular species that are the same length are not necessarily the same age, however, for individuals vary in how fast they grow. Perhaps one feeds more often or more efficiently than another; perhaps it has grown up in a colder habitat and has therefore grown larger though more slowly; perhaps it has survived parasitic infection; perhaps it is genetically capable of more rapid growth as a result of differences in metabolic enzyme activity. But such variation is characteristic of most populations. We can only propose a likely age for a fish of a certain size in a particular species. To confirm the age of an individual fish, we can look at the annual growth rings in its scales or in its otoliths, calcareous stones suspended in parts of its inner ear. What we would find is that individuals, in almost every species, ride different trajectories to sexual maturity and beyond.

After eggs are fertilized in the water above a school of spawning fish, they are swept along and supported by the ocean currents as they develop. After they hatch, they remain in the plankton, feeding as fish larvae on the small zooplankton around them in the water. In turn they are preyed upon by any larger predator that might be there as well—for instance the immense schools of herring or related pelagic fish that then in turn are fished by humans. Relatively few fish larvae survive and grow large enough to drop out of the plankton as juveniles—about one in a million for cod. Looking rather like miniature adults, they then search for schools of their own size and species if they are pelagic fish, or for an appropriate benthic nursery habitat if they are groundfish.

At some point—again, at a certain size but at an uncertain age that varies from species to species—it joins the adult population or at least begins to behave in a fashion similar to that of adults, schooling or foraging in places that fishers know they should be, and they become vulnerable to human predation for the first time.

SCHOOLS, STOCKS AND POPULATIONS

If fish didn't school, many of the commercial fisheries in the world's oceans would not exist. The schools may be immense. The smaller pelagic species, such as herring, sardines, anchovies and pilchards, form schools of many millions or even billions, and the predators they attract include seabirds, seals, whales, other larger fish and fishing fleets. Sometimes the predators share information about a school. For instance, schools of tuna in the Pacific drive schools of

smaller fish to the surface as they prey on them from below; seabirds see the surface turmoil and arrive to feed on the fish driven to the surface by the tuna; tuna
boats watch for seabirds diving into the water and encircle the school in a purse
seine to catch the tuna feeding on them. Everyone watches everyone else.

People in the business of managing fish talk about stocks of fish. An unattractive word, "stock." But it does emphasize the way we look at fish—as commodities, protein, resources, something to earn an income from or to eat. They
are, of course, all of these things. They are also highly evolved, diverse, adaptive
organisms that spend their lives in diverse habitats, mostly as predators, often
in schools or in less obvious groups that may be called populations. Fisheries
biologists call them stocks.

A group, such as a school or a bunch of adjacent schools, is recognized as a
population. As long as there is frequent movement of individuals between
schools, gene flow between the schools remains high, and the group of schools
is really one large population. But such a group of schools may live in a particular region, separated from other similar populations by enough space that
genetic flow between them is reduced. Each of these potentially large populations may then be distinct from other populations, even a little different genetically. And each of these populations then becomes what fisheries people call
stocks. Stocks are managed separately, for otherwise it could be possible—
these days far too likely—that an entire stock could be eliminated, fished out,
and then not be replaced. The herring on Georges Bank are a good example of a
separate stock that was almost fished to extinction while more northern stocks
of the species remained relatively healthy. Stocks of fish vary greatly in size, and
what is appropriate management for one could be terminal for another.

COMMUNITIES

No species is an island, to paraphrase John Donne. Every species lives in a
community of potential competitors, prey and predators; every community
has producers, getting their energy from sunlight, herbivores that eat the producers, and predators that eat the herbivores and smaller predators. The interactions between species are often subtle and complex, as each species adapts
not only to the physical aspects of its environment, such as fluctuations in temperature and salinity, but also to the abundance and the activities of many of
the species it shares its habitat with. These observations may seem obvious, but
the marine world is not easily accessible. Biologists know some of it by direct
observation through scuba diving and small submarines, but not very much.
They know part of it by dragging up dead or soon-to-die pieces of it which
they may have a chance to study in some detail. Biologists examine the gut con-

tents of the species of the community and try to piece together the predator-prey interactions that are occurring. They develop a general picture of the community, and that really is quite a remarkable achievement.

THE GROUPS MOST FISHED

Despite the great diversity of types of bony fish, over the millennia we have learned to fish with most enthusiasm and success for five groups. The first group includes two closely related families; one includes herring, sardines and pilchards, and the other includes anchovies and anchovetas. Fish in this group, particularly those living in cooler waters, have the greatest number of individuals within a species and form the largest schools. These fish school near the sea surface, feeding on plankton. Their silvery scales scatter the light coming from above, and their compressed bodies make them less visible from below, both adaptations that give them perhaps a little more protection from predators foraging for them from below. Schools concentrate in coastal waters, where upwelling water brings valuable nutrients to the surface and ensures dense supplies of plankton. If they aren't fished as food for humans or as fish meal, they are usually preyed on by larger fish that are in turn fished by humans. As a result, their importance to the global fisheries is very great. Because of their relatively small size, their potential for truly immense numbers (imagine a billion or several billion fish in a single school) and their vulnerability to both fishing pressure and environmental changes, they are particularly likely to go through typical boom-and-bust cycles. Peruvian anchoveta made up more than 15 per cent of the world catch before the stock collapsed in 1972, a reminder of how a relatively small number of species may dominate the world catch.

The second group is the family that includes the salmon that live in northern temperate waters of both the Atlantic and Pacific Oceans. Loved for their fine taste, texture and colour, they breed in freshwater streams and lakes, usually grow there for a while and then migrate to the ocean, where they grow much faster because the small fish they prey on are much more abundant there. The largest of the salmon is the chinook, a Pacific species that may grow to 1.5 metres (5 feet) in length if it isn't captured first. Although they don't form schools as herring or tuna do, they aggregate in large numbers during their migrations back to their home streams to breed and are easily hunted then. Because of their size, taste and texture, they are far more valuable than the herring.

The third group is the cod family, a small family of about fifty-five species. Most of them grow large enough to be worth fishing for, forming large schools close to the bottom. Probably the biggest is, or was, the too-easily-caught Atlantic cod. True cod, and the closely related pollock, haddock and hake, swim just off the bottom, cruising for crabs, mollusks and small fish that often are juveniles of their own species. Although northwestern stocks of the Atlantic cod are now protected from commercial fishing as a result of the Canadian moratorium, the Alaskan pollock remains one of the largest of the world's fisheries.

The family of mackerels and tunas makes up the fourth group. Again, there are only about fifty species, and they comprise less than 10 per cent of the total weight of fish caught each year. They are so favoured by American and European markets, however, that they are worth a lot more than 10 per cent of the world catch. They are the top carnivores in the surface waters of the open sea, hunting in high-speed schools for schools of smaller fish and sometimes squid. They are adapted in many ways for sustaining high swimming speeds, and in fact most tuna are warm-blooded, an unusual characteristic among fish.

The fifth group consists of three families of the flatfish order, which are easy to recognize because of their bizarre shape and features. They lie on the bottom on one side, which is white and lacks an eye, whereas the upper side is dark, often the colour and pattern of the substrate the fish lie on, and it bears both eyes. When foraging, they swim close to the bottom in search of prey; most feed on invertebrates, but the large halibut species feed on other fish. Flatfish start off life as properly bilateral symmetrical larvae, but as they become juveniles and settle to the bottom, one eye amazingly migrates across the head to lie beside the other eye, and the fish lies on its now eyeless side, growing into a flatfish. Plaice, flounder, sole and halibut—all live in relatively shallow water on the continental shelf, often in very large numbers, in many parts of the world, and trawlers drag the bottom for them wherever they are known to live.

WHERE WE FISH

The sea varies immensely in its ability to support large populations of fishable fish or invertebrates. Some regions are almost deserts, whereas others are extraordinarily productive. Distant-water fleets of fishing nations are of course attracted to the most productive places, wherever they are. As a result, fleets gather where upwelling of nutrient-rich water occurs, where the continental shelf is very extensive and where tuna schools migrate.

In the surface waters of the open sea, nutrients that result from the metabolism and decay of plankton and pelagic fish usually sink into the deep, cold and dark depths, and such surface waters cannot support much life. In some regions, however, the deep, cold, nutrient-rich seawater is forced to the surface again as a result of the often complex interactions of ocean currents with each other and with bottom topography. Then the surface waters sustain huge plankton blooms, which feed the smaller pelagic fish such as herring, sardines and anchovies. Rich sites occur off northwestern Africa, in the southeast Atlantic off the coast of newly independent Namibia and, richest of all, in the southeast Pacific off the coasts of Peru and Chile.

The waters overlying the continental shelves are also rich in nutrients, for they are relatively shallow, stirred by ocean currents, river runoff and, where the coast is more enclosed, by strong tides. The most extensive and richest continental shelf regions are in the northwest Atlantic, dominated by the famous fishing banks lying between Cape Cod and Newfoundland; the northwest Pacific, around the Gulf of Alaska and the Bering Sea; the southwest Atlantic, where huge squid stocks have been found and are now fully exploited; and the South China Sea between Taiwan and Indonesia.

Fisheries biologists have identified at least sixteen major fishing regions in the world (Figure 3). Each has a distinct combination of temperature and currents, influenced by the shape of the landmasses adjacent to it or in its waters and by the extent of the continental shelf below it. As a result, each also has a distinct community of species adapted to its conditions. And each has been explored and exploited to varying extent by human fishers.

The Northwest Atlantic Region lies along the east coast of North America and extends north to include the nutrient-rich waters along the west coast of Greenland. It includes the fishing banks that enclose the Gulf of Maine as well as the Grand Banks off Newfoundland. The groundfish that are of commercial interest are cod, pollock, haddock and hake, of the cod family, and flatfish such as the winter and yellowtail flounder. The pelagic species hunted are Atlantic herring, menhaden, mackerel, swordfish, migrating Atlantic salmon and the northern bluefin tuna. The invertebrates of value are the giant scallop, the American lobster and, recently, green sea urchins, scooped up to send to Japan, where their gonads are a delicacy. Despite the decline or crash of the stocks of several species that has closed down much of the salmon fishery and the groundfisheries over the banks during recent years, the potential for the region remains great. Before the recent stock depletions and crashes, about 4 million onnes a year were caught by the U.S. and Canadian fleets and the distant-water fleets from Europe and Asia. But no one expects the fish stocks to recover to allow fishing at that level ever again.

The oldest overfished region in the world is on the other side of the North Atlantic. The Northeast Atlantic includes the shallow and very rich North Sea, the continental shelf west of the United Kingdom and the waters adjacent to the Scandinavian countries, including the isolated Faroe Islands between Norway and Iceland. At its peak, 13 million tonnes of fish were caught each year. Cod, haddock, pollock (called saithe), whiting, Norway pout, lings and

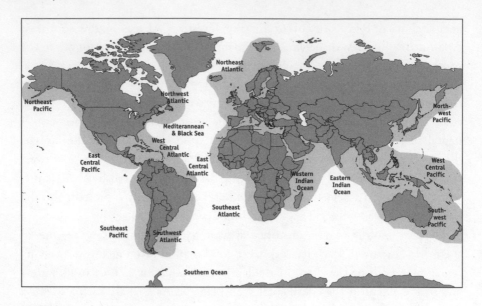

FIGURE 3

The Major Fishing Regions. Fisheries biologists have divided the world's oceans into distinct fishing regions. Each region is characterized by a particular group of fish and shellfish that are of commercial interest.

tusk have dominated the groundfish catch. Herring, once closely associated with the growth of United Kingdom and Scandinavian cultures, has only recently partly recovered from its collapse in the 1960s. Managing the North Sea and other European waters that so many nations share is proving to be a particularly complex challenge.

Four other Atlantic regions are still developing and are generally poorly understood and barely managed. The most developed region is the Southeast Atlantic, along the coast of southern Africa. In the Southwest Atlantic, the management of the Argentinean coast, embracing the Falkland Islands, has been confounded by political tensions. Both the West Central and East Central Atlantic Regions contain many species of commercial interest, but none of them in the large numbers found in temperate latitudes, and poor documentation and management make estimates of the total catch difficult.

The final Atlantic region is the Mediterranean Sea and the Black Sea, with its long history of fishing. During the past two decades the human impact on these two mostly enclosed seas has become a cause of great concern. The problem is not only the increase in the fishing but also the increase in contaminants flowing in from the many rivers. In addition, far too many countries share jurisdiction over the various stocks. Decline of fish in the Black Sea has been particularly steep, but the Mediterranean is in similar danger.

The Indian Ocean is the least exploited of the world's oceans. Both the Western Indian Ocean and Eastern Indian Ocean regions are undergoing continuing development. Most of the fishing is by the coastal states, but foreign fleets now intrude, mainly in search of tuna, which are now fully exploited there as elsewhere.

Travelling eastward into the Pacific Ocean, the Northwest Pacific Region is the most productive in the world. Japan, China, Russia, North and South Korea and Taiwan fish the same groups that support the North Atlantic fisheries. About 25 million tonnes a year, 30 per cent of the world catch, are caught: Alaskan pollock (4 million tonnes a year just for this species, which is made into the surimi so loved by the Japanese); Pacific salmon species, now largely depleted; and smaller pelagic species such as saury, herring, jack mackerel, sardines, anchovies and chub mackerel.

Across the ocean, the Northeast Pacific, extending from Oregon to Alaska, is now managed completely by the United States and Canada. This partnership ought to make management far more successful than in most other regions, but it doesn't necessarily. About 3 million tonnes of fish come in each year. Until the 1930s, Pacific halibut dominated the catch, and since its crash it has recovered only to support a small albeit valuable fishery. Now Pacific salmon dominate the coastal fisheries, which south of Alaska are in crisis. In the Gulf of Alaska, groundfish such as flatfish, hake and cod, and pelagic herring are fished competitively and often dangerously. There as well Alaskan pollock are heavily fished to support the Japanese market.

The West Central Pacific is a huge region, including the island nations of the South Pacific, Indonesia, the Philippines, Malaysia and Thailand, along with the rich Gulf of Thailand and the South China Sea. As in the tropical Central Atlantic, many species are fished, and few are truly numerous; but the very valuable tuna, especially skipjack tuna, are fished by every nation whose economic zone they cross as they migrate back and forth across the Pacific. Another 5 million tonnes of fish per year are caught here.

The shelf is narrow along the Pacific side of Central America, the region called the East Central Pacific, which the United States shares with the fishing nations of Central America, particularly Panama, Mexico and Ecuador. Fishers go after the usual pelagic species, such as the California sardine and the northern anchovy, and they also hunt for the tuna that migrate in from the West Pacific. The United States has been a difficult neighbour for Central America, particularly when it comes to the tuna, and conflicts between them continue.

The Southwest Pacific is partly open ocean but reaches Australia and includes New Zealand, and it has long been fished by the fishing nations to the north, Japan and the former Soviet Union—mainly for tuna. Now with the collapse of the Soviet Union and the inactivity of much of its distant-water fleet, not to mention the problems brought on by the extension of economic control to 200 miles offshore, the million tonnes of fish caught each year is increasingly caught by the local coastal countries.

The Southeast Pacific, which includes the coasts of Peru and Chile, is another matter. The cold Humboldt Current drives north along that coast, resulting in some of the world's most nutrient-rich, productive waters. The Peruvian anchoveta was driven to collapse by overfishing and the warming effects of El Niño. It has slowly recovered, however, and is fished again along with other pelagic species, such as South American pilchard and Chilean jack mackerel, and groundfish such as the Chilean hake. Once again, the catch for the region is in excess of 15 million tonnes a year. Like well-known fish stocks in the North Atlantic and North Pacific, these fish are all fully exploited, unable to sustain any increase in fishing pressure without risk of collapse.

The final major fishing region is the Southern Ocean, circumscribing Antarctica. There are not many fish worth making the trip for, though some stocks have been found and quickly fished almost to oblivion. But krill, which are pelagic shrimplike crustaceans, live in seemingly endless schools in the Southern Ocean, providing food for what fish there are and for the remaining baleen whales, which for the most part were killed in the whaling years. The diverse seals and seabirds of the Antarctic region in turn eat the fish that eat the krill, so the krill support quite an extraordinary ecosystem. Distant-water fleets have also shown interest in the krill in the past couple of decades for possible human consumption. If the krill were heavily fished, the ecosystem would certainly collapse with it. Since krill are hard to keep fresh and to process, however, and the distance from the possible markets is great, excessive harvesting of krill may not occur. Moreover, protective regulations may at least limit the attempts at overharvesting, though nobody is on hand to enforce these regulations.

Over the past two centuries, a gradual shift in fishing in the various regions has occurred as fish stocks have been exploited and distant-water fleets developed. From the North Atlantic the fleets moved first to the North Pacific, from there to the South Atlantic and South and Central Pacific, and finally, more recently, to the Indian Ocean. Only the fisheries of the Indian Ocean remain less than fully exploited. There is nowhere else left to go.

THE MAJOR SPECIES

A fishery is a fishing industry focussed on a particular species or group of closely related species. The five largest fisheries of the last decade have not been of particularly high value per fish. All are relatively small pelagic fish: the

Japanese pilchard, the South American pilchard, the Peruvian anchoveta (making a comeback), the Chilean jack mackerel and the Alaskan pollock (Figure 4). These five are all fished to about the same extent, about 4 to 6 million tonnes of each species per year, for a total of about 24 million tonnes out of the total global catch of marine species of 80 million tonnes. Of the five, only the Alaskan pollock, which is in high demand for the surimi market of Japan, is of reasonable value per fish. The first four species, which are used mostly for producing fish meal to feed to pigs and poultry, have about 10 per cent of the average unit value of other fished species, such as cod, flatfish, tuna and salmon; Alaskan pollock is worth about one-third the average of these other species; and the five species combined, making up more than a quarter of the total global catch, comprise only about 6 per cent of the total value—certainly poor value for effort. Fished heavily, these species, like other small pelagic fish, are likely to oscillate most in stock size as they are buffeted by the small but critical and unpredictable changes in their environments.

Fishing fleets have swarmed after these pelagic species because the market for fish meal is increasing and because more valuable species have become harder to find. Although the total tonnage of fish caught per year has increased, the value of the total hasn't. Greater efforts have been made to catch them, and the cost to fishers and fishing nations has risen. The result is more effort, more fish but smaller, less valuable ones and greater cost for the effort and greater debt. The situation is hardly sustainable.

THE INVERTEBRATES

Although fish dominate both the marine harvest and the news reports about the fishing industry, the global fisheries include a variety of invertebrates. Two groups dominate the invertebrate fisheries: crustaceans and mollusks. Other invertebrates are eaten (the French and Japanese eat just about anything, such as sea urchin gonads and sea cucumber skins), and there are local small but thriving fisheries, such as the recent boom (but heading for a bust) fishery for sea urchins in the U.S. northeast.

Among the crustaceans, we like to eat shrimp, crabs and lobsters. We like their taste so much that we are willing to pay a lot for them. They are so valuable—often too valuable for the fishers who catch them to be able to afford to eat them—that they may be considered a luxury food. The expense of lobsters and crabs is in part understandable, because they can be harder to catch in large numbers than fish. But shrimp are trawled up with considerable ease, along with much less valuable fish, which are then dumped overboard by shrimp trawlers everywhere.

Among bivalve mollusks, we have a gourmet taste for oysters, abalone,

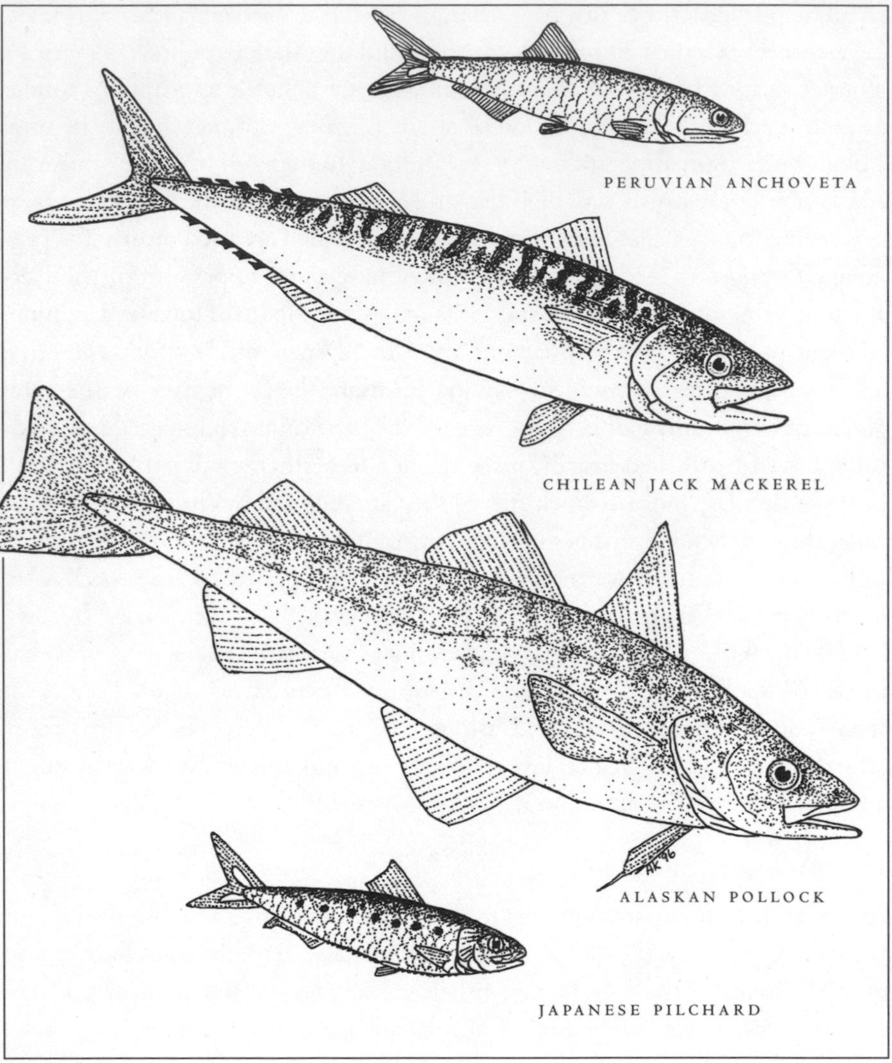

FIGURE 4

The Most-Fished Species. *Just a few species account for much of the total world catch of fish. Three of them are pelagic—the Peruvian anchoveta, the Japanese pilchard and the Chilean jack mackerel—and are fished along the productive coast of South America or in the Southeast Pacific. The Alaskan pollock is a groundfish that is abundant in the North Pacific.*

mussels, scallops and clams, but the largest fishery is for squid, those most unusual of mollusks. The more familiar bivalves are dug for, dragged for and in some places cultured. The squid are trawled for, as if they were just another schooling species of fish.

So, although only 10 per cent of the tonnage of marine species harvested each year is made up of these invertebrates, they are worth over 30 per cent of the total value of the global marine catch. Another way of looking at the high value of the invertebrates is to look at the ranking in value of all harvested species or groups of species (Table 2.1). Together, shrimp, crabs and lobsters are the most valuable. Tuna are next, and then the squid family. Despite the huge numbers that are caught, the herring family is next, comprising a little over 5 per cent of the total value. The flatfish family, the cod family (before the collapse of the Atlantic cod fishery), scallops and other mollusks, and salmon follow. These eight groups of species account for over 60 per cent of the value of the total annual harvest. Although a number of species are lumped together in this analysis, the point remains that some species are far more valuable than others, and not many species altogether dominate the world catch.

≈≈≈≈≈≈≈≈≈≈≈≈≈≈≈≈≈≈≈≈≈≈≈≈≈≈≈≈≈≈≈≈≈≈

TABLE 2.1
Most Valuable Groups of Fish and Invertebrates

	% of total world catch	% of total value
Shrimp, crabs, lobsters	4.6	20.0
Tuna	4.9	9.7
Squid family	3.1	7.6
Herring family	30.4	5.4
Flatfish family	1.4	4.9
Cod family	4.6	4.9
Scallops and other bivalves	2.6	4.9
Salmon	1.1	4.7

≈≈≈≈≈≈≈≈≈≈≈≈≈≈≈≈≈≈≈≈≈≈≈≈≈≈≈≈≈≈≈≈≈≈

Herring, sardines, anchovies and pilchards—all small pelagic fish of the herring family—therefore make up 30 per cent of the total catch but little more than 5 per cent of its value, while invertebrates make up less than 10 per cent of the total catch but over 30 per cent of its value. A few species, or groups of similar species, make up the bulk of the global catch. The more valuable species are the ones most likely to be overfished; the least valuable ones are most likely to vary widely in numbers as they respond to changes in sea temperature or food

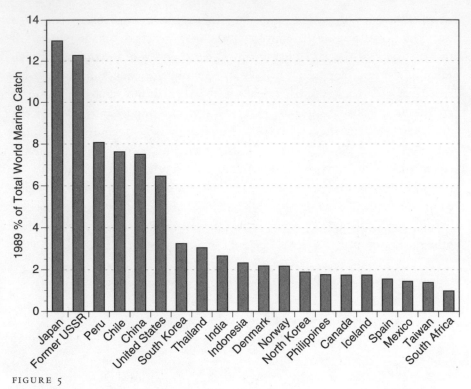

FIGURE 5

The Countries That Fish Most. Only six countries account for more than 50 per cent of the world catch, while fourteen more countries catch another 30 per cent of the total. Source: FAO.

sources. Like it or not, this describes the economics of the global fisheries, even though it doesn't sound reasonable.

THE FISHING NATIONS

The world continues to be divided into developed, developing and underdeveloped nations, at least by the UN. Twenty countries do most of the fishing; of these, nine are developed and eleven are designated as developing countries (Figure 5). Over the past two to three decades, the catch by the developed, industrialized countries (Canada, Iceland, Denmark, Norway, Japan, the Republic of South Africa, Spain, the former Soviet Union and the United States) has increased, but not nearly as rapidly as the catch of developing countries. The developing countries in this list of the top twenty are Chile, China, South Korea, India, Indonesia, Mexico, Peru, the Philippines, North Korea, Taiwan and Thailand.

The two groups now split the total catch fairly evenly, but their methods can be strikingly different. Developing countries usually depend on small-scale fisheries, using small boats, and for the most part they remain in their 200-mile

Exclusive Economic Zones (EEZS), an expanse of sea beyond their territorial limits granted to them by the 1982 UN Law of the Sea. Only South Korea, Taiwan and, most recently, China have significant distant-water fleets. The developed nations, in contrast, are quite likely to have large vessels and large fleets, and they fish offshore with sophisticated and expensive technology. The designation of developed and developing nations remains arbitrary, however, for the coastal fisheries of Newfoundland have hardly become very sophisticated, and Taiwan and South Korea are hardly struggling, nonindustrial nations.

In addition, things change very rapidly. The distant-water fleets of the former Soviet Union operated with large deficits and large subsidies. Most of the fleet now belongs to Russia, but the subsidies are hard to sustain, the patterns of fishing are shifting, and the intensity of fishing is declining. Spain continues to fish where it can; it overfished the Cape hake for twenty years but left the African coast after Namibia became independent and gained control of its own 200-mile EEZ. Meanwhile, China is expanding its distant-water fleet and is fishing far from its own coastal waters. Japan's fleet has largely moved out of the Northeast Pacific, pulling much of its fleet into its EEZ, while extending into the Southwest Atlantic and other parts of the Pacific. South Korea and Taiwan work the Northeast Pacific but have also gone after the squid of the Southwest Atlantic and tuna in the Pacific. Always shifting, the distant-water fleets continue to press for fish wherever they can fish legally, or even illegally.

JUST A COMMODITY?

We have probably lost most, if not all, of our sense of the symbolic or mystical nature of fish. They have become a commodity, a greater global source of protein for humans than beef, pork or poultry. As stocks decline in every ocean, and as more nations join the race to catch them with more sophisticated equipment, the focus on fish as just another commodity is likely to increase. Yet every recreational fisher, everyone who raises aquarium fish and everyone who has watched the fish on a coral reef knows that they are more than this. Every species is exquisitely adapted to its environment, honed by time, competition and natural selection. In the fight a striped bass gives to an angler, in the elaborate breeding behaviour of salmon, in the extraordinary migrations of tuna and in the awesome size of schools of anchovetas lie reminders of how complex and fascinating fish really are, food though they be. Santiago, the old man in Hemingway's *Old Man and the Sea*, knew the beauty, majesty and mystery of the giant marlin that he struggled with for three days. Although he killed it nonetheless, he deeply respected what he had killed.

CHAPTER 3

THE AMAZING NEW LAW OF THE SEA

In earlier ages conflicts between nations over fish were settled by war.

D. H. Cushing

THE PROVIDENT SEA

The United Nations Law of the Sea is one of the most remarkable achievements in the history of international law. In late 1994, when thirty-three wars sputtered along around the world, all within countries and not between them, and when a chilling 1 per cent of the world's population were refugees from these wars, the United Nations Law of the Sea went into force and shone like the proverbial beacon in the night. Achieving it took forty years of negotiation between countries that often have had little in common, including, as they do, the undeveloped, the developing and the developed nations. People who began the negotiations are old or dead; generations of negotiators have come and gone. Presidents Kennedy, Johnson, Nixon, Ford, Carter, Reagan, Bush and Clinton, each with his own particular perspective, have come and mostly gone. The cold war abruptly ended, shifting the relationships between the negotiating countries in the process. A process of negotiation that should have collapsed, that should never have worked, has afterall succeeded. It provides an alternative to war and some hope for the survival of global fisheries as the race for fish reaches its greatest intensity. The Law of the Sea was unnecessary as recently as fifty years ago. It is vital now.

THE DISTANT-WATER FLEETS INVADE

For many millennia, ever since humans began fishing for fish with nets and lines, the sea was considered an endless resource to fish from and to dump our waste in. No country had offshore exclusive fishing rights. Whether along the coasts of Europe or of South Pacific islands, communities may have protected the inshore waters in their immediate vicinity, but beyond the few kilometres of inshore water the sea could not easily be protected, and therefore no one owned it. Exclusive rights did not exist. A few centuries ago, the territorial limit that a country could defend as its exclusive territory settled at 3 miles, a marine league, about the distance a cannon could shoot at that time. This boundary did not change until well into this century. Beyond the 3 miles lay the high seas, no territoriality, no regulations, open access to everyone.

≈≈≈≈≈≈≈≈≈≈≈≈≈≈≈≈≈≈≈≈≈≈≈≈≈≈≈≈≈≈

For many millennia, ever since humans began fishing for fish with nets and lines, the sea was considered an endless resource to fish from and to dump our waste in.

≈≈≈≈≈≈≈≈≈≈≈≈≈≈≈≈≈≈≈≈≈≈≈≈≈≈≈≈≈≈

Unrestricted, unlimited access to fish populations outside the 3-mile territorial waters continued until World War II. During the war, offshore and distant-water fishing in vulnerable places like the North Sea dropped off radically. As soon as the war ended, though, fishing began to expand enormously, everywhere.

The distant-water foreign fishing fleets began to appear not long after the end of the war, and they ranged the world. The Soviet and Japanese fleets grew to be the largest, but the Spanish and Eastern European fleets were also substantial. Even countries such as Poland, without much of a coastline to fish from, developed a distant-water fleet to compensate. The fleets pushed into places they had never been before and drastically increased both the pressure on the resident fish populations and the resentment of coastal fishers.

In those early postwar years, new, more effective nets and trawls were developed to drag over the sea bottom. Equipped with filleting machines and immense freezers, and able to convert offal into fish meal, large stern trawlers could therefore remain on fishing grounds as factory ships. The first of these factory ships arrived on the Grand Banks from Britain in 1954, and two more arrived from the Soviet Union in 1956; by 1958 three dozen more had arrived from the Soviet Union. Now that fish meal was valuable as a supplement to poultry food, pelagic fish everywhere instantly became worth hunting. The echo sounder and sonar, which could search ahead of a ship and were developed to hunt for submarines in the war, were adapted to hunt for schools of fish. A new age began; the old rules couldn't hold.

The Japanese had extended their fishing fleets through the Pacific well before

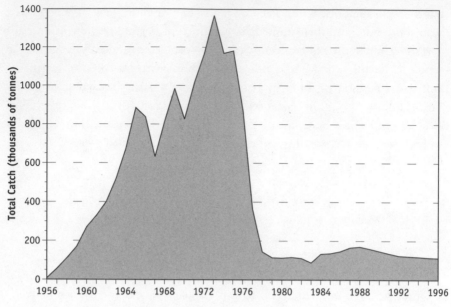

FIGURE 6

The Soviet Catch in the Northwestern Atlantic. Between 1960 and 1976 the Soviet fleet caught an extraordinary number of groundfish of a variety of species. Their catch plummeted after Canada declared a 200-mile exclusive zone in 1976 and evicted most of the foreign trawlers.

World War II. After the war their fleets grew steadily once again and, with new trawlers and factory ships, spread through the South and East China Seas and north onto the broad shelves of the Sea of Okhotsk and the Bering Sea. They trawled up the groundfish of the North Pacific; as stocks diminished in the west Pacific, they moved east into the Bering Sea and fell upon Alaskan pollock. Closer to Japan, they fished for pelagic species. Tuna boats spread through the subtropics to help serve the new American lust for tuna. Smaller numbers of trawlers turned up along the coasts of Africa, New Zealand and Indonesia. And in the North Pacific, Japanese vessels fished for Pacific salmon on the high seas, far from land.

Like the Japanese fleet, the Soviet fleet fished the world. With their freezer factory trawlers, the Soviet ships hunted for Atlantic cod, Alaskan pollock, and Antarctic fish and krill. They ranged from pole to pole, but they had the greatest destructive impact on the fishing banks off the northeast coast of North America (Figure 6). This was a new scale of fishing, and no population of fish could withstand the pressure.

Soon distant-water fishing fleets were in every ocean. They came from Spain and Portugal, Denmark and Norway, the United States and the United Kingdom, Poland and East Germany, Bulgaria and Romania. Fleets from Ghana worked along the African coast; fleets from Thailand fished off Bangladesh and in the South China Sea. South Korean ships took up distant-water tuna fishing. Coastal countries everywhere felt the pressure and did not like it.

RESISTANCE GROWS

The first true threat to the freedom of the seas came from Chile. In 1947, Chile announced, outrageously as far as most of the rest of the world was concerned, that it owned the water above the seabed, as well as the seabed, for a distance of 200 miles offshore. Chile wasn't protecting its fish stocks or its continental shelf and had no interest in its immensely deep seabed. But at the time, Chile was a whaling nation, hunting the whales of the Antarctic. It wanted to clear the new, postwar factory ships of other whaling nations out of its coastal waters, and this unilateral declaration achieved that goal. Curiously, Chile's whaling industry only wanted a 50-mile exclusion zone, but it got a zone 200 miles wide. It could as easily have been 50 or 300 miles, but international law often emerges from arbitrary action.

Ecuador and Peru had supported Chile in its declaration, and each declared a similar jurisdiction for the same offshore distance—Peru later in 1947, Ecuador in 1951. For them, tuna and anchovetas, not whales, were the reasons for their actions. The anchovetas were becoming recognized around the developed world as an excellent source of fish meal for poultry and pigs, and Peru wanted to develop the fishery on its own, a good plan, considering that it would develop into the planet's most valuable fishery before it crashed to oblivion in the early 1970s.

Unfortunately, tuna migrated into the coastal waters of the two countries and then migrated out again. Ecuador and Peru wanted exclusive rights to these fish, but no other countries, particularly not the United States, would grant a coastal nation possession of such a valuable fish stock. In response to Peru and Ecuador's position, the American Tunafishermen's Association was soon created to protect the rights of American tuna boats to fish anywhere they damn well pleased on the world's oceans. Distant-water fleets everywhere felt threatened.

Several years after the unilateral action by the South American countries, Iceland also decided to protect itself from the intrusions of foreign fleets and provoked the first of its several famous cod wars with Great Britain. Iceland is a small, highly developed country, tied loosely to Scandinavia and Europe but isolated from the rest of the world. Its economy has long been dependent on fishing, and on cod especially. Just after World War II, when there were not yet any fishing trawlers in the region, cod became unusually plentiful. The increase occurred not only because the fish had recently been underfished but also because recruitment of juveniles into schools had probably been unusually high. In 1952, Iceland extended its jurisdiction from 3 to 4 miles offshore; Britain objected. The British ambassador to Iceland at the time, Sir Andrew Gilchrist, wrote in his book *Cod Wars and How to Lose Them* that "with two hostile fleets about to go into action against each other, the scope for diplomacy was somewhat limited. . . . One of the difficulties at this time was that the Icelanders, who were (in our view) the aggressors did not look like the aggressors." Iceland deployed its navy; shots were fired. In 1958, it extended the limits to 12 miles, and in 1961 the British signed a treaty recognizing the new limits, ending the first cod war. As Sir Andrew noted, "nothing could conceal that this was in fact a massive Icelandic victory."

After the collapse of the North Sea herring fishery in the 1960s, Britain, Germany and Belgium sent their fleets where fish could still be easily caught, including the coast of Iceland. In response, Iceland protested that the fishing pressure on the cod was too great for the stocks to withstand and extended its fishing zone to 50 miles. Sir Andrew wrote: "For the record, the Second Cod War (which began when the Icelanders proclaimed a 50-mile limit) was settled on 13th November, 1973, the outcome being a further reduction of British fishing efforts, as measured by available sea areas and working periods, the tormented British trawler fleet being given this time only a 2-year grace period under these restrictive conditions."

Finally, Iceland complained that even with 50 miles of protected sea, the cod stocks were still being depleted, and once again extended offshore jurisdiction, this time to 200 miles, initiating the third cod war with the United Kingdom. Iceland had both a navy that was strong enough to patrol and protect the expanse of sea and the will not to back down; it also had the growing support of other coastal countries hoping to extend their own fishing zones. The British conceded defeat in 1976. Foreign fleets were now excluded from an area of water twenty times larger than the landmass of Iceland. A rather remarkable precedent, set by the three South American countries thirty years previously, had now been just as remarkably extended by Iceland.

Conflicts arose elsewhere as fish stocks dropped. In 1964, Canada increased its jurisdiction over fisheries from 3 to 12 miles and in 1971 made that 12-mile limit its full territorial zone. In 1975 it banned Soviet ships from Canadian ports, threatening to do the same to Portuguese and Spanish fleets. The jurisdiction had not yet extended to 200 miles in Canada, but with the events in Iceland, everyone now expected it to happen.

THE UN TRIES, FAILS, THEN FAILS AGAIN

During this time of growing unilateral actions and potential conflicts, the newly established UN quite properly recognized that it had a responsibility to help resolve the disagreements about who owned how much of the high seas. Preparations for a meeting began in 1950; the first UN Conference on the Law of the Sea (UNCLOS I) was held in Geneva in 1958, followed by a second conference in 1960 (UNCLOS II). Both were remarkably ineffective. Most countries were not yet ready to abandon their historic rights, and they were not yet ready to agree on issues relating to fisheries protection zones or on access by military and commercial craft to coastal waters. New or landlocked countries did not like the UN provisions that would prevent them from exploiting the coastal resources of other nations. Countries with distant-water fleets wanted to continue to fish where they wanted. Other countries thought that the proposed provisions did not give them enough control over their coastal waters. In the end, the key decision to extend territorial waters for fishing was not made. Many ambiguities were written into the document that emerged, and far too few states subsequently ratified it. It encouraged unilateral assertions and even provoked subsequent conflicts, such as the third cod war between the United Kingdom and Iceland. Nonetheless, it was a start.

As the perception grew that the sea had its limits as a source of food and receptacle for waste, new needs also developed. New technology made offshore exploitation of seabed resources possible, particularly for oil in the short term, but in the more distant future for rich mineral deposits, such as manganese nodules scattered over the sea bottom on deeper parts of the continental shelf. Owning the rights to seabed resources became another source of disagreement, and conflicts arose between countries in the South China Sea, in the Aegean Sea and around the Falkland Islands near the southern tip of Argentina. The land beneath the sea began to look increasingly valuable.

At the same time, the cold war was flourishing, and heavily armed U.S. and Soviet naval fleets roamed the world, displaying their power to each other and to others. They made it clear that they should be able to go where they wished, that open sea routes had to remain open, that international straits could belong to no one. By the late 1960s, the international community understood that the growing conflicts needed diplomatic resolution before they got worse and made diplomacy more difficult. As well, in 1967 the disastrous breakup of an oil supertanker, the *Torrey Canyon*, on the south coast of Britain, gave everyone a scare about coastal pollution, increasing the urgency for international rules. A gradual consensus emerged, leading to yet another UN Conference on the Law

of the Sea, which brought all nations together once more to debate the ownership of coastal waters and their resources. An event of unprecedented scope, it
has changed the map of the world profoundly.

THE THIRD ATTEMPT SUCCEEDS, MORE OR LESS

Plans for the Third United Nations Conference on the Law of the Sea, UNC-
LOS III, actually began as soon as UNCLOS II failed. The conference began in
1974. In 1982, eight years and three U.S. presidents later, 159 nations and international agencies present at the conference signed the final document, called the
UN Convention on the Law of the Sea. Almost tragically, the United States, the
United Kingdom and Germany, active participants in the negotiations of the
previous decade, couldn't accept a critical part of the convention, which concerned deep-seabed mining, and they refused to sign.

To become binding international law, the convention then needed to be
ratified by the governments of sixty countries. Gradually countries ratified it,
at the rate of about six a year, but the emerging pattern couldn't have looked
more unworkable. Underdeveloped and developing countries saw the clear
advantages and protection that the convention gave them, and their governments ratified it. Even landlocked states found reason to ratify it. As the number approached sixty, however, only two developed countries had ratified the
Convention: Iceland and Yugoslavia. Yugoslavia has shattered since then, and
Iceland remains uniquely isolated. Nonetheless, in November 1993, Guyana
became the sixtieth country to ratify the convention, and twelve months later,
in November 1994, it became international law, twenty years after the formal
opening of the conference.

No one really believed that the new Law of the Sea would survive without
the backing of the developed countries, for those were the countries with the
power and resources to make the law stick or founder. Although they would
not ratify the convention because of their problems with the provisions about
deep-seabed mining, among other concerns, the developed countries still
accepted much of the rest of the convention. In 1976, the United States passed
its own Magnuson Act, establishing a 200-mile fisheries zone in order to protect and conserve its coastal resources; in 1986, it reauthorized the act, indicating which provisions of the UN convention it would comply with and which it
would not. The United Kingdom passed a series of laws during the 1980s,
establishing some of the critical provisions of the convention. Other developed
states took similar action. But as the years passed, despite the growing consensus, it seemed likely that the proposed Law of the Sea would be a colossal fail-

ure, with unofficial agreements eroding and unravelling, and countries once again going their unilateral and essentially greedy ways.

WHAT THE LAW OF THE SEA DOES

The UN Convention on the Law of the Sea is not exactly an exciting document to read, but it covers most of the problems countries may face in their interactions anywhere beyond the traditional 3-mile territorial limit. It established a 12-mile territorial sea for coastal nations, guaranteed passage of all ships through international straits, prohibited dumping of industrial waste on the continental shelf and considered matters related to military passage, pollution and mining. The most critical provision of the convention, however, recognized that each coastal country had a further qualified territory extending another 200 miles offshore. Called either an Exclusive Economic Zone (EEZ) or an Exclusive Fisheries Zone (EFZ), every country moved to implement it, even those who had refused to sign the document at the end of the conference, and even though it had not yet been ratified into law.

The convention gives each coastal country the rights to natural resources, along with other jurisdictional rights, throughout its EEZ. Other countries still have freedom of navigation and overflight by aircraft, key points for those with aircraft and tankers, as well as for navies and air forces. Since the primary motivation of the whole effort was for coastal countries to gain control of their own coastal fisheries and regulate or ban distant-water fleets, such limited jurisdiction over the EEZ seems to satisfy most of the participants. Even though the convention remained unratified by enough countries until 1993 for it to become international law, most acted as if this part of the convention were customary law: almost everyone, from the United States to the Pacific island countries, accepted it as common practice. International courts, including the International Court of Justice, applied provisions of the convention in resolving territorial disputes between neighbouring countries, again despite the fact that the convention as a whole was not yet international law. A surprising increase in harmony emerged, reflecting customary law.

WHO WINS AND WHO LOSES?

This common practice had an immense impact on every coastal country. Some countries became instant winners, on a huge scale; others gained modestly; and yet others, with extended distant-water fleets but short coastlines of their own, became instant losers. A small island country in the Pacific such as Kiribati or Fiji suddenly had an EEZ hundreds of times larger than its landmass. Distant islands belonging to continental countries also suddenly became invaluable, as each expanded to include a large piece of exclusive ocean. The United States, with Guam, the Marshall Islands, American Samoa and Hawaii, controlled much of the Pacific, along with the seas associated with Alaska and its other continental coastlines (Figure 7). Canada, with its own endless coastline, not only won some endless ocean to go with it, but some of that ocean contained the bountiful fishing banks around Newfoundland. Islands that extended a country's jurisdiction did have to be habitable, which has led to attempts at inhabiting some quite uninhabitable rocks or islets sticking out of the ocean.

Countries that lost include Japan, the one developed country most dependent on fish as a source of protein for its people. It gained plenty of ocean adjacent to its string of islands, but it lost unlimited access to the rest of the world's seas, where its distant-water fleets had worked over the preceding decades. And countries such as Poland and Germany, with hardly any coastline to speak of, can simply no longer consider themselves fishing nations. The fleets of the former Soviet Union have struggled to survive, and with the breakup of the Soviet empire, they are unlikely to recover. South Korea, however, is doing better than ever, at least in part because of its emergence as a developed country, able to sustain an expanding fleet. Some distant-water fleets have moved to other seas or to other regions where enforcement is less strict or where they can make tolerable arrangements with coastal countries. Others have retooled for working in fisheries in the expanded EEZ of their own country. Japan has been a good example of both, pulling its fleets out of U.S. and Canadian EEZs, negotiating fishing rights in the EEZs of Pacific island countries and retooling some of its fleets for fishing in the Japanese EEZ.

Obviously the EEZs of adjacent countries overlap, and resolving the resultant conflicts has challenged the mediation abilities of all involved as they try to draw fair boundary lines in the sea. The United States and Canada could not agree about who owned how much of Georges Bank, off Cape Cod. France owns a couple of islands in the Canadian Gulf of St. Lawrence and demanded a large part of the adjacent fishing banks. The eight European States with at least a claim to a piece of the North Sea have had to develop a most complex agreement on who can use how much of the available fish populations in that remarkably rich yet vulnerable sea. Similar complex arrangements have divided the Mediterranean, Caribbean and China Seas. The countries involved have resolved most of these conflicts peacefully, through negotiation or through the International Court of Justice. The odd loose cannon still exists, such as North Korea, really the last player still playing by its own secret and mysterious rules.

FIGURE 7

The Exclusive Economic Zones of the United States and Canada. Both Canada and the United States took control of very large exclusive zones, but the United States did particularly well because of its island possessions from the Aleutians to Hawaii and on into the South Pacific.

RESPONSIBILITIES INCREASE

This is nothing less than a global revolution of ocean ownership. When all the lines are drawn 200 miles offshore of all the world's coastlines, 36 per cent of the sea is enclosed, and with it 90 per cent of exploitable fish stocks. Whereas just several decades ago fleets could go anywhere, they now go only where they are invited, and they are invited fewer and fewer places. Coastal countries now have responsibilities that a few decades ago most would have considered pipe dreams. Whether they can carry the responsibilities is another question.

The new Law of the Sea allows each coastal country to manage its fisheries, setting the total amount of fish of any species that may be caught; to propose appropriate management and conservation programs; to promote optimal use of the fish resources, which often means allowing other countries to fish for any surplus in return for fishery-related benefits such as access fees. These are not easy responsibilities, and they remain full of the uncertainties that have pushed fish populations into decline in the days before EEZs existed. Who knows what the optimal use of a fish resource is? And access fees can be very tempting to those countries lacking the ability to overfish their own resources without outside help.

≈≈≈≈≈≈≈≈≈≈≈≈≈≈≈≈≈≈≈≈≈≈≈≈≈≈≈≈≈≈≈≈

When all the lines are drawn 200 miles offshore of all the world's coastlines, 36 per cent of the sea is enclosed, and with it 90 per cent of exploitable fish stocks.

≈≈≈≈≈≈≈≈≈≈≈≈≈≈≈≈≈≈≈≈≈≈≈≈≈≈≈≈≈≈≈≈

In any case, the result has been that countries have taken control of their own fisheries, up to 200 miles offshore. Despite the departure of many of the distant-water fleets, and certainly contrary to all expectations, the fish populations in most EEZs have continued to decline.

THE DEVELOPED NATIONS ARE RELUCTANT

It does seem paradoxical that so many countries have behaved as if the convention had established international law that all should adhere to yet at the same time refused to sign the convention when UNCLOS III ended in 1982 or in the years since have refused to consider it for ratification. Why haven't developed states ratified it, or why have they waited so long to ratify?

The main reason concerns seabed mining. Seabed mining is still really an endeavour of the future. No doubt the seabed is rich in oil deposits and mineable minerals, and not just the manganese nodules that litter its surface. Twenty years ago it looked as if the seabed would begin to be mined sooner rather than later. Now it looks as if it will happen later, decades from now at best, and the urgency of agreeing to the details of such exploitation has greatly diminished. At the close of the UN conference in 1982, however, mining still seemed possible, and the developed countries clearly could not accept the proposals. It seemed that the costs and risks of mining would be borne by the developed countries (those that could afford the excessive investment) but that the profits would be widely shared. It just wasn't clear if the developed nations could act or profit under such constraints; President Reagan refused to have the United States sign the convention in 1982, and the United Kingdom and Germany refused as well. Developed nations that did sign the convention in 1982 then declined to ratify it in the years that followed.

Without ratification by the developed countries, the Law of the Sea had little hope of success even as it approached its sixtieth ratification and in fact already seemed to be crumbling. By 1992, nineteen countries had set territorial limits of 20, 30, 35, 50 and even 200 miles instead of the 12 miles agreed to by the convention. With such creeping extension of territorial jurisdiction, it looked as if the whole thing could unravel. In addition, many countries ignored many provisions of the convention, adopting only those that were convenient. The developed countries had to find some way to consider ratifying the convention despite their misgivings about seabed mining, and they had to find it soon.

SEABED MINING IS RENEGOTIATED

Talks on the seabed issue began in 1983, almost immediately after the end of the Third UN Conference on the Law of the Sea, but they progressed poorly. Then the political tensions in the world eased with the end of the Cold War, President Reagan left office, and the urgency of agreeing about how to mine the seabed in the distant future seemed rather silly. Even though the countries that had ratified the convention were reluctant to compromise, most countries thought that it was unnecessary to attempt to finalize the regulations for seabed mining; they believed that the question should be postponed until such mining actually became economically viable. The consultations continued. Finally, in July 1994, the General Assembly adopted a new resolution concerning deep-seabed mining, with 121 voting for it, none against and 7 abstaining. Virtually all industrial states have since signed the 1994 Seabed Agreement, for it eliminates the constraints that so bothered them in the 1982 Convention. With such broad support, the obstacles to ratification by the industrial countries have evaporated. Another extraordinary step had been taken in the long process to make real an international law of the sea.

The role of the United States has, as always over the past century, been pivotal. Its refusal to sign or ratify the 1982 convention could have sunk the deal. Its endorsement of the 1994 Seabed Agreement means that it too will ratify the convention. It should have ratified it in 1995 but didn't, and it would have ratified it in 1996 if only Jesse Helms had let it out of his committee and if election-year politics hadn't interfered. Other countries continue to accuse the United States of excessive self-interest, but that apparently is the prerogative of a superpower, especially when it is the only one left on the stage. Other developed countries have ratified it, however—first Germany, Australia, Argentina and Italy and then, in 1996, France, New Zealand, Norway, Sweden and Ireland. By late 1996, 109 countries had ratified it, including India and China. The rest of Europe, the Russian Federation and Japan, all are likely to follow through and ratify the convention over the next year or two. Even Canada should soon sign, if it can only focus on something besides its own internal politics.

THE CHALLENGE CONTINUES

Coastal countries expected increases both in fish catches and in employment when the distant-water fleets left. Both occurred, but they didn't last long. In most places heavy fishing pressure continued, a result of open access to all coastal fishers and management policies that didn't work. As a result of misreporting and other cheating by fishers, continued ignorance of the true underlying biological complexity by biologists, unexpected recruitment failures of the fish and unpredicted environmental changes, successful management remained as elusive as ever. The closing of major cod, groundfish and salmon fisheries in North America in the early and mid-1990s—the most devastating step a government can take—emphasizes just how total the failure of management there has been, with no foreign fleets to blame except those still fishing in international waters, beyond the 200-mile limit.

Still, the UN has given us the Law of the Sea. Most of the countries on this planet have agreed to abide by its provisions, no matter how much they disagree about everything else. It has been forced on all of us by our conflict over a critical and dwindling source of protein. Everyone recognized that we had no choice but to change what we were doing. The fish have continued to decline despite the changes in the laws, but this certainly does not mean that the law is badly flawed. The law provides a framework for action; it identifies who has what responsibility for protecting the fish populations from decline. It radically reduces conflicts between countries, though it cannot influence the conflicts that remain between the various constituencies within each country. As flaws or limitations are found—such as the difficulties in dealing with deep-seabed mining, management of highly migratory species and straddling stocks, marine mammal destruction by drift nets and other gear, and bycatch wastefulness—further new agreements are emerging. We have a vehicle to help us manage what we have. We are learning that the responsibility that comes with the vehicle is complicated and considerable.

PREDICTING THE UNPREDICTABLE

While it is true that the statistics of the world's fisheries are better now than they have ever been, it is also true that they are still incomplete and riddled with guesses, inadvertent errors, omissions, and even, perhaps, perjuries.

Peter Larkin

AN EPITAPH FOR THE CONCEPT
OF MAXIMUM SUSTAINED YIELD

"It ain't easy counting fish. It ain't easy and it never will be."

Fisheries biologist, quoted
by A. C. Finlayson
FISHING FOR TRUTH

Pity the fisheries biologists. Their job is to estimate the number of fish in a stock that should be safe to catch. They can't see the fish, yet they are somehow expected to figure out how many there are, what sizes they are and how many can be caught without diminishing next year's catch. Fisheries biologists work with mathematical models based on assumptions that they know could be wrong, for many features, such as growth, reproduction and mortality rates, even in species that have been fished for centuries, may be poorly known. Fisheries biologists depend on counting techniques that they know are anything but perfect and rely on information from fishers reporting their catch, knowing that they may be lying, or misreporting, as the euphemism goes. Fisheries biologists know that the regulations proposed to enforce their estimates will be broken in most imaginative ways by the fishers who believe them to be intrusive. And they are all too aware of the impact of unexpected, unpredictable environmental events, such as shifting sea currents or the onset of an El Niño, that can radically affect reproductive success and the future size of the stocks in ways that can be only guessed at.

As scientists, as ecologists, fisheries biologists have also long since learned to live with uncertainty and to accept the fact that their best estimate of stock size even at the best of times is still likely to be within 30 per cent, plus or minus, of the real stock size. Through long experience they know that both

≈≈≈≈≈≈≈≈≈≈≈≈≈≈≈≈≈≈≈≈≈≈≈≈≈≈≈≈≈≈≈≈

So pity the fisheries biologists. They can't be certain, and their best estimates will likely be misunderstood, misused and perhaps abused.

≈≈≈≈≈≈≈≈≈≈≈≈≈≈≈≈≈≈≈≈≈≈≈≈≈≈≈≈≈≈≈≈

fishers and politicians have little patience with such uncertainty. As a Canadian government scientist, Brian Morrissey, said on behalf of fisheries biologists, "Well, there you're drawing a firm line with a very unsteady hand. There is an expectation of certainty. And we have become the focus for frustration and unhappiness when we can't provide certainty." The biologists know, in fact, that whatever their estimates may be, the highest estimate of the stock size that they offer will be considered the one to go with. Moreover, managers and politicians may ignore the numbers because they are more concerned about the local employment of the fishers. Virtually every politician knows that to take away someone's job is to also lose that person's vote.

So pity the fisheries biologists. They can't be certain, and their best estimates will likely be misunderstood, misused and perhaps abused. They would probably like to catch all the fish, count them and say, there, that's how many there are, and for once in their lives be certain of their numbers.

Fisheries biologists are, nonetheless, absolutely essential to the fishery. No matter what management scheme a community, country or group of countries uses, it depends on knowing what the total allowable catch of a particular stock of fish should be. The total allowable catch, enshrined in the fisheries literature as TAC, usually indicates the most fish that can be harvested without reducing the size of next year's stock of reproducing individuals; it supposedly allows for sustained fishing of the stock into the future. The total allowable catch proposed by the fisheries biologist can be accepted, exceeded or ignored; it can even be wrong. It usually varies from year to year as biologists change their estimates; it can even change within a fishing season if the biologists have enough information and bureaucratic backing to make a change. Despite the uncertainty, despite the inaccuracy and abuse, a fishery has no future without catch restrictions that can be proposed and adjusted when needed. And only the much maligned fisheries biologists can do the job.

To make their estimates, they need to know as much as they can about the life history of the fish concerned. When and where does it breed? Where does it spend its time as a juvenile? At what size or age does it become recruited into the adult, fishable population? How old is it when it becomes sexually mature, and how big is it then? How fast does it grow after that? How many eggs does a female produce when it spawns for the first time? How long does it continue to reproduce? How does its mortality rate change as it grows from juvenile to young adult to older adult? How sensitive is it to environmental fluctuations in temperature and abundance of food? What does it eat, and what eats it? What other species compete with it for the same food? When fisheries biologists can't answer these questions, and that can happen often, they have to guess and then guess at how accurate their guess is likely to be.

RECRUITMENT OF JUVENILES

Fisheries biologists are especially concerned about the recruitment of juveniles into the adult population. After remaining in the plankton as larvae and then perhaps in some nursery habitat as young fish, juveniles eventually join the adults and are said to have been recruited into the fishable population. Fisheries biologists have put a great deal of effort into trying to understand what influences the numbers of juveniles that are recruited into the fishery each year, for only then can they predict how large the fishable population is likely to be and so advise the managers and everyone else about how large the total allowable catch for the next year or two should be. Recruitment, though, varies more than growth rates do and is a topic of much frustration. How many hatched young survive their planktonic life? How many find a suitable nursery habitat or school? How sensitive are they to yearly shifts in currents and temperatures? Why do the numbers that are recruited vary by orders of magnitude from year to year? Questions beget questions. Scientists live with uncertainty, but nobody really likes it.

UNCERTAIN ESTIMATES

Although biologists undertake quite complex stock assessments for many fisheries, their estimates of stock size are often greatly influenced by observations of the rate at which the fish are caught. One of the ways that biologists estimate how many fish are in a population is by evaluating what fishers bring to shore. The more fish that are brought to shore per trip, the larger the fish population is estimated to be. This method should work reasonably well provided that the means the fishers use to search for fish don't change, but of course they do. To find a school of fish, fishers usually search with sophisticated echo sounders and sonars and for pelagic species may even use spotter aircraft. With experience they can not only detect a school by its echo but also get a good idea of what species it is, how big the school is and even what size of fish it includes. Over the past few decades, fishers have become increasingly able to find exactly what they want to catch. And an interesting problem emerges. If fishers improve their fishing ability, catching more fish for less effort, the fisheries biologists need to know about it. Otherwise the fisheries biologists will estimate that the population is considerably greater than it really is. They may then allow a higher rate of fishing to continue than the real population of fish can sustain. The population can crash before anyone realizes it is even in decline.

This is, in part, what happened to the huge Norwegian herring stocks during the 1960s. Although in 1956 more than 1.5 million tonnes of the herring were caught, by 1971 the harvest had shrunk to an abysmal 30 000 tonnes. The crash occurred for a variety of reasons—that is true of almost every stock decline—but certainly a major reason was that during this period fishers were able to locate the schools of herring increasingly easily, using the improved techniques of echo sounding. They were able to keep catch rates high even during the decline of the stock, and as a result, the stock appeared to fisheries biologists to be declining much more slowly than it really was.

THE COMPLEXITY OF COMMUNITIES

When fishers harvest one species, the abundance of another species almost always changes. Because cod eat capelin, a large capelin fishery on the east coast of North America would have devastated the cod stocks if we hadn't found other ways to devastate them. In the Antarctic, as a result of the overhunting of the great krill-eating baleen whales, populations of pelagic fish, seals and seabirds have increased and smaller whale species, such as the minke, have become much more numerous. In other places, fishers have decided that their fish stocks are declining in part because other predators are too abundant. Cod fishers believe that harp seals eat the cod; Maine lobstermen think that harbor seals interfere with the lobsters; abalone fishers of the Pacific coast blame the resurgence of sea otters for the decline of their harvest. In all these cases, the fishers wish to have the numbers of predators competing with them reduced, either through a bounty system, by culling or perhaps through the development or extension of a commercial hunt. Because of the protection given marine mammals by the U.S. Marine Mammal Protection Act and the resistance of potential markets to any trade in marine mammal products, the fishers face many obstacles. Right or wrong, though, their concerns emphasize how important it is to recognize the role other species play in influencing stock size.

Unfortunately, biologists are often ignorant of the real complexity of the community. They know only a little of what truly occurs. They are most familiar with shallow, near shore communities, in areas most accessible to exploration. Farther offshore, or in more remote areas, they know increasingly less, sometimes enough to be tantalizing, never enough to let them announce with certainty how the community works. Even with species that are fished intensively, such as herring and tuna, and that have been subjected to a vast amount of research, they still cannot answer questions about how discrete the stocks really are and how far migrations actually occur, let alone the much more difficult questions, such as those concerning the intensity of species interactions and how they may affect the size of the population that fishers may wish to harvest.

The complexity is also a result of the changing feeding habits of growing fish. For instance, as larvae in the plankton, cod eat copepods and euphausiids; when they hit the bottom substrate as juveniles, they eat worms and prawns; as they grow larger, they eat crabs and mollusks; and finally they eat fish such as capelin or juvenile cod if they are available. Such shifts in feeding preferences are certainly typical of most fish species.

Tropical communities offer even greater challenges. Far more species live there, and far fewer individuals of each species exist. The same general rules of competition and predation no doubt occur, but they are likely to result in far more complex interactions. Systems set up to manage the relatively small number of species that dominate a temperate region community of fish may have little relevance to a diverse community in the tropics.

UNPREDICTABLE ENVIRONMENTS

Fish are also sensitive to physical changes in their environment in ways that probably haven't even been considered yet. They are certainly very sensitive to temperature changes. Unexpected shifts in temperature of just a few degrees may be enough to change a life history, cause failure of those born in a particular year to grow successfully, shift the prey and predator relationships or cause the population to move somewhere else, seeking the appropriate temperature. Ocean currents also shift from year to year and season to season, and migrating species often follow the currents. Oceanographers make estimates about future currents and temperatures based on patterns of the past, though they are all too aware of the limitations that such forecasting involves. And sizes of fish populations bounce around wildly, seemingly almost randomly, as the fish react to changes in their environments.

The smaller pelagic fish such as herring, sardines and anchovies are especially sensitive to such changes and are likely to oscillate widely in population size, irrespective of human fishing. Off the California coast, in the California Current, we have in this century seen the rise and crash of the California sardine, followed by a rapid increase in the size of northern anchovy populations. The sardine collapse, which was so dramatic, is still the subject of debate. Did overfishing alone cause it? Did a change in the environment or some interaction with the anchovies also contribute to the collapse? The historical record, based on fish scales found in the sediments off the California coast, suggests that the numbers of these two species fluctuated for many centuries before human fishers existed, and these fluctuations seem to be correlated with temperature changes over that period. Identifying historical patterns is difficult, though, for establishing past events is far trickier than describing current ones.

To predict what a fish stock will do depends on being able to predict temperatures and currents, and making these predictions is like trying to predict the weather: there is simply no way of knowing what the season-long temperatures are going to be or whether the currents will shift a little. With shifts in temperature come shifts in abundance of food, shifts in growth rates, shifts in metabolism, shifts in community structure and increasing uncertainty in the predictions.

Some predictions, however, are possible no matter what. Scientists can predict that another El Niño will occur within a window of several years, and they can predict the range of effects it will have. But they are unable to predict how long it may last or how extensive it may be. If its effects are light, water temperatures along the west coast of the United States may not increase enough to have an obvious impact on inshore fisheries. If its effects are severe, like those of the El Niño that occurred in 1982–83, it may persist and raise the sea temperatures too much for the small pelagic fish to remain, and a whole cascade of effects may occur: yellowfin tuna may leave coastal waters, seabirds may not lay eggs, and changes in weather that are somehow connected may occur around the planet, ranging from winter rainstorms and flooding in California to a warm winter in Ontario to intense monsoons in the Indian Ocean.

The more common that unpredictable events such as these turn out to be, the more we are forced to admit the role that chance must play in affecting the sizes of fish populations. If climatic events are unpredictable, and if they play a reasonable role in determining recruitment of juveniles, growth, mortality or breeding success in a fish population, then no predictive model will ever be correct for long. More likely it will be correct by chance—hardly what anyone wants to hear.

COMBINED UNPREDICTABILITY

Where does this leave us? Recruitment of juveniles into the adult population varies, even under stable conditions, and predictions of the number of juveniles that will be recruited are rarely accurate. Unpredictable environmental changes, particularly in sea temperature, may affect stock size. Changes in food and predators may also affect stock size. The result is uncertainty that will not disappear, no matter how hard the modellers model. To deny the uncertainty would be absurd, but it still provokes resistance and argument from politicians and fishers.

Talented biologists and statisticians are trying to predict the size of various fish stocks, but they simply cannot predict the unpredictable. The problem is too complex, and too many assumptions about all aspects of the fishery have to be made. There is no alternative to great uncertainty. We might as well learn to live with it.

MAKING ESTIMATES ANYWAY

Despite the problems and uncertainty, estimates of stock sizes must be made, or we will manage fisheries in the worst possible way, waiting until they collapse, then closing them down completely and hoping they recover. Once again the familiar cases of Atlantic cod, other Atlantic groundfish, North Sea herring, and parts of the Pacific and Atlantic salmon fisheries come to mind, along with other fisheries that have collapsed around the world over the past few decades.

Since the need to manage fisheries emerged early in this century, fish have been managed one stock at a time, without regard to changes in its prey, predators and competitors. This approach isn't as misguided as it might sound. Because we know so little about these other factors, it has been as reasonable to ignore them as it would have been to try to make estimates about them.

For the past decades, fisheries management in most parts of the world has been guided by the principle of maximum sustainable yield (usually referred to as MSY), the maximum number of fish that can be harvested from a fish stock, year after year, without driving it into decline. A few species have survived this policy reasonably well, such as lobsters in the Gulf of Maine and some of the Atlantic herring stocks, but for the most part it has driven fish stocks to dangerously low levels. The maximum sustainable yield for a particular stock depends on the age that individuals are recruited into the harvestable population, their subsequent growth rate and natural mortality, and the reproductive success of each year class (all those born in a particular year), and it assumes stability of environmental conditions over the years.

The idea is that a stock may be fished to the point where fishing and natural mortality are balanced by recruitment of juveniles and the population size stays constant. Inevitably, however, as a fishery develops, the larger fish are caught first, and the average size of fish in the population declines. As time passes, the fish that spawn are more likely to be spawning for the first time, destined to be caught before they have a chance to spawn again. Sometimes a year class of first-time spawners fails to show up and become recruited into the harvestable stock. This phenomenon, called recruitment failure, may occur for environmental reasons. Perhaps changes in water temperature or food supply during the fish's early years, or their first year, reduced their numbers. Fisheries biologists try to stay aware of such natural declines and adjust the maximum sustainable yield to accommodate them. But they have to know a lot about the stock at all times, requiring time, funding, hard work and honest fishers. Quick response by the biologists and managers may protect the stock from a sudden decline, but far too often the decline occurs before anyone has noticed the recruitment failure or before managers have taken any action on warnings provided by the biologists. Recovery of a stock then becomes difficult without a massive and certainly unpopular decrease in fishing.

≈≈≈≈≈≈≈≈≈≈≈≈≈≈≈≈≈≈≈≈≈≈≈≈≈≈≈≈≈≈≈

*The past decades have taught us that no maximum
sustainable yield is really sustainable.*

≈≈≈≈≈≈≈≈≈≈≈≈≈≈≈≈≈≈≈≈≈≈≈≈≈≈≈≈≈≈≈

A stock can also decline or crash because the fish are caught before they get a chance to breed for even their first time. Everyone knows this is about the most short-sighted error that could occur in a fishery, and yet a fishery is often discovered and developed before the biology of the species involved is sufficiently understood and the minimum size at which the individuals first breed is identified.

The past decades have taught us that no maximum sustainable yield is really sustainable. At some point an unexpected change in sea temperature, food supply or number of predators will cause recruitment failure. The maximum sustainable yield turns out not be sustainable after all, and the stock will decline. Less productive stocks will disappear under the fishing pressure that other stocks still tolerate. As a management tool, maximum sustainable yield has certainly been far better than no management, reducing the fishing pressure in many fisheries. But it has been inadequate. It has set fishing limits too high and usually failed to enforce whatever limits it did set. Unable to compensate for the unpredictability of fish, it has also ignored the other confounding effects of human economic, social and political concerns.

Recognizing that a management system has severe limitations is one thing. Finding better alternatives is another. There has, for instance, been some enthusiasm for something called optimal sustainable yield (usually referred to as OSY), which incorporates biological, economic, social and political concerns into a plan designed to bring maximum benefit to society from the fish stocks while taking into account the effects that harvesting may have on other species. The problem with this policy is that it has to deal not only with unpredictable fish stocks but also with equally unpredictable and hard-to-manage humans. It is certainly an improvement over management by maximum sustainable yield in its recognition of some of the interactions between the various species. Thus, the harvest levels that are set are lower and the fish stocks ought to have a greater chance of survival. But optimal sustainable yield still depends on an understanding of the underlying biology of the fish, which is characterized by uncertainty and ignorance. Because it also depends on even more uncertain economic and social predictions and assumptions, it remains very difficult to implement. Melding the various concerns to achieve some optimum level of fishing will always be very difficult, for as the fisheries biologist Peter Larkin has further commented, "Your optimum is unlikely to be the same as mine."

Maximum sustainable yield works best where single species are abundant and can be captured without harvesting, intentionally or otherwise, other species. But how do biologists advise tropical fisheries, where few species have that kind of abundance and fish communities are made up of far more species? How do biologists advise trawlers, who indiscriminately drag up everything in the way of their trawls, throwing back dead everything they don't want or are not licensed to keep?

Despite the flaws that everyone seems to recognize, despite the attacks the management system has received from fisheries biologists themselves, maximum sustainable yield has survived as a management tool. Acknowledging all the other influences that should be included has made many other models hopelessly complex, impossible for all but their creators, statisticians all, to understand. Managers, fishers, politicians and many biologists find them simply unusable—possibly accurate, who knows—but of no real practical value. Most fish are still managed one species at a time; biologists know each species interacts with other species but hope that those interactions largely cancel each other out. The human side of the equation gets more complicated, not less, as we learn more about the cultural traditions of fishing communities and the resistance of fishers to change or loss of their way of life.

The only management system mentioned in the 1982 UN Law of the Sea was maximum sustainable yield. A number of modifications and alternatives have been proposed over the past decade, ones that would reduce the fishing level to some point below maximum sustainable yield by establishing a different reference point. One that has been adopted widely in both Canada and the United States is known as the Fo.1 rule. It refers to the level of fishing where adding one more boat to the fishery would result in increasing the total catch by only 10 per cent as much as the very first boat in the fishery would have caught by itself when it first started to fish. This is an attractive model because it takes into consideration the economics of the fishery without the difficulty of searching for the optimal sustainable yield, and it is more conservative than the maximum sustainable yield, providing the fishery with a wider margin of safety. Nonetheless, all the models remain based on uncertainty, rely on unlikely honest reporting by fishers and involve statistical manipulations that nonspecialists will often not understand. Fisheries biologists have to convince too many people that one particular model is better than others. Proposals to kill maximum sustainable yield as a management tool began to surface in the mid 1970s, and the alternative, more conservative reference points have been tested, for instance in the Northwest Atlantic fisheries. Since stocks there continued to decline anyway—partly because the reference points have often been ignored—confidence in the new models is not particularly great. Around the world, maximum sustainable yield lives while biologists seek new ways to protect the fish stocks.

MULTISPECIES MANAGEMENT AND LARGE MARINE ECOSYSTEMS

So we have an interesting situation. Single-species management is usually ineffective, and since it is based on inadequate data, it is often wrong. But trying to manage a bunch of interacting species is just too complicated. Moreover, in multispecies management the uncertainty is compounded. For these reasons, it is a very tough sell.

Even so, multispecies management remains attractive, if only because it has to be closer to the truth than single-species management. Once again, though, the underlying theory has evolved in cold-water habitats, where the number of interacting species is relatively small. It is much more difficult to model interactions in the tropics, where far fewer individuals of each species exist but interact with far more species, both competitors and predators.

Multispecies management may still be a dream, but it is a worthy dream. Like any management system, it has to go through the familiar steps of planning, data gathering, implementation, and then feedback and adjustment before fisheries scientists will know whether it is a viable approach or not. Mostly it is in the planning stage, with some data available from some regions of the world and very little from others.

At least enough is known to identify the regions that might be possible to consider as whole units. Forty-nine of these regions, called Large Marine Ecosystems, have been identified, covering the coastal waters of the world. Some occur over shallow areas of the shelf, where there is much vertical mixing of nutrients in the water and productivity is high. The U.S. Northeast continental shelf is an example, as are the East and West Greenland shelves and the Yellow Sea. Other regions are associated with particular coastal ocean currents that also result in upwelling of nutrients and high productivity as they are deflected away from the coast. The Humboldt Current, along the west coast of South America, and the California Current are examples of such productive currents. Still other regions may be semi-enclosed seas, such as the Baltic Sea and the Mediterranean Sea.

The proposed Large Marine Ecosystems vary greatly in size. The smallest is the Faroe Island plateau, about 200 000 square kilometres (77 000 square miles) lying midway between Britain and Iceland (Figure 8). The other extreme is the South China Sea, embracing 3 million square kilometres (1.16 million square miles). The seaward boundary of these ecosystems occurs where the fish biomass abruptly drops off, usually at the edge of the shelf. The idea is that each of these ecosystems is an independent unit, with its own characteristic species and its own human traditions of fishing activities, as well as human-provoked stresses such as pollution and coastal habitat loss.

Interest in managing Large Marine Ecosystems comes from what we have seen happen when overfishing occurs and an entire ecosystem becomes much less commercially valuable. For instance, as Georges Bank off Cape Cod has been stripped of its valuable groundfish, such as cod and haddock, the number of less valuable species, such as skates, spiny dogfish and sand eels, has exploded; the total biomass may remain much the same, but the species of fish are quite different. The same thing happened several decades ago in the North Sea, where cod, haddock and plaice (another flatfish) were overfished and replaced by less valued Norway pout, sprat and sand eels. Getting the Georges Bank ecosystem back to its original state may be quite difficult, for the skates and dogfish prey on juvenile cod, haddock and flounder. Must we somehow create enthusiasm for a large-scale fishery for the skates and dogfish and

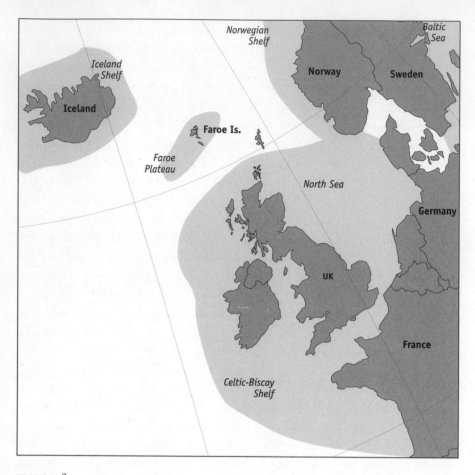

FIGURE 8

Examples of Large Marine Ecosystems. *Six Large Marine Ecosystems have been identified in the Northeast Atlantic. Although they range greatly in size, they have the potential to be managed as discrete units.*

thereby reduce their numbers while we continue to protect the groundfish we far prefer from our fleets? Probably so.

An ecosystem, like any of the Large Marine Ecosystems, may undergo profound change not only in response to highly selective fishing preferences but also in response to climate changes. For instance, in the Northeast Pacific, the abundance of zooplankton appears to change over years and decades, influenced by how strong the winter winds are in the northern Gulf of Alaska. When the winds are strong, the Subarctic Current flowing east across the Pacific speeds up, and zooplankton become more abundant. When the Subarctic Current approaches the coast of North America, it splits into the Alaska Current, flowing north, and the California Current, flowing south. If the surface winds drive more of the surface water and plankton to the north, as they do at present, salmon in the coastal waters of Alaska have ample food, and populations thrive there. At the same time, less of the plankton-rich surface water flows south in the California Current. Coupled with heavy fishing pressure and destruction of breeding habitats, a decreased food supply in recent years has caused salmon stocks in the California Current to crash along with sardine and anchovy populations. When the wind systems change, however, and more productive waters flow south instead of north along the coast, the pattern should change and Alaskan stocks should decline while stocks from Washington to California should increase. Sometime in the coming decades, we'll probably have a chance to see if these predictions come true.

Examples such as these emphasize just how important it is to take into account a whole ecosystem, made up of many interacting species and dependent on climatic events that may affect their food supplies, growth rates and mortality. If we ignore these complexities, we are probably destined to repeat the experiences of the Northeast Atlantic and the North Sea.

There are many obstacles to managing at this scale. Not the least is that most of the forty-nine Large Marine Ecosytems are shared by two or more coastal nations. Fourteen are each contained in the Exclusive Economic Zone of just one nation—for example, the New Zealand shelf, the Iceland shelf and the various shelf regions along the east coast of North America and along the coasts of Greenland. Six others are shared by just two countries each, including the California Current Marine Ecosystem (shared by the United States and Mexico) and the Gulf of Alaska Marine Ecosystem (shared by the United States and Canada). But the Caribbean Marine Ecosystem is shared by thirty-eight countries, the Mediterranean by eighteen, the South China Sea by ten, the Persian Gulf by eight. In some of these, cooperative management of ocean resources is virtually hopeless.

Despite political realities, some limited Large Marine Ecosystem management is under way. Seventeen of the eighteen nations bordering the Mediterranean are planning the management of that very vulnerable sea (Albania is the holdout); the Great Barrier Reef, under the control of just Australia, may be protected from overfishing and pollution now that it is thought of and managed as one large ecosystem; Namibia and South Africa are planning ways to protect the Benguela Current Ecosystem from overfishing and inappropriate fishing; in the Yellow Sea Marine Ecosystem, China has introduced shrimp to compensate for the decrease in fish; and China and South Korea are negotiating ways to manage the whole Yellow Sea ecosystem (North Korea, like Albania, remains uninvolved in international agreements).

Given the grim history of fisheries, ecosystem management is probably the way we have to go. To manage Large Marine Ecosystems, however, fisheries biologists will need more accurate biological information, they will need to deduce what they can about historical changes associated with climate change, and their current crop of sophisticated statistical models will have to be tested with care. The challenges and the risks are huge, for uncertainty and ignorance about the biological interactions increase with the size of the ecosystem in question. Managing Large Marine Ecosystems may seem like a nightmare to fisheries biologists who now find single-species management already very difficult. Errors in management will affect many species and many fishers, not just a single species and those who fish for it. A compromise is to manage fisheries now as much as possible in light of multispecies and ecosystem considerations, and not attempt the impossible.

THE PRECAUTIONARY PRINCIPLE

For all types of management—maximum sustainable yield, optimal sustainable yield and whole-ecosystem management—ignorance of the biology of the species of commercial interest and uncertainty about what influences the sizes of their populations remain discouraging obstacles. And yet somehow decisions must and will be made about how to manage both species and ecosystems.

≈≈≈≈≈≈≈≈≈≈≈≈≈≈≈≈≈≈≈≈≈≈≈≈≈≈≈≈≈≈

Where there is significant risk of damage to the environment, users must take precautionary action to limit the potential risk of damage even where scientific evidence is inconclusive.

≈≈≈≈≈≈≈≈≈≈≈≈≈≈≈≈≈≈≈≈≈≈≈≈≈≈≈≈≈≈

There is growing interest in the precautionary principle among environmentalists around the world. This principle states that where there is significant risk of damage to the environment, users must take precautionary action to limit the potential risk of damage even where scientific evidence is inconclusive. This action involves risk prevention, cost effectiveness, ethical responsibility for maintaining the integrity of natural systems and recognition of the fallibility of human understanding. The precautionary principle presumes that when humans interfere with natural ecosystems mistakes can be made, yet it allows policy formulation in the face of uncertainty. It recognizes that uncertainty is unavoidable but that uncertainty should not be used as an excuse to ignore protection measures. Action should be anticipatory rather than defensive, and the onus should be on those who propose actions that might be harmful. The precautionary principle has now been endorsed repeatedly; it is part of the Rio Declaration on Environment and Development of 1992: "Where there are threats of serious or irreversible damage, lack of full scientific certainty shall not be used as reason for postponing cost-effective measures to prevent environmental degradation."

The precautionary principle is a new idea. Its wording is vague, and it is just beginning to be implemented in fisheries such as the Atlantic herring fishery. But it acknowledges uncertainty in a way that is new, and its potential application to fisheries management is considerable. There are growing proposals on how it can be made workable—for instance, by forcing users to pay assurance bonds up front, getting them back only when it is clear that no damage to the environment or resource has occurred.

Exciting though the precautionary principle is as a way to protect our resources while we exploit them, it is of limited use. Its intent is to hold the fort until scientists understand more and can reduce the uncertainty. There is, in fact, no reason to expect the uncertainty to decrease, but adopting the precautionary principle would at least give the fisheries and the ecosystems a greater chance of long-term survival.

CHAPTER 5

BREAKING THE RULES

"Every fish counts and we are charged with protecting them."

> National Marine Fisheries
> Service officer, quoted by
> Brad Matsen, "Law and Order"
> NATIONAL FISHERMAN

"The enforcement people come on board loaded for battle, toting guns. It makes people feel uncomfortable and resentful."

> Longline fisher in the
> North Pacific, quoted by
> Brad Matsen, "Law and Order"
> NATIONAL FISHERMAN

THE NEED TO CHEAT

Fish may be unpredictable and therefore difficult to manage, but humans may be even more difficult to manage. Fishers understandably have little faith in fisheries regulations, particularly when they hear the uncertain predictions of the biologists. No fisher will willingly stop fishing for fish that are clearly declining if other fishers keep fishing. No fisher will obey regulations if the regulations appear to be stupid or if they are unlikely to be enforced or if the penalties are worth the risk. Fishers, like most other people, don't like to be managed at all. They may like it even less than most of us, for freedom from bureaucracy and from the constraints of a 9-to-5 job is at least one of the factors that drive many to the sea to fish to start with. Is there a fisher anywhere who hasn't broken regulations? Probably not. As a result, it is all the more difficult to manage a fishery.

Nobody likes being constrained by rules, even in cultures that are accustomed to the intrusion of rules into daily life. The more rules there are, the more likely it is that they will not be equitable, no matter how fair they are intended to be. As a fish population begins to decline, as the fishing pressure on it increases, regulations to protect it become increasingly essential, more numerous, more constraining and less fair to more people. It doesn't matter whether the regulation comes from the government or from the local village or cooperative, rules are rules.

≈≈≈≈≈≈≈≈≈≈≈≈≈≈≈≈≈≈≈≈≈≈≈≈≈≈≈≈≈≈≈

Is there a fisher anywhere who hasn't broken regulations? Probably not.

≈≈≈≈≈≈≈≈≈≈≈≈≈≈≈≈≈≈≈≈≈≈≈≈≈≈≈≈≈≈≈

As rules proliferate, cheating can be an excellent strategy for survival. A good cheater gets the benefits without incurring all of the costs—a free lunch. The cost is in getting caught, and fishers weigh the seriousness of the penalty of getting caught against the rewards of escaping detection. We may cheat on our taxes, on our adherence to traffic regulations, on our diets. We may cheat as recreational fishers, poaching or exceeding limits when we can get away with it. We expect lawyers and accountants to help us find ways around the laws. We may bribe our way out of expensive situations or for access to contracts or to persuade people of influence to assist us. We know the world works this way, though we seem to be offended by cheating and graft and corruption whenever it surfaces. Cheating is as deeply ingrained in us as an option for action as any of our other traits; it comes with intelligence and imagination. To be human is to try to get away with something, to break the rules.

So we may cheat out of frustration and anger with the rules that constrict us, finding them to be intolerable, unacceptable, placed in our way by people who are in authority but who are ignorant of the reality of our lives and problems. We may cheat because we are greedy for the rewards that success may bring us. But there is more to it than that. We also cheat because of the risk. There is a sense of challenge, of excitement in getting away with it.

Nowhere is cheating more likely or tempting than in a highly regulated fishery. Boat skippers have resisted almost every regulation thrown at them, ignored as many as they have dared and circumvented others. Where the fishing season has been restricted to a certain number of days, skippers may increase the size of their vessels or nets. If a vessel cannot exceed a certain length, it can be made to go faster with a more powerful engine. If nets have to have a certain mesh size, a skipper may line it with a second net that effectively reduces the mesh size and catches more abundant smaller fish. When an inspector boards the vessel, a skipper may produce the book kept for inspectors, keeping hidden the book of actual captures. When unloading their catch on shore, skippers may under-report their catch by as much as they think they can get away with. When they catch fish of a size or species that the regulations forbid, they may consider selling them on the black market to willing buyers onshore. When two adjacent coastal countries, such as the United States and Canada, argue over where the new ocean boundary between them should lie,

≈≈≈≈≈≈≈≈≈≈≈≈≈≈≈≈≈≈≈≈≈≈≈≈≈≈≈≈≈≈

Nowhere is cheating more likely or tempting than in a highly regulated fishery.

≈≈≈≈≈≈≈≈≈≈≈≈≈≈≈≈≈≈≈≈≈≈≈≈≈≈≈≈≈≈

skippers may fish both sides knowing nothing will happen to them until the two countries finally agree on the boundary. Even when the boundary is agreed upon, they can cross it anyway, expecting to escape detection or to outrun a patrol boat that might turn up on radar. They can also fish at night, when detecting them becomes even more difficult.

ENFORCEMENT OF REGULATIONS

Regulations are only as good as the ability to enforce them, and enforcement is difficult. Patrolling coastal waters that extend offshore for 200 miles, whether by patrol boats or aircraft, is expensive. If the EEZ is very large, or if the coastal country has few resources, detection of cheating can be almost impossible. Putting observers on board fishing vessels to monitor the catch is also time-consuming and expensive and is hardly considered a friendly act by the fishers. Governments must make a significant investment in a fishery to cover the cost of enforcement, a cost the fishers certainly don't want to bear but increasingly may have to. Some of the regulations can now more easily be enforced with the new technology that allows satellites to monitor where every vessel is fishing, another intrusion fishers are displeased with.

Enforcement is effective only if fishers are persuaded that they are relatively likely to get caught, that if they are caught they will be convicted and that if they are convicted the penalty will be severe. Only rarely are all these criteria met. Even when skippers are caught in foreign waters and their vessels are detained, they have to believe they may not get their vessels back or that the fine will be catastrophic; if they only risk losing the value of what they may have caught illegally, or if the fine is small, they probably consider the risk worth taking. Even in their own coastal waters the likelihood that they will be detected and convicted and the size of the penalty determine how far fishers will go in testing, bending and breaking regulations.

For this reason, penalties are likely to increase. Patrol boats of many coastal countries are now armed or carry armed boarding parties to enforce fisheries regulations. Iceland, Norway, Canada, France, the United States, New Zealand and Australia are all prepared to use force. Fishing vessels are not likely to ignore patrol boats or fishery officers, as Spanish vessels did in 1986, when they

≈≈≈≈≈≈≈≈≈≈≈≈≈≈≈≈≈≈≈≈≈≈≈≈≈≈≈≈≈≈≈≈≈

Enforcement is effective only if fishers are persuaded that they are relatively likely to get caught, that if they are caught they will be convicted and that if they are convicted the penalty will be severe.

≈≈≈≈≈≈≈≈≈≈≈≈≈≈≈≈≈≈≈≈≈≈≈≈≈≈≈≈≈≈≈≈≈

transported Canadian fisheries officials halfway back across the Atlantic from the Grand Banks before releasing them. Fishers who have been caught face increasingly large fines, and they may lose their catch, their fishing gear and valuable fishing time. They may also face losing their licences for periods of time related to the extent of their offence. Where management is community based, they may face unbearable social ostracism.

Still, the cost of enforcement remains a burden for a coastal country, and everyone assumes that no matter how extensive the surveillance, some fishers will continue to fish illegally and avoid detection. Economists have proposed a variety of contradictory suggestions, but one model that is attracting interest proposes that surveillance could be cut back, provided that conviction rates and penalties remain high.

GEAR WARS

Fish are hunted with seine nets, which encircle them; gillnets, which are hung in the water and entrap the fish by their gills; longlines bearing baited hooks; trawls, which drag nets through the water; and a great diversity of pots and traps. Sometimes they are hunted at the same place by fishers using different gear, and conflicts develop between the fishers over who has the right to fish there. Often these conflicts are resolved, if not amicably, at least without violence. Occasionally the conflicts are less easily resolved, and fishers again cross the line into criminal action.

When conflict over gear does erupt, it usually involves destroying the gear and sometimes the vessel, but people are only rarely harmed or killed. The conflict usually erupts over territorial rights or when one group believes another is taking an unfair amount from a fish stock. Trawlers are often involved, for fixed gear such as traps or gillnets, which are used extensively in inshore fisheries, are particularly vulnerable to trawlers intent on expanding their operations into inshore waters.

There are many examples of serious gear wars, but one that occurred in Indonesia during the past few decades indicates how great the stakes may be. Indonesia is a huge country of 13 000 islands sprawled across more than 2000 km (1250 miles) of ocean, straddling the equator. It is a populous nation of 180 million people, and fish provide about 60 per cent of the high-quality protein that people eat. Each coastal community has fished its immediate inshore area for as long as people can remember, setting traps and nets, fishing from small boats they paddle, sail or, more recently, hook small outboard motors onto. They fish for groundfish and pelagic fish and for the abundant shrimp that live near and on the bottom. Several hundred thousand boats head out daily to fish.

For a time, though, during the 1960s and 1970s, it looked as if the coastal communities and fishers would lose their way of life, for during the 1960s, trawlers arrived. They were 20 to 30 metres (60 to 100 feet) long, financed by the small Chinese minority (Chinese make up 3 per cent of the population of Indonesia but run a disproportionate amount of the commerce). The trawls scooped up immense amounts of fish and shrimp so efficiently that more and more trawlers arrived to cash in on the bounty. The small-boat fishers found they could not compete, and many quit fishing and tried to find employment on shore.

As the number of trawlers along the more productive coasts eventually rose to 1300 vessels, they began to trawl up not only the larger sizes that they could sell but also the juvenile stages, along with unwanted species (trash fish), and ground them into fish meal. For the first time the fish and shrimp declined in numbers, for no fishery can sustain that kind of plunder. They also trawled up much of the fishing gear set by the small-boat fishers.

The small-boat fishers finally went to war with the trawlers. Sometimes they attacked them with Molotov cocktails, and a few trawlers throughout the region were sunk. The Indonesian press got involved, describing the conflicts and the hard times the small-boat fishers faced. The director general of fisheries intervened, deciding that trawlers should be limited to areas more than 7 kilometres (4.3 miles) offshore. As well, only a limited of number of trawlers were given licences to fish.

These regulations should have solved the problem, allowing the two kinds of fishing to coexist. But the regulations didn't work. The trawlers simply ignored them. They trawled at night, when the shrimp were easier to catch and the trawlers couldn't be seen. They trawled where they wanted, as close inshore as the fish drew them. They moved from port to port, and most of them fished without licence to do so. They cheated without hesitation, for the regulations were too difficult to enforce over such a long coastline, and too much money could be made too quickly to stop fishing.

Luckily or not, Indonesia is a military dictatorship. Armed with pressure from the press and plenty of evidence that the conflicts between small-boat fishers and trawlers were going to escalate, President Suharto banned all trawlers from coastal waters. With the might of the military to back it up, the decree worked wonderfully and the trawlers disappeared. The number of small-boat fishers increased, and although the fish and shrimp populations have not necessarily recovered, the conflict was resolved. It was not an unpopular act of intervention.

Gear wars involve the same problems that any illegal actions within fisheries involve. Regulations exist and are ignored. If the violators cannot be detected and the regulations cannot be enforced, they are meaningless. Few places have the luxury of calling in the navy to act as enforcers, though they may often wish they did.

In California, trawlers sell undersized halibut to buyers on shore waiting in small trucks and cars. Abalone poachers on the same coast masquerade as scuba divers. Meanwhile, in Maine a new technique makes it possible to detect whether a female lobster has been scrubbed with bleach to remove her eggs. But even as fisheries officers get better at catching cheaters, fishers find new and imaginative ways to avoid detection. Whether they are deep-water trawlers or recreational anglers, fishers examine the laws and weigh the benefits of cheating and the costs of getting caught. Unless they are faced with heavy-handed enforcement by fisheries officers—or by a navy—the temptation to break the rules can be irresistible.

CHAPTER 6

WASTED FISH AND DESTRUCTIVE GEAR

Billions of investment dollars and purchased politicians swing a lot of weight, but if this kind of fishing is really hammering the ocean ecosystem, we have to put a leash on it.

From an editorial on the U.S. factory trawlers in NATIONAL FISHERMAN, October 1996

Catching fish for food or fish meal or even for recreation is one thing. Catching fish only to kill them and toss them back into the sea is quite another. Yet fishers catch vast numbers of fish that they simply do not want. These fish are usually the wrong species, either of little market value or not what that particular fishing boat is licensed to catch. Sometimes they are the right species but not the right size for marketing. Whatever the reason, probably 30 per cent of the fish caught around the world are thrown back. This figure varies according to the kind of gear the fishers use, the particular type of fish or shrimp they are searching for, the regulations they are trying to meet or avoid, the time and place they are fishing, and their experience as fishers. Whatever the reason, every year billions of fish are caught but not kept. Many of these fish spend a fair amount of time on deck while fishers sort for the preferred species and sizes, or they are caught by their gills in driftnets or damaged in other ways by the gear. As a result, they are thrown back dead or dying. The fishing industry calls them the bycatch (Figure 9).

The waste is colossal. Besides the billions of individual fish, this waste also includes many thousands of dolphins, porpoises, sea turtles and seabirds that get tangled in the nets every year and drown. The destruction of these other

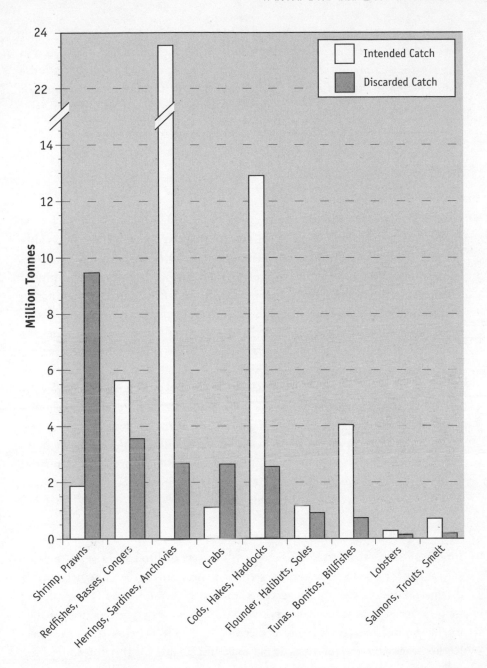

FIGURE 9

The Global Bycatch. *Vast amounts of fish are discarded dead back into the sea as fishers harvest more valuable species. By far the worst offender is the shrimp fishery. Source: Greenpeace report on UN statistics.*

marine vertebrates is intolerable, and fishers are being forced to modify their nets and their methods in order to exclude or release unharmed the mammals and turtles that are unfortunate enough to have been captured along with the fish. The marine turtles are of special concern, for their populations are not large enough to withstand the increased mortality caused by driftnets and

≈≈≈≈≈≈≈≈≈≈≈≈≈≈≈≈≈≈≈≈≈≈≈≈≈≈≈≈≈≈≈≈≈

Whatever the reason, every year billions of fish are caught but not kept.

≈≈≈≈≈≈≈≈≈≈≈≈≈≈≈≈≈≈≈≈≈≈≈≈≈≈≈≈≈≈≈≈≈

trawls. In the 1970s the death rate of porpoises in the purse seines of tuna fishers was so great that some of the species that were caught most frequently became endangered. Prodded by environmentalist groups, outraged U.S. consumers forced the tuna fishers to modify their purse seines to allow captured porpoises to slip out of the nets before the tuna were hauled in. Everyone agrees that the bycatch of unwanted fish and other unlucky marine vertebrates must be reduced, yet it persists. It is even called a necessary evil, the cost of managing any fisheries. How could this possibly be true, and if true, how can it be acceptable?

Fishing methods are of course designed to kill fish. The challenge facing all fishers is to try to catch the particular species or sizes of fish that can be legally marketed without catching species and sizes that are of little value or are illegal to sell. Every method of fishing, whether with longlines, purse seines, trawls, or gillnets and driftnets, kills unwanted animals. Some methods, however, are especially inefficient and destructive. Large-scale driftnet fishing and bottom trawling are the ugliest, the most indiscriminate and therefore the most irresponsible methods of catching fish.

LARGE-SCALE DRIFTNETS

Imagine a ship of 300 to 400 tonnes, with a crew of fifteen to twenty, able to stay at sea for one to two months, setting its nets once a day. The nets, called driftnets, come in five to ten sections, each 5 to 10 kilometres (3 to 6 miles) long. When set, the entire net is 25 to 55 kilometres (15 to 34 miles) long, hanging like an invisible curtain 10 to 15 metres (30 to 50 feet) below the sea surface. Radio beacons at each end of the net make it possible for the ship to find the net again. Once set, the net drifts through the sea, unseen by all that swim into it. Fish smaller than 15 centimetres (6 inches) or so in width or height might swim through unscathed. Larger fish become entangled, caught by their gills.

A driftnet is simply a very long gillnet. Fishers have probably used gillnets for some thousands of years, for even small ones can be very effective and are easily set by a couple of fishers from a small boat. Now they are used in many coastal and high seas fisheries to catch pelagic fish and squid. In the past, when the nets were made of heavier twine, fishers could not manage a very large gill-net, and few nets were more than a few kilometres long. With the development of strong, light plastic filaments in the 1960s, larger nets became possible, and in the 1970s the first large-scale, 50-kilometre (30-mile) driftnets were set.

Such large-scale driftnets are now illegal in the world's high seas, banned because of their unselective destruction of unwanted fish and marine mammals, marine turtles and seabirds. Driftnet fisheries began in the North Pacific in the late 1970s as vessels from Japan, Taiwan and South Korea fished for squid. Because the nets were so efficient at straining fish and squid from the sea, a much smaller crew was needed than with other methods of fishing. The remarkable efficiency of the nets has itself provoked opposition, for fishers from the same countries using other fishing methods have felt unable to compete with driftnet fishers. During the late 1970s and 1980s, when distant-water fleets were losing access to distant-water fishing regions as coastal countries proclaimed and enforced their 200-mile EEZs, they still needed to continue to supply their home markets, which were ravenous for fish. Large-scale driftnet fishing could supply these markets cheaply and efficiently.

Although the driftnet fishers set their nets for squid in the North Pacific, they also caught and discarded Pacific salmon along with thousands of marine mammals and seabirds and attracted world attention to their nets. The Japanese driftnet vessels seem to have been the worst offenders. In 1989, the first sanctioned multinational observers went to sea with some of the Japanese driftnet fishers. Because these observers had various amounts of training and experience and recorded what they witnessed in varying degrees of detail and accuracy, their reports are not completely reliable. Nonetheless, it seems that in 1990 the Japanese fleet harvested over a million squid, discarded over 30 million fish known as pomfret and killed an additional 140 000 salmon, 270 000 seabirds and 26 000 marine mammals. These numbers don't include "dropouts," or fish that fall off the nets before they are retrieved. Nor do they include the impact of ghost nets, nets that are lost yet drift on, entangling fish, birds and mammals for months before finally breaking apart. And they don't include the practice, on vessels lacking observers, of discarding fish that have been caught for species or sizes that are more valuable. Considering all of these factors, the waste becomes too large to defend to anyone.

The protests against high seas driftnet fishing in the North Pacific came from two directions, and both were powerful in that they engaged the United States in helping to ban the nets. The salmon fishers of Alaska, British

Columbia, Washington and Oregon, along with some environmental groups, organized themselves to protect their coastal salmon fisheries from high seas fishing. Believing that the high seas interception of salmon, by intent or as bycatch, was harming their coastal fisheries, they wanted the gillnet salmon fleet and the squid driftnet fleet banned from the North Pacific high seas. Even though Japan had agreed to cease fishing for salmon in the North Pacific high seas after 1986, Japanese ships, along with Taiwanese vessels, were still thought to be out there fishing illegally; the nets they set for squid had a reputation for killing too many salmon. Banning the practice of driftnet fishing in the high seas would be a strong signal to the world and would protect the salmon.

The other player in the growing movement to ban the use of large-scale drift-nets was Greenpeace. Greenpeace, and other environmental groups, focussed on the killing of the seabirds, dolphins, porpoises, seals and sea turtles entangled in the driftnets. Many people are far more sensitive to the needless death of animals like these than to the wasteful death of a few million fish. By widely advertising the killing of marine mammals and seabirds, Greenpeace made the large-scale driftnets sound like walls of death, emptying the high seas.

During the mid-1980s, the Japanese and Taiwanese also brought large-scale driftnets to the South Pacific and the Indian Ocean to fish for tuna. There, as in the North Pacific, the bycatch was immense. Twenty-seven species of dolphin and one species of porpoise were vulnerable to becoming entangled in the nets, and an estimated 100 000 dolphins drowned annually in the nets. Other whales, seals, sea lions, sharks, unwanted tuna species, mackerel species, leatherneck turtles and petrels also died in the drifting nets.

Although the bycatch associated with large-scale driftnets became well known and attracted criticism and protest, it was really the extraordinary efficiency of the nets that finally halted their use. The South Pacific island countries worried that distant-water fishing fleets and their driftnets would so deplete tuna stocks that they themselves would not be able to develop a viable fishery in their own EEZs. They argued that the fish would soon be overfished, leaving little for anyone. They refused to help vessels that were engaged in drift-net fishing, and they pushed other countries, including the United States, to put pressure on Japan, Taiwan and Korea. Greenpeace again attacked the use of the nets, as it had in the North Pacific, intent on achieving not just a regional ban but a global ban.

The UN then joined the conflict, adding to the pressure to restrict driftnets. With U.S. backing, it held the Convention for the Prohibition of Long Driftnets in the South Pacific in 1989 and proposed banning all nets longer than 2.5 kilometres (1½ miles). Japan, always sensitive to such criticism and fearful of losing what access it still had to fishing regions, announced in 1991 that it would ban large-scale driftnet fishing on the high seas. In 1992, a total global moratorium began.

Japan and Korea never agreed that the bycatch was that much of a problem and have kept calling for more research; they have continued to believe that more data, along with greater care in when and where the long nets were set, would establish that the nets were taking unfair criticism. Korea was distinctly unenthusiastic about the moratorium, wanting to continue to fish for North Pacific salmon with the nets. The inclusion of Taiwan in the UN agreement was tricky because China has refused to acknowledge Taiwan's independent existence and Taiwan wanted to link its agreement to stop large-scale driftnet fishing with diplomatic recognition by the Pacific island countries. Despite these difficulties, the moratorium took place.

This does sound like a success, and it is. Driven by politics and self-interest rather than conservation or concern about the bycatch, the moratorium on the use of large-scale driftnets still eliminated one of the most destructive of indiscriminate fishing methods on the high seas. Where there are still some large-scale driftnets in use, particularly by Italy in the Mediterranean Sea, the threat of economic sanctions should be enough to force the fishers to pull the nets out of the water.

Smaller-scale driftnet fishing—setting nets up to 2.5 kilometres (1½ miles) long—still continues, along with extensive use of smaller gillnets. The nets may be set less frequently in high seas regions, but they remain a favoured fishing method in coastal waters around the world. There they are often set in densities great enough to be even more damaging than the large-scale driftnets ever were. They remain just as indiscriminate, the bycatch just as great. Driftnet fishing remains destructive at any scale.

THE GILLNET BAN IN U.S. INSHORE WATERS

The fishers in the coastal waters of the United States have come under increasing pressure to use more environmentally safe gear. In 1990 voters banned the use of gillnets from waters within 3 miles of shore along California. Since then, the coastal states of the Gulf of Mexico have done the same, though the proposed ban failed in Washington. The harvest of finfish such as sea trout and mullet has dropped dramatically in the inshore waters of the Gulf of Mexico states, and the white bass and halibut catch in California is down about 50 per cent.

This is not simply a victory for responsible environmentalism, however. Much of the pressure to ban the nets has come from recreational fishers who would like to see commercial fishing eliminated in state waters or limited to

rod-and-reel fishing. The outcome of the bans has also not been what the voters might have expected. In Florida, the state paid out $25 million to help the
fishers who were put out of work by the gillnet ban, a cost the voters in the
state had not known about. In California, Mexican fishers bought the gillnets
that the California fishers could no longer use, caught more fish, upgraded the
quality of their catch and have continued to supply the Californian restaurants.

Two issues are involved here, and unfortunately they have become mixed
together, no doubt intentionally. Who should have the greater access in inshore
waters to the available fish—recreational or commercial fishers? And what is
the most responsible method of fishing? The use of gillnets, like the use of
larger driftnets, deserves careful assessment, for gillnets are just as indiscriminate in their catch as driftnets. If their bycatch is great, then banning them is
warranted. But to ban them because they compete for the fish that recreational
fishers want sole access to is pure politics and has little to do with the rational
management of a fishery. In the meantime, as a chef in Louisiana, quoted by the
journalist Brad Matsen, has said, "The gillnet law is so offensive, it will destroy
a fishing culture."

TRAWLING

Almost as destructive as large-scale driftnet fishing is bottom trawling. Bottom
trawlers drag their nets along the bottom substrate, scraping up everything that
lies on it, often destroying bottom habitats in the process. Bottom trawling is
by far the most efficient way to catch groundfish and shrimp, but like driftnet
fishing, it catches without discrimination unless it is fitted with devices that
exclude some of the unwanted catch. Raising the temperature in the local gear
wars around the world, the trawlers also easily trawl up smaller gear such as
traps and fixed nets set in inshore waters, a most unpopular form of bycatch.
Even though it kills few marine mammals or seabirds, bottom trawling has
received very bad press since it was first used. In 1366 British fishers petitioned
against the use of bottom trawls, angered by the damage the nets did to both
fish and bottom habitats. In 1499 trawls were banned in Flanders, in 1583 the
Dutch banned shrimp trawling in the estuaries of Holland, the next year France
banned them completely, in 1631 Britain followed suit.

In every case the complaints were the same. Then, as now, bottom trawling
created the world's most wasteful fisheries and scoured the bottom substrates.
The trawlers still protest that the damage and the waste are overestimated and
demand to see some evidence that they do any permanent harm to the bottom
habitats. There are areas, such as the North Sea, where probably every stretch
of bottom is trawled at least once every year, and yet the sea still remains pro-

ductive. The Gulf of Maine was also trawled increasingly after 1976 until the recent reduction of groundfishing, but no one knows how much of the collapse should be blamed on overfishing, on the wasteful bycatch or on the damage to bottom habitats. The campaign that Greenpeace mounted against factory trawlers in the Pacific Northwest region of the United States in the late summer of 1996 drew a great deal of attention to the issues of habitat damage and excessive bycatch, but the arguments would have been stronger had Greenpeace had better data on the extent of the damage. Until video cameras clearly document the extent of the damage, the disagreement will persist.

≈≈≈≈≈≈≈≈≈≈≈≈≈≈≈≈≈≈≈≈≈≈≈≈≈≈≈≈≈≈≈≈≈

Bottom trawlers drag their nets along the bottom substrate, scraping up everything that lies on it, often destroying bottom habitats in the process.

≈≈≈≈≈≈≈≈≈≈≈≈≈≈≈≈≈≈≈≈≈≈≈≈≈≈≈≈≈≈≈≈≈

The bycatch discarded from trawlers can be enormous. By far the worst case involves the shrimp fisheries. Shrimp are trawled for in relatively shallow inshore waters, particularly in the subtropics, where the trawlers also come into conflict with other fishers using other methods. Because of their fine taste and texture, shrimp are unusually valuable, a luxury food shipped to markets and restaurants in the more affluent parts of the world. Unfortunately, when one species becomes so much more valuable than those caught with it in the trawling nets, the bycatch escalates. Where shrimp are fished, they are picked from the catch and the fish captured with them are discarded. The fish bycatch, discarded dead back into the sea, is often as much as eight times the weight of shrimp that are kept. Even when the fish are of relatively high value, they will be dumped because the shrimp are still more valuable and storage space on the boats is limited.

Although shrimp trawling is the world's most wasteful fishery, bottom trawling for groundfish produces a discouragingly high bycatch as well. In most places where deepwater flatfish are trawled up, at least as many fish are thrown back dead as are kept. Many of those discarded are juveniles of the very species that are fished for, an absurd situation in a managed fishery.

The bycatch will never be eliminated, but it surely can be reduced. Careful use of echo-sounding equipment can target a school and reduce the bycatch of unwanted species. This is especially true in midwater trawling, where the nets are dragged through the water well off the bottom, but it should also be possible in bottom trawling. Agreeing to use wider-mesh nets will allow smaller species and smaller individuals of the targeted species to escape. Attachments to the leading edge of the nets, called turtle excluder devices (TEDS) and bycatch reduction devices (BRDS), can also be of some help in keeping turtles and fish such as red snappers out of the shrimp trawls. The trawlers hate these devices, for they doubt their effectiveness and they are convinced that the devices reduce their catch by about 50 per cent.

Whether they like the devices or not, U.S. shrimp trawlers are being forced to use them. There is a strong sense that if U.S. fleets have to use the devices, foreign fleets should have to do so as well. Several organizations (including the Sierra Club, the Earth Island Institute and the Humane Society) pressed for a U.S. ban on shrimp imports from any of the other seventy countries that trawl for shrimp unless they too adopt turtle excluder devices. The ban came into force in May 1996, but it has been challenged by India, Malaysia, Pakistan and Thailand, four of the countries most affected by the ban. Similar pressure is growing in the United States on behalf of other bycatch reduction devices. New and improved designs will emerge as testing of the devices continues, and the trawlers may find ways to live with them more comfortably. We will have to find further ways to reduce the bycatch where it is greatest, however. We may even have to stop eating the shrimp and eat the discarded fish instead.

DISCARDED FISH

The fish that are not kept may be species that the fishers do not have a licence to catch, or they may be species of low market value, impossible to sell for a profit. They may be the right species but smaller than the minimum legal size the fishery allows. Or they may be the right species but go beyond the quota allotted to that particular boat. In all cases, if the fishers obey the regulations, the fish are thrown back, and most if not all are dead.

If a boat is licensed to catch one particular species but not others, the bycatch escalates again. In the Bering Sea, trawlers seeking Alaskan pollock also catch and discard Pacific halibut and chinook salmon, reducing what the inshore coastal fishers for those two species can hope to catch. In the North Sea in 1985, trawlers kept 500 million haddock but discarded 460 million fish that were too small or were of other species. In the hake fishery in the Bay of Biscay and the Celtic Sea, more fish are discarded than the 100 million or so usually caught each year.

Fish are also discarded because they are unpopular in the home markets. Danish and Dutch ships throw back 80 per cent of the whiting (a codlike fish) they catch in their trawls, about 50 000 tonnes per year, because they are unable to sell them domestically. In contrast, the French trawlers keep a much higher percentage of the whiting they catch, since they can sell the fish in French markets.

One of the more bizarre cases of dumping fish involves Spain, which tends to disregard regulations more than most other countries. When Spain entered the European Union in 1994, it was allowed to catch only seven of the twenty species controlled by quotas in EU waters. Spanish ships caught everything, kept the seven allowed species and discarded the rest, an enforced waste. In 1996 Spain gained full rights to the EU fisheries and can now keep the species it has had to throw back.

Unfortunately, many absurdities remain, often a result of regulations intended to conserve fish stocks. A common practice in controlled fisheries is called high grading. Increasingly in many fisheries, a boat is allowed to catch a maximum total weight of a particular species. At the same time, fish of a certain size, usually the largest ones, are likely to be more valuable than others. To make the most profit under such circumstances, fishers will keep fishing until they catch the optimal-sized fish, dumping what they may have already caught in order to make room in their quota for the more valuable catch.

SOLUTIONS

A large bycatch is likely to occur whether the fishery is an open-access unmanaged fishery or a highly regulated one that depends on allocating a total allowable catch among participating fishers. No one likes the situation, for the waste of fish makes no sense when we are worrying about overfishing and conservation. As more fisheries operate under quotas, the bycatch will continue to plague us. The EU recognizes that its rules force fishers to discard fish and accepts that cost in the belief that to do otherwise would encourage even more damaging practices with even graver consequences.

This situation sounds like admission of a failed fisheries policy. Since we really can't afford to accept a high bycatch as a necessary byproduct of a regulated fishery, managers are looking for other solutions. Certain gear types may be prohibited, escape panels and other bycatch excluders may be added to nets, mesh size may be increased to allow smaller individuals to escape, and more efficient gear may be developed. But improved gear will probably not be any more selective of the species it catches than older gear, and dumping of discarded fish will continue, even if it is reduced. In 1990, Norway decided to ban discards completely; everything a boat caught had to be landed. To offset the ban on discards, however, the fishers have argued that they should have higher quotas allotted to them. The arguments continue; the situation is changed but not resolved.

The problem with all of these measures is that they are difficult to enforce. Moving to larger mesh sizes is costly because targeted fish are lost in the process, and anyway, the widely used diamond mesh, which can seem large enough to allow undersized fish to escape, closes up rather nicely under pressure and catches them anyway. Boats can dump unwanted fish without being seen. It is far easier to dump illegal fish at sea than to try to avoid catching them in the first place. Any optional regulations of course are ignored. Discards are supposed to be reported in some places, but not in others. For example, they must be reported in high seas waters under the jurisdiction of the North Atlantic Fisheries Organization but not in EU waters. No matter what, misreporting is easy. Announcing that the bycatch must be reduced to a certain level isn't helpful without a reliable way of monitoring and enforcing the rule.

The dilemma then persists. Around the world we waste too much of what we catch using the more unselective gear of drift nets and trawlers. Open access to fisheries will result in a high bycatch. Regulating a fishery through quotas—understandably popular among managers, since it involves the least contention and intervention on their part—ensures that the bycatch will remain high. Gear improvements will help, and any kind of enforcement will as well, but more than that will have to change. When a management system condones waste, even as the least of several evils, everyone in the fishery will sense the implications. How can we expect conservation to be successful when waste is considered legitimate? And how can we expect fishers to accept other regulations when they are forced to discard fish every time they pull in their nets? Until we find a way to resolve the bycatch problem, reducing it to a minimum that is consistent with an attitude of conservation, it remains a signal that our management of the fisheries is unsuccessful.

CHAPTER 7

THE DESTRUCTION OF COASTAL HABITATS

He spoke of the dreadful burden humanity was throwing upon this inland sea: effluvia from the sewer systems, poisons from the plants, industrial waste from the entire Susquehanna Valley, the garbage of the small-boat fleet, the awful pressure of human beings, each year more insistent, less disciplined, more wasteful, less attentive.

James Michener, CHESAPEAKE

As if overfishing and unpredictable natural environmental stresses aren't enough to cause fish stocks to decline and crash, there is a third, more troublesome problem. Most of the fish and invertebrates that are harvested commercially around the world spend part or all of their life cycles in coastal waters, where they find food and protective cover in estuaries, mangrove forests, kelp beds, sea grass beds, coral reefs and other coastal marshes and wetlands. Wherever these habitats are close to human development—and that means most of the temperate, subtropical and tropical coasts—they are threatened with contamination by pollutants and outright destruction by the other, conflicting needs of human populations.

As these habitats disappear, their communities of fish, invertebrates and marine plants diminish with them. Reversing this process is going to take more than international laws and conservative and precautionary management. Many countries are looking for ways to protect what is left of damaged coastal habitats and reclaim some of what has been lost, but they face immense difficulties.

Half of humanity lives within 100 kilometres (60 miles) of the coast. In some regions, such as Southeast Asia, two-thirds of the population lives that close to the coast. Most of the world's largest cities lie on the coast. Urban populations continue to explode, and the coastal cities creep ever outward, absorbing more coastline, draining coastal wetlands to make them habitable for humans and usable for industry. The wastes and contaminants produced by the cities are colossal in variety and abundance and are difficult to treat or control under the best of conditions. Rivers carry industrial and agricultural

≈≈≈≈≈≈≈≈≈≈≈≈≈≈≈≈≈≈≈≈≈≈≈≈≈≈≈≈≈≈≈

Half of humanity lives within 100 kilometres (60 miles) of the coast.

≈≈≈≈≈≈≈≈≈≈≈≈≈≈≈≈≈≈≈≈≈≈≈≈≈≈≈≈≈≈≈

contaminants, as well as huge sediment loads, and kill the estuaries they drain into. Oil spills endanger every port and coastline where there is tanker traffic. Between the cities along the coasts, the increasing population threatens the coastal habitats with further destruction and contamination. No coastal habitat is safe; no coastal habitat is protected from potential catastrophic contamination or destruction.

COASTAL CONTAMINANTS

Contamination of estuaries and coastal waters comes in many guises, from many sources. It often originates far inland and is carried by the rivers to the sea. Pulp and paper mills dump chlorinated organic compounds, used in the bleaching process, along with other toxins into the rivers. Pesticides used in both forestry and agriculture seep with the groundwater into the rivers. As the rivers flow through land cleared for agricultural use, they pick up more and more sediment along with nutrients that come from fertilizers. In the coastal harbours, where industrial development is usually concentrated, other contaminants join the increasingly lethal cocktail—particularly PCBs and heavy metals, such as lead, zinc, cadmium, copper and mercury, which are damaging to living organisms even in low concentrations. Where human waste exceeds the capacity of local waste-treatment facilities, the rivers, harbours and adjacent coast become contaminated with partly treated sewage and the pathogens that accompany it.

New Bedford, on the coast of Massachusetts, is a good example of what can happen even where the technology and facilities ought to be in place. Until the groundfish stocks on the nearby Georges Bank crashed and forced much of the fishing fleet out of business, New Bedford was the most active port in the United States for fisheries. The cost of this success has been great, though. In the mid-1980s, when the New Bedford harbour still was at its busiest, it was also so severely polluted that it had to be closed to all fishing. Its sediments were loaded with PCBs, compounds that are known to be carcinogenic to fish.

Poorly treated sewage and waste water compounded the problem. Harbours everywhere where there is similar activity are equally polluted, from Halifax and Vancouver in Canada to New York City, Buenos Aires, Cape Town and Tokyo.

POLLUTION OF THE ESTUARIES

Estuaries tend to be densely inhabited by humans, sites of intense development for settlements, ports, industry and marinas for recreational boats. Wetlands are diked and drained for agricultural use, and submerged eelgrass and turtle grass beds are smothered by sediment or die because suspended sediment cuts off the light they need to grow. The fish and invertebrates that use the grass beds and wetlands for food and for protective cover have nowhere to feed or hide. Larger species that in turn depend on these fish and invertebrates for prey must leave to search elsewhere. Migrant species that return each year to breed in the estuaries or swim up their tributaries to breed have little to feed on, are harmed by the contaminants they swim through and often have no breeding habitats left to them.

San Francisco Bay is the largest estuary on the west coast of the United States, and its history is all too typical. In the last 150 years, 60 per cent of its water surface has been lost as 85 per cent of its wetlands have been filled. Contaminated by toxins and overrun by species introduced accidentally in the ballast of arriving vessels, it no longer supports commercial fishing. The days that Jack London evoked so well in *Tales of the Fish Patrol* are long gone.

The sediments that rivers carry and then dump into the slower-moving waters of the estuaries and the adjacent coastal regions can destroy fish and their habitats even if they are not contaminated with toxins and sewage. They may clog the gills of the fish; they cause an increased turbidity that may decrease or inhibit photosynthesis; they may simply bury ecosystems. The amount of sediment load varies with the density of human population more than it does with the size of the estuary. The Ganges River, draining about 100 000 square kilometres (39 000 square miles) of farmland and harvested forested land, dumps more than 1.5 billion tonnes of sediment into the Bay of Bengal each year, five times what the Amazon River dumps into the Atlantic Ocean each year, even though the Amazon drains a far greater area. Such a load of sediment deposited in the Bay of Bengal each year does in fact result in emergent spits of land that are suitable for renewed mangrove settlement and growth. But land is at such a premium for the human population that people move onto any land that emerges. Mangroves don't have a chance to colonize and stabilize the sand spits, and the human habitations are often washed away in the next monsoon.

CHESAPEAKE BAY

If protection and recovery of estuarine habitats is possible, it ought to occur in Chesapeake Bay. It is the largest estuary in the United States and for its size it has been as productive as any place on earth, famed for its fisheries for oysters, blue crabs and fish, particularly striped bass. It has also been subjected to two centuries of increasing human settlement, including the growth of the cities of Washington and Baltimore, and in the process it became polluted by the runoff from the agricultural and industrial development along its watersheds. The overload of nutrients as a result of fertilizers and animal wastes from poultry farms, the accumulation of herbicides and other toxins, and increasing amounts of sediment—all threatened to destroy the fisheries that had been so successful.

To make matters worse, in the 1930s a virus pandemic obliterated most of the eelgrass in Atlantic coastal regions, and a vital estuarine habitat was lost. It recovered in many places elsewhere in the temperate Atlantic, but not in the Chesapeake. There the greater turbidity from all the sediment as well as the herbicides carried into the bay by the many rivers prevented the eelgrass from regrowing. With the loss of the submerged grass beds, fish and invertebrates lost a nursery habitat to hide and feed in, and other, larger fish and waterfowl lost a habitat rich in food resources.

The major fisheries of the Chesapeake all declined. The eastern oyster harvest crashed from 20 000 to 3000 tonnes in the late 1980s and is now at about 1 per cent of the abundance it once had. It has been overharvested, managed as an open-access fishery; it has lost most of its preferred habitat because of the pollution and sedimentation; and it has suffered from disease, a result of parasitic infections and of the extraordinarily high concentrations of pathogens in the bay. Now shorter harvesting seasons and a few sanctuaries protect the species, but there is little left to protect. Other species of commercial interest, such as blue crabs and striped bass are recovering, however, and the bay is not yet dead. Nonetheless, the algal blooms are frequent, the bottom layers of the bay often become anoxic, devoid of oxygen, and any bottom-living animals then simply die.

Protection of the Chesapeake marine habitats from pollution is difficult. Its 150 tributary streams and rivers come from six states, although predominantly from Maryland and Virginia. Research on the problems afflicting the bay, begun in 1975 and initiated by the U.S. government, identified strategies to control the runoff of nutrients and toxins, to protect remaining wetlands and to prevent further shoreline erosion. Maryland, Pennsylvania and Virginia, along with the District of Columbia, the Environmental Protection Agency and an assortment of local citizens and businesses, have agreed to attempt to revive the bay, hoping to cut nutrients by 40 per cent by the year 2000, to control the discharge of toxins and to increase the extent of coastal wetlands. Despite this agreement, agricultural runoff has continued to increase along with the population and the development of the shoreline, and the nitrogen load is not shrinking. Maryland, which has jurisdiction over most of the upper half of the bay, has tried to limit the pollution by restricting development, farming, mining and logging from within 300 metres (1000 feet) of tidewater and wetlands. The overall intent is good, but the potential for conflict with all these other activities remains great. The grass beds, nurseries for fish and crabs, are slowly recovering, however, and that is an excellent sign, indicating greater water clarity. With sustained technological management, the bay should gradually recover, or at least not deteriorate further.

≈≈≈≈≈≈≈≈≈≈≈≈≈≈≈≈≈≈≈≈≈≈≈≈≈≈≈≈≈≈≈≈

*N*o coastal habitat is safe; no coastal habitat is protected from
potential catastrophic contamination or destruction.

≈≈≈≈≈≈≈≈≈≈≈≈≈≈≈≈≈≈≈≈≈≈≈≈≈≈≈≈≈≈

Another sign of recovery is that striped bass are returning to the bay in reasonable numbers to spawn, largely because of a very aggressive hatchery program. The return of striped bass is a rare success story, expensive though it has been. Stripers swim close to the beaches along the Atlantic coast as they migrate to the estuaries to breed. Commercial fishers seined for them close to shore as well as fishing for them in offshore, federal waters. They caught millions of fish and sold them at high prices to the restaurants along the coast. Anglers fished for them in the estuaries and from the beaches, valuing them for the fight they put up and for their size. Then the stock crashed after its peak year of 1973, and the various states along the coast from Maine to Florida progressively restricted the commercial catch. Maryland eventually closed the Chesapeake to all commercial fishing for stripers, and in 1990 fishers were also banned from federal waters.

The stocks have recovered more quickly than anyone expected, and the Chesapeake stripers were declared to be fully recovered in January 1995. That doesn't mean that the commercial fishery will reopen, however. For many decades recreational fishers have argued strongly that commercial fishers of striped bass should be restricted from inshore waters, and their voice is now more powerful than ever before. Although federal officials were ready to reopen the fishery to commercial fishers at least in federal waters, the recreational fishers have succeeded in delaying the action. They blame the commercial fishers for the crash of the stocks two decades ago, but the commercial fishers maintain that estuarine pollution was as much to blame as overfishing. The recreational fishers will probably at least succeed in keeping commercial fishers out of state waters, including the Chesapeake. They may not succeed in extending the ban to federal waters, but it is clear that managers are going to have to listen to them as they make decisions on appropriate management. As journalist Kirk Moore has written, "although the majority of striped bass are caught in state waters, commercial fishing advocates say the ban in federal waters is proof that sport fishermen and their allies are trying to put a political lock on the species—if they haven't succeeded already."

The Chesapeake is ailing. Great effort and cooperation may allow it to partially recover, and fish such as striped bass may be able to breed there again without the help of fish hatcheries. As with the Red Queen from *Alice in Wonderland*, it is a case of running hard to stand still. Unfortunately, many other estuaries around the world are also contaminated and filling with sediment. In many of them there is little immediate hope of reversing the processes that are making them poisoned eutrophic soups of algae and bacteria, unfit for most other organisms.

OIL CONTAMINATION

Oil pollution is a threat to the inshore habitats of all coastlines, such as marshes and wetlands, and every port. Much of it originates from land-based sources such as cars, machinery and industry. About 30 per cent of it comes from small spills and dumps from tanker and shipping operations. These spills and dumps, which happen all the time and seem almost impossible to control, pollute most harbours and most of the highly trafficked waterways. Only about 13 per cent of oil pollution comes from major spills, but these are particularly damaging because of the sheer volume of oil deposited over a relatively large area. From the *Arrow* in Nova Scotia in 1970 to the *Exxon Valdez* in Prince William Sound in Alaska in 1989, the consequences for the affected coasts have been dramatic. In each case the local fisheries had to close down until the fish and invertebrates again became both edible and abundant enough to harvest.

Offshore drilling for oil presents yet another risk for coastal fish and fishers. There appear to be great reserves of oil in areas where fish abound—for instance, in the North Sea (though the oil there is now almost all used up), off Atlantic Canada and off California. In other places, such as the Beaufort Sea and the coast of Newfoundland, ice-fast coasts in winter make exploration even more hazardous. The safeguards for the fisheries that might be affected by the drilling or by associated spills are rarely adequate.

The effects of a spill or of drilling operations may be minor, but they may also be devastating. They may include large amounts of sediment resulting in very turbid water, fouling of nets, impeded fishing and decline in fish numbers. Spilled oil may be toxic to the fish, may induce sublethal effects on behaviour, may result in tainted fish flesh and will certainly cause disruption of the fishing

≈≈≈≈≈≈≈≈≈≈≈≈≈≈≈≈≈≈≈≈≈≈≈≈≈≈≈≈≈≈≈≈

Spilled oil may be toxic to the fish, may induce sublethal effects on behaviour, may result in tainted fish flesh and will certainly cause disruption of the fishing community.

≈≈≈≈≈≈≈≈≈≈≈≈≈≈≈≈≈≈≈≈≈≈≈≈≈≈≈≈≈≈≈≈

community. North Sea exploration for oil curtailed fishing in the area of the platforms. Drilling on Grand Banks (the Hibernia project) is also likely to disrupt fishing, even if it doesn't affect the already depleted stocks of groundfish. On Georges Bank, also probably rich in oil, there will be no further exploratory drilling because of such risks, a moratorium that should last into the next decade at least.

OTHER CONTAMINANTS

The litany of contaminants goes on. For example, plastics litter the coastlines of the oceans and drift in the open seas in the form of durable netting fibres, containers and bags; cargo and cruise ships dump bags of garbage filled with plastics; in U.S. coastal waters, half of the plastic litter comes from recreational boaters. The plastic netting fibres entangle and entrap fish, seabirds, marine mammals and turtles. Other plastic litter gets mistaken for food and chokes the feeder. And plastic is made to last, perhaps a few hundred years.

Probably in response to the higher amounts of nutrients in coastal waters, red tides have become more common. A red tide is a bloom of single-celled organisms called dinoflagellates, which give the water a reddish tint when they occur in sufficient concentrations. They are also toxic and kill the fish that eat them. The widespread manatee deaths that occurred in winter 1996 along the southeast coast of the United States also seem to have been caused by red tides. Bivalve mollusks suck in the dinoflagellates, and although they tend not to be killed by the toxins they ingest, anything that eats the bivalves risks being poisoned. All along the coasts of the world red tides are occurring with greater frequency. More and more of those coastlines have to be closed to harvesting of shellfish, and increasing numbers of fish kills as a result of red tides are reported.

THE VULNERABLE TROPICS

The coastlines of the tropics and subtropics are especially vulnerable to destruction of the habitats that support the fish populations. The tropical coasts of the world are in general characterized by human poverty, dense and growing human populations, and few ways of controlling pollution.

Three coastal habitats are critical to fish populations and the communities they live in, and all three are disappearing with alarming speed. Mangrove forests line the protected coasts, sea grass beds extend along these coasts in shallow water, and coral reefs lie offshore. All three habitats support a great diversity of fish and invertebrates. Mangroves and sea grass beds provide shelter and nurseries for many species that are of commercial interest; they also trap sediment carried in the runoff from the land, protecting the offshore reefs from siltation that could smother them. If these three habitats did not provide protection and food, most of the tropical and subtropical species would not survive. The tropics differ from the temperate regions, where nutrients are recirculated to the surface and seasonal explosions of planktonic organisms occur and nourish the immense schools of pelagic fish. Most of the surface water in the tropics and subtropics is impoverished, since the nutrients sink too deeply into the water to be used and are lost. A coral reef, one of the world's most productive ecosystems, is usually surrounded by unproductive, almost desertlike conditions. The loss of the coral reefs, mangrove forests and sea grass beds is nothing short of disastrous. Even where there may be resources to limit the loss, the loss may still be great; in Singapore, where the waterfront has been cleaned up at huge expense, all the mangroves, most of the seabeds and 95 per cent of the coral reefs in the region have been lost.

The coastal mangrove forests are shrinking everywhere. From South Florida and much of the Caribbean to the coasts of Africa, South Asia and Southeast Asia, the destruction and degradation of mangrove forests has been intense. More than half of the world's mangrove forests are gone, and in some places, such as Vietnam and other coastlines in southeast Asia, they may completely disappear within a few years. They have been cleared, drained, diked and filled as more and more land is demanded for people to live on, for ports to build on, or for agricultural use for sugar cane fields or rice paddies. They have been cut for fuel where people have few alternatives for a fuel supply. They have been replaced by shrimp farms because the value of the shrimp on the world

market is irresistibly great, too great for the people who farm them to be able
to afford to eat them themselves. Only the mangroves of the more remote,
largely uninhabited, oceanic islands remain unthreatened.

Even more vulnerable are the coral reefs. They are easily damaged by heavy
seas, heavy rains, turbid water, freshwater runoff from the land, cold seas and
seas that remain very warm for too long. Some of the nutrients they need come
from the organic matter leaking out of the mangroves and sea grass beds. They
provide food and cover for an extraordinary variety of fish, about a third of the
species that have been described, and many of these have been fished for millennia by the fishers of the local coastal communities.

≈≈≈≈≈≈≈≈≈≈≈≈≈≈≈≈≈≈≈≈≈≈≈≈≈≈≈≈≈≈≈≈

*Three coastal habitats are critical to fish populations and the communities
they live in, and all three are disappearing with alarming speed.*

≈≈≈≈≈≈≈≈≈≈≈≈≈≈≈≈≈≈≈≈≈≈≈≈≈≈≈≈≈≈≈≈

Now the reefs are under heavy attack. Few remain healthy and undamaged. In
a survey of 630 reefs made in the 1980s in Philippine waters, only 10 per cent
appeared undamaged; this situation is probably typical of the more densely
populated parts of the Indo-Pacific. Damage from sedimentation is the greatest
problem, reported by fifty countries that have coral reefs in their coastal waters.
Most of this sedimentation can be correlated with increased land and shore erosion and the loss of the coastal mangrove forests and sea grass beds. Particularly
in the Indo-Pacific, where they are most extensive, coral reefs are also subject to
outright destruction. In many places they are mined for lime and cement. They
are also blasted apart by fishers using dynamite to get fish out of the reef—the
fish are stunned and easily collected, but the dynamited section of the reef is
destroyed. Dynamite fishing is illegal in most places, yet it continues on the
reefs of at least forty countries. Damaged coral reefs are very slow to recover,
much more so than sea grass beds or mangroves. Once destroyed, it isn't clear
that they can ever recover.

REVERSING THE DAMAGE

The damage to coastal habitats is so extensive and its economic and biological
implications are so obvious that coastal countries around the planet are taking
action to try to recover what has been lost and protect whatever may remain.
Now that the causes of this degradation and destruction have been identified—erosion, sedimentation, sewage pollution, industrial and urban expansion
and its accompanying contaminants, destruction of mangroves and coral reefs,

and the resulting decline in fisheries—it should be possible to prevent them. In particular, two initiatives have some potential: integrated coastal zone management and marine reserves.

A hundred or more programs in integrated coastal zone management are running in different parts of the world. These programs are intended to develop coastal resources in a sustainable manner, involving participation of both government and stakeholders. The programs are very ambitious and are intended to strengthen local and national management, to protect natural habitats and species, to control land-based pollution and runoff, to limit mining and excavating, to rehabilitate degraded resources, to develop rational allocation of the various resources and to resolve the conflicts between people who are competing for use of the coastal resources. Areas of high biological diversity need to be protected. Sewage disposal needs to be improved. Further destruction needs to be halted. Around the South China Sea, Brunei, Indonesia, Malaysia, the Philippines, Singapore and Thailand are all developing pilot projects. Six East African countries (Madagascar, Mauritius, Mozambique, Seychelles, Tanzania and Kenya) have agreed to make integrated coastal zone management government policy. Sri Lanka has a national conservation strategy. Canada and the United States continue to explore ways to both initiate and implement coastal zone management at regional and national levels.

Although such programs are easily agreed to, they may be almost impossible to implement, for the underlying socioeconomic problems can seem insurmountable. How exactly will poverty be reduced and sustainability of resources be increased where the population is dense and growing and the standard of living is low? Even where the standard of living is high, as it is around the Chesapeake, the conflicting pressures of the competing commercial interests in the region make coastal zone management slow, difficult and usually ineffective. To work, coastal zone management must have two vital ingredients: the local communities have to be committed to long-term care of their resources and must be willing to give up short-term gains; and the government must have the political will to act, to make tough decisions that will certainly be unpopular. How likely are these ingredients to exist?

A more manageable approach, which is really part of any coastal zone management program, is to establish marine reserves. Marine reserves were first established in the mid-1970s, and now every coastal state has established some or is planning to. Hundreds exist, set up along all types of coastlines, and they include coral reefs, kelp forests, subtidal and intertidal habitats, mangroves, salt marshes and sea grass meadows. Marine reserves vary in size from a protected kelp forest or coral reef to the largest of them all, the Great Barrier Reef.

The Great Barrier Reef Reserve really crosses the line into a coastal zone management program, however, for it allows different kinds of activity on different parts of the reef and acknowledges the various interests of tourists and fishers.

Marine reserves don't demand the broad agreement and bureaucratic complexity involved in a national coastal zone management program, but they still require care and include conflict. They usually need to allow some balance of use, with limited access by commercial or recreational fishers and by tourists. Because a reserve will restrict people from using an area they have traditionally had access to, it must seem to provide greater benefits than costs. Most of the opposition comes from fishers.

The benefits of a marine reserve are related to protecting fish stocks. A reserve ought to protect a spawning stock, letting females grow larger and produce far more eggs as a result. It ought to restock adjacent habitats where fishing persists. A network of coastal marine reserves ought to result in increased species diversity. A reserve should also act as a kind of insurance against the failure of other management methods, and since enforcement of regulations should be relatively easy, management of a reserve should not be expensive. If the benefits are clear to the local communities, then they can probably manage the reserves without further intrusion by government. If the community doesn't see the benefits, then poaching is as likely as ever to be a problem; in a marine reserve in Tonkin Bay in Vietnam, for example, dynamite fishing continues.

No matter how reasonable this approach sounds, however, there is as yet little strong evidence that marine reserves do actually increase the yield of the fisheries that they are intended to protect. They certainly should help. But are they enough? Mangroves are being replanted now that they are recognized as valuable and vital component of tropical coasts. Perhaps we can think of them as indicators of environmental health—as they grow, if they grow—we have a clear sign of a reversal that is absolutely essential. But estuaries must be inhabitable, ports must be cleaner, sewage must be treated properly even if only by lagoon impoundments, and contaminants must be reduced. None of these achievements will be worth much, however, if the population continues to explode and encroaches further upon the vulnerable and fragile coastline habitats that support so many of the coastal fisheries that the coastal communities depend on. There are likely to be 10 billion humans by 2030. It is essential that most of the increase not end up on the coastlines of the world, yet that is where most of the cities are.

CHAPTER 8

THE EFFICIENT SOLUTION

Earth has resources for everyone's need, but not for everyone's greed.

Attributed to Mahatma Gandhi

One of the troubles of our age is that habits of thought cannot change as quickly as techniques, with the result that as skill increases, wisdom fades.

Bertrand Russell,
quoted by Fikret Berkes
COMMON PROPERTY RESOURCES

Let's start with a few assumptions. Open-access, competitive fishing never works. It leads to overfishing and overcapitalization, fish disappear, the fishers lose money and then they lose their jobs—the dismal cycle of boom and bust. Although as individuals we know perfectly well what is going to happen, as groups of competing individuals we take as much as possible before others get there first. Because of the competition and the need to make a profit wherever and whenever possible, the competing fishers ignore regulations protecting the fishery or discover imaginative ways to get around them. Greed and competition drive us on to the famous tragedy of the commons, destroying that which we share.

This is the grimmest of pictures. The fish disappear, and we don't come out of it looking particularly bright. Economically, open-access fishing is madness. Regulations must be imposed by government, but to work at all they must be enforced, and the cost of enforcement can be high. Economists point out that even if fishers adhere to the regulations for using only certain types of gear, avoiding nursery grounds and protecting spawning fish, the competition still increases until the costs that a fisher pays for boat, crew, gear and fuel are not balanced by the value of the fish that are caught. The fishery becomes a money-losing proposition for everyone, government and fishers.

Fisheries economists have offered a few solutions. One of them is privatization, giving fishers the same kind of property rights that farmers have had for so long. In a privatized fishery, only a restricted number of fishers have the right to fish and each fisher is guaranteed a certain proportion of the total catch. Both features are essential. More than just a licence system is necessary, for without further controls, those lucky enough to have the licences are still likely to sink into the same competitive, overcapitalized hole, as they catch as many fish as time, equipment and regulations permit. A licence system has been well tried in many places   for example, in British Columbia's salmon fisheries and the Georges Bank groundfish fisheries, where heavy fishing pressure by the licensed fishers contributed to the stock crashes.

For the fishery to be privatized along the lines proposed by the economists, it is equally important that each licensed fisher be given a limit or quota of fish to catch, for then the total catch can be controlled and the stock should not be overfished. At the same time, much of the competition between the fishers disappears as they stop fishing when they reach their quotas. Fishers should no longer be tempted to overcapitalize, for they no longer need faster vessels, larger nets or stronger engines to get to the fish more quickly and then catch them more efficiently when they find them. Because the number of fishers is restricted and they have less need to invest in a great deal of equipment and vessels, those lucky enough to be doing the fishing actually ought to make a profit. The overfishing and overcapitalization that has destroyed so many fisheries should be eliminated. The stocks of fish should be relatively stable.

This probably sounds too good to be true, and it certainly is. The frightening prospect is that unless this management system is watched and controlled very carefully, fewer and fewer fishers are likely to do an increasing amount of the fishing. The fish stocks may still not survive, and the fishing communities may perish.

INDIVIDUAL TRANSFERABLE QUOTAS

Privatization, involving fishing licences and limited quotas, is under way in many parts of the world. The licensed fishers are left to figure out how to catch their allotted quotas as economically as possible, quite a different situation from the pressure to overcaptalize in fisheries where such individual fishing quotas don't exist. To make the system work most efficiently, the economists propose that individuals should be able to sell their quotas or to buy those of other fishers. They predict that the most efficient fishers would then gradually accumulate the quotas, while the less efficient fishers would gradually sell their quotas.

When the quotas become transferable in this way, the economist's models work best. Fishers who catch their quotas most efficiently remain in the fishery. In such a system of individual transferable quotas, it is hard to imagine how

≈≈≈≈≈≈≈≈≈≈≈≈≈≈≈≈≈≈≈≈≈≈≈≈≈≈≈≈≈≈≈

Economically, open-access fishing is madness.

≈≈≈≈≈≈≈≈≈≈≈≈≈≈≈≈≈≈≈≈≈≈≈≈≈≈≈≈≈≈≈

very many individual fishers would be able to remain in the fishery, for they would soon be in competition with firms that are able to fish more economically. Soon few individual fishers would be left, replaced by firms competing with other firms in buying and selling the quotas. And eventually the most efficient firms would end up doing all the fishing. If the economics of fisheries were the only consideration, this would be a logical endpoint. Since fleets of vessels that belong to fishing firms rarely come from local fishing communities, the local communities face the prospect of being unable to harvest the fish that may have sustained them for many generations. As Russell Cleary, acting director of the U.S. Commercial Anglers Association, has commented, "If the privatization steamroller that the National Marine Fisheries Service is pushing prevails, America will be left with about as many family owned and operated fishing businesses as it now has family owned and operated oil wells."

Fisheries managers still have a critical role to play in a fishery that has become privatized and subjected to individual transferable quotas. They still must set a total allowable catch for every fishery. Total allowable catch is always an estimate buffeted by ignorance about the fish, by unpredictable environmental events and by decisions made in the political arena, where it remains unusual for fish to have much leverage. Still, the total allowable catch can be adjusted downward to protect a fishery from decline when the evidence warrants and the political will exists. The quotas given to the fishers each year can then be set as a percentage of the total allowable catch so that if the fishery is declining each fisher would then be allowed to fish for a smaller amount of fish. The combination of individual transferable quotas and an adjustable total allowable catch really ought to work quite well, so long as we focus on economic efficiency.

But privatization does not solve all the problems. Familiar ones persist, and new ones emerge.

SOME PROBLEMS

Cheating is certainly one of the problems that doesn't disappear. In the name of efficiency, fishers will do best to catch the most valuable of the species that they hunt for. Almost always these are the largest individuals. What do fishers do if their holds are filled with fish that aren't the largest, and they come upon a school of larger ones? The best move for the fishers is to dump the load already caught and catch the larger fish instead, getting better value for their quota. This practice is known as high-grading and is especially likely to occur if a boat has a quota. Bycatch is also likely to become an even larger problem as fishers discard everything not included in their quotas.

The waste from high-grading and bycatch can be controlled. Monitors or observers can ride the boats—at great cost to whoever pays for enforcement—to ensure that high-grading doesn't occur. In addition, fishers may be able to arrange deals with each other so that those who exceed their quotas need not dump the excess but can sell or trade it to those who haven't filled their own quotas yet. In fisheries where several species at once are trawled up and a different quota exists for each species, the situation is more complicated. Fishers can perhaps swap quotas, rather than dump species they are not supposed to catch. Again, close monitoring might be necessary, and nobody really thinks that every boat can be monitored. Despite the costs and the complexities, the dumping and waste must somehow be dealt with, through monitoring the vessels and tinkering with the quota arrangements.

The far greater problem is the potential loss of traditional fishing practices, however. With the efficient economies of management by individual transferable quotas, far fewer fishers will be out there fishing, and few of them are likely to be local inhabitants. Under these circumstances, traditional fishing, where it still exists, will simply cease. Unless there are ways to protect them, traditional fishing communities will lose their traditions, without any particular reason to hope that they will ever recover them. The inhabitants of these communities may have to seek new ways of employment, they may require financial assistance from their government, and they may have to leave their communities to seek employment in the cities. This is exactly what has happened to communities that have become the victims of the overfishing caused by open-access fisheries management, familiar from the coast of China in the South China Sea to the ports of Newfoundland. The only difference is that where management is by individual transferable quotas, the fish stocks should remain sustainable instead of crashing. The cost to the local communities will be the same, for the fishers will be unable to fish.

This grim picture is not necessarily inevitable, for there may be ways to limit the impact of privatization and to protect some of the traditional fishing

≈≈≈≈≈≈≈≈≈≈≈≈≈≈≈≈≈≈≈≈≈≈≈≈≈≈≈≈≈≈≈

With the efficient economies of management by individual transferable quotas, far fewer fishers will be out there fishing, and few of them are likely to be local inhabitants.

≈≈≈≈≈≈≈≈≈≈≈≈≈≈≈≈≈≈≈≈≈≈≈≈≈≈≈≈≈≈≈

communities. Most current management by individual transferable quotas is still in its experimental stage, under way in places where traditional methods and communities may not be so affected. As it spreads, it will need to be constrained and carefully monitored.

SUCCESS STORIES: NEW ZEALAND AND ICELAND

Just where is management by individual transferable quotas occurring? Only two countries, New Zealand and Iceland, have converted almost completely to this kind of management. Other countries are definitely interested and have started to use it in a few fisheries. Still others are about to try something, or are planning to do so.

In New Zealand waters, fishers had free access to fisheries until the late 1970s. Faced with the usual events of overfishing, overcapitalization and excessive government regulation, managers tried a few experiments using individual tranferrable quotas in some of the fisheries. Then, in October 1986, they formally introduced management by individual transferable quotas to most of the country's fisheries—certainly all of the important ones. Initial allocations of parts of the quota to both individual fishers and fishing companies were based on their catches in previous years. At first these allocations were in absolute amounts of fish, a strange decision considering that the natural fluctuation of a population could reduce its numbers and fishers taking their allocated tonnage of fish could once again quickly push the stock to the edge of extinction. Recognizing the error, in 1990 the managers changed allocation amounts to fractions of an adjustable total allowable catch. If the total allowable catch for the next fishing season had to be reduced to protect the stock, or if it could be increased because of the increased recruitment of fish into the stock, the absolute amount of fish each fisher caught shifted down or up accordingly, but the percentage of the total each fisher caught remained the same.

New Zealand managers made the change to individual transferable quotas management a clean one, eliminating ambiguities wherever they identified them and adjusting the rules over the years to cope with unexpected intricacies that the fishers noted. The basic rules are simple. Those who own a quota of a fish stock have the right to fish a fixed proportion of that stock forever, in perpetuity. If they want to sell part or all of their quotas, they can. If they want to buy quotas from other fishers who are willing to sell, they can. The fishers have negotiated additional rules. For instance, they are now allowed to trade quotas, especially where they fish for several species at once in a multispecies ground fishery. They are allowed to overrun a quota by 10 per cent and reduce their quota the following year in compensation. And they can exchange their quota of one species for the overcaught portion of their quota for another species. These measures are not always in the best interests of the fish, but they do reduce wasteful dumping of fish, and they are rational attempts to make the system work.

Has it worked? It is at the least a modest success. Some reduction in fishing has occurred. Some companies have increased their quotas by buying the quotas of less efficient fishers. The profitability of fishing has increased. Even the value of owning a quota has increased. These are all trends in the direction the managers are trying to lead the fisheries.

At the same time, enforcement is difficult, excessive quota overruns still occur, and the bycatch and high-grading problems remain acute. The estimates of total allowable catches have been inadequate for some species and not adjusted downwards where they should have been for some other species. In the trawl fishery, where twenty-nine species are fished, the fishery is perhaps too complex to have any hope that it can be successfully managed.

New Zealand's experiments are well documented, but Iceland was actually the first to convert a fishery to management by individual transferable quotas. International free access to the rich fisheries on the continental shelf around Iceland ended in 1976, when the country unilaterally gave itself a 200-mile exclusive fishing zone. To try to control the enthusiastic Icelandic fishers, managers set overall catch quotas, sold fisheries licences, tried to restrict fishing and began to establish quotas for individual vessels.

It started with herring. Herring had declined alarmingly in the early 1960s, and a total allowable catch was established for the first time in 1966. The decline continued anyway, so a moratorium on herring fishing began in 1972. In 1976, a small fishery was allowed to reopen and vessels were given individual quotas. Then, in 1979, herring became the first fishery to be managed through individual transferable quotas, developing the basic rules that New Zealand used a few years later. In 1980, the managers began to manage capelin in the same way; in 1984, they extended the system to include the groundfish; in 1990, like New Zealand, they agreed to manage all their fisheries through individual transferable quotas.

As with New Zealand, the sense is that management by individual transferable quotas has improved the fisheries, sometimes quite substantially, gradually reducing both overfishing and fleet overcapitalization. Certainly the herring fishery has improved, for fishing has decreased while the total catch has increased; fewer fishers are harvesting fish from a growing herring population. Because the changes in the other fisheries have been more gradual, reflecting a kind of trial-and-error learning, the results are still inconclusive. A few more years of stable regulations are necessary to show whether fishing there is also declining and whether overinvestment in the fleet has been eliminated. So far, however, it seems that the amount of fish discarded remains a problem that still needs to be resolved, although it isn't any greater than it was in earlier years. More interesting to those watching from around the world, enforcement appears to be moderately successful, paid for by the fishers at a rate of 0.2 per cent of the value of what they catch. The experiment seems to be working, despite some social opposition to it.

INITIATIVES IN OTHER PLACES

Although other countries have introduced individual transferable quotas or are planning to do so soon, in most cases it is too soon to tell whether the new management is working well or has just raised as many problems as it has tried to solve. There are perhaps now about fifty fisheries managed through individual transferable quotas around the world.

In Australia, which is not a major fishing country but has an immense EEZ in its surrounding 200 miles of coastal seas, individual transferable quotas have reduced the level of fishing on the bluefin tuna while increasing the profitability of the fishery. Individual transferrable quotas have been introduced in other Australian fisheries and are likely to spread through most of the rest of them. Chile and Peru will also soon shift all or most of their fisheries to management by individual transferable quotas. Meanwhile, on the coast of British Columbia a quite remarkable and successful experiment with Pacific halibut is under way.

THE CASE OF PACIFIC HALIBUT

Pacific halibut live on the coastal sandy bottoms from California to the Bering Sea. For the most part, they are fished in the Gulf of Alaska and along the coast of British Columbia. They have the potential to live a long time and to grow large; there used to be individuals as old as a hundred years, weighing 225 kilograms (500 pounds) or more. In recent years few have been caught weighing more than about 27 kilograms (60 pounds), and most have been far smaller, as we would expect in a fully exploited fishery where most fish are harvested not long after they reach sexual maturity.

≈≈≈≈≈≈≈≈≈≈≈≈≈≈≈≈≈≈≈≈≈≈≈≈≈≈≈≈≈≈≈≈

Change is a lot more acceptable when there
don't seem to be any other options.

≈≈≈≈≈≈≈≈≈≈≈≈≈≈≈≈≈≈≈≈≈≈≈≈≈≈≈≈≈≈≈≈

Until 1990, fishers raced to fish for Pacific halibut in increasingly dangerous and competitive fishing derbies, forced into the race by shorter seasons each year. In 1982 the season lasted sixty days; in 1990 it lasted only six, open for one to two days at any one site along the coast of British Columbia. In an attempt to control the fishing, the fishery was limited to 435 licensed vessels beginning in 1979. The licensed fishers increased the size of their crews, invested in better, more efficient electronic gear and fishing equipment, and fished harder. A few vessels sank in rough weather they shouldn't have been out in, gear often was lost, and the amount of bycatch grew. Over the same time, the budget to support government monitoring and enforcement of regulations decreased.

When everyone agrees that a fishery is heading into a terminal catastrophe, they are more likely to change how they manage and fish it. Change is a lot more acceptable when there don't seem to be any other options. In 1991, Canada brought in individual vessel quotas. All licensed vessels that had participated in the 1988 and 1989 seasons received quotas. The season was extended to eight months, allowing a new and more valuable market of fresh, rather than frozen, halibut to open. Processors protested because they lost business, and the crew members' union protested because crew sizes shrank again. Observers hired to validate the catch of each vessel were paid by a surcharge of 20 cents per kilogram (9 cents per pound) of halibut caught. Stiff penalties were established for those caught cheating, including forfeiture of the complete vessel quota.

At first, fishers could not buy or sell their vessel quotas. Then, in 1993, it became possible to transfer some quotas, a limited form of management by individual transferable quotas. In the past several years, about a hundred vessels have dropped out of the fishery as fishers have transferred their quotas, and there is little doubt that the management will evolve into one of fully divisible and transferable quotas similar to those of New Zealand and Iceland.

From 1990 to 1995, as halibut management in British Columbia developed, the U.S. halibut fishery continued unchanged, an open-access race involving three to four thousand vessels in the Gulf of Alaska, as dangerous and absurd as any fishery anywhere on the planet. Observing the apparent success of the Canadian shift to individual transferable quotas, the U.S. fishery is now changing as well. Over the next several years it will metamorphose into a system of individual transferable quota management. The changes are not popular with the fishers, for the quotas have been allocated to boat owners rather than boat skippers, causing the fishers to fight the new management system in the courts, so far unsuccessfully. At the same time, a portion of the harvest is also allocated to the coastal fishing villages of western Alaska in an attempt to protect them from economic collapse. Still, many vessels will drop out of the fishery, fewer fishers will work the boats, the season will expand, overcapitalization of the vessels will decrease, individual fishers should start to make a profit at fishing, and the race should end. The fish may even recover.

THE ATLANTIC WRECKFISH FISHERY

The United States is experimenting with individual transferable quotas, although there is now a moratorium on any new initiatives. In 1989, mid-Atlantic surf clam and ocean quahog fisheries were the only U.S. examples of this type of system. In 1992, however, the Atlantic wreckfish also came under management by individual transferable quotas. The history of this fishery is quite an extraordinary one, for it has compressed into less than a decade what has often taken many decades in other fisheries.

The wreckfish is one of the marine basses, rather like a grouper, and it is marketed as a kind of grouper. It lives out on the Blake Plateau, 75 kilometres (47 miles) off the coast of Georgia in about 500 to 800 metres (1600 to 2600 feet) of water. The fish was unknown until the mid-1980s, when swordfish longliners accidentally caught some while trying to retrieve lost gear from deep water. They pulled in an abundance of fine-looking, 14-kilogram (30-pound) fish, and a new fishery was born.

The fishery opened, as most new fisheries do, without regulations. An explosive boom fishery began. In 1987, two vessels harvested 13 600 kilograms (30 000 pounds) of wreckfish. In 1988, six vessels brought in 136 000 kilograms (300 000 pounds). In 1989, twenty-five vessels caught 900 000 kilograms (2 million pounds), and that became forty vessels and 1.8 million kilograms (4 million pounds) in 1990. The catch in 1990 would have been even higher, except that regulations finally came into play about two months into the season. Besides establishing a total allowable catch, the regulations included the usual ones of limiting access and closing the fishery during the spawning season; biologists were learning enough about wreckfish to provide their familiar form of advice.

Yet in those several years following discovery of the wreckfish stock, the fishery had already become another derby. The price of the fish dropped, the conflicts between fishers increased, and the fleet became overcapitalized—all in three to four years. Because the fishery was so far offshore, there was little hope that enforcement would be effective. Because the bycatch in this fishery was relatively little, and because there was no recreational interest in the species, since the fishery was so new, fisheries managers realized that it was an excellent candidate for management by individual transferable quotas. The management of the fishery wouldn't be confused by interference with fisheries of other species, nor would other politically powerful groups, such as recreational fishers, have to be considered.

In 1992, after only four years of explosive growth, management shifted to individual transferable quotas. For a vessel to be allowed to remain in the fishery, it had to have caught at least 5000 pounds (2268 kilograms) of wreckfish in both 1989 and 1990. Each vessel was given an initial limited share of the total catch, but fishers could begin buying and selling their quotas immediately. Although it will take another decade to be sure of the effects of such a change in management, the early information indicates that fishers are transferring ownership of quotas, that the number of vessels fishing for wreckfish is decreasing and that fishers are starting to make more money.

There may still be problems. The fishers leaving the fishery are probably moving to fish for other deep-water and inshore species such as groupers, snappers and tilefish. If so, they are developing an unregulated, multispecies fishery, and another more complex boom may occur. The experience of Iceland, New Zealand and Australia indicates that it is difficult—perhaps impossible—to establish management by individual transferable quotas in a piecemeal fashion. But it may be instructive to look at what actually happened in the wreckfish fishery—or rather at what didn't happen. In a classic boom-and-bust situation, it didn't bust.

AN EARLY EXPERIMENT: CANADA AND HERRING

After a decade of experience, we are starting to understand what the rules have to be for individual transferable quotas to work. One way to assess how important those rules are is to look at a case where they were only partially implemented and thus failed. Canada's well-intentioned attempt to manage its Atlantic herring stocks is one such example.

Canadians fished for Atlantic herring around the Atlantic Provinces for about a hundred years before 1960, supporting a small canned sardine industry. In the 1960s, when the herring began to be used as fish meal, large purse seiners began arriving in the Maritimes and removing large volumes of fish. In 1975, in an attempt to increase the market value of the fish as food for human consumption again, the minister of fisheries prohibited fishing for herring for fish meal. The fishers were resistant to losing the fish meal market, and the quality, price and numbers of fish continued to fluctuate as they had for the previous decade. Clearly some other action had to be taken.

By 1983, Canadian managers realized that the herring fishery would become stable and viable only if the fishing fleet could be reduced and if each boat had a quota. They introduced a formal system of transferable quotas, but with a number of restrictions. It allowed for the sale and purchase of individual boat quotas, but quotas could not be subdivided, and the whole scheme was set up on a trial basis, for ten years only. The managers hoped to cut the number of boats in half while doubling their quotas, making it profitable to be a herring fisher. To keep the employment level as high as possible, despite the anticipated reduction in number of vessels, individual boats were not allowed to accumulate quotas; each boat could own no more than 4 per cent of the total allowable catch. In other words, individual transferable quotas would really not be owned for very long, for ten years passes very quickly, nor would they be truly transferable beyond a very limited degree.

But for reasons both unsurprising and unexpected, the fleet was not reduced, quotas were not raised, and profits for the fishers did not increase. By 1992, the number of boats in the fishery did indeed drop, but only from forty-nine to thirty-nine. Many of the remaining boats were replaced. After ten years the boats were, on average, 3 per cent longer, 60 per cent larger and 28 per cent more powerful, and they were usually equipped with modern refrigeration facilities for keeping the fish cool. Instead of downsizing the fleet, a classic case of overcapitalization continued. Why would this happen when the fishers couldn't increase their quotas or their percentages of the total allowable catch? We expect overcapitalization to occur in open-access systems, not those using individual transferable quotas.

One reason was the unexpected emergence of a new market for herring, or at least for their eggs. Herring roe, when salted, is a favourite traditional end-of-year present for Japanese people to give each other. Sometimes it is flavoured with brandy, peppers or a variety of sauces. During the 1980s, Canadian Atlantic herring became one of the best sources of roe. For a short four to six weeks late each summer and autumn, the fishers raced for the fish, which were far more valuable as a source of roe than they were in any other way. Considering that only the roe, making up about 6 per cent of the weight of the herring, was sold, the fishery was remarkably wasteful. The fishers lobbied hard for increases in the total allowable catch, and therefore for larger quotas, and tended to get them. The fishers also noted that enforcement was slack and misreporting quite easy; they were able to under-report their catches by more than 50 per cent.

≈≈≈≈≈≈≈≈≈≈≈≈≈≈≈≈≈≈≈≈≈≈≈≈≈≈≈≈≈≈

*A*ny *fishery management system will fail if too many aspects are unstable,*
if cheating is extensive, if stock estimates are far too high or the total
allowable catch is unreasonably inflated.

≈≈≈≈≈≈≈≈≈≈≈≈≈≈≈≈≈≈≈≈≈≈≈≈≈≈≈≈≈≈

Instead of becoming more efficient under the influence of this limited version of management by individual transferable quotas, the fishery was subjected to competitive overfishing and overcapitalization. The very features that were supposed to be reduced raged on as fiercely as ever. Misreporting, that wonderful euphemism for cheating, made trying to purchase more quotas less interesting to the fishers. Why purchase more quotas when misreporting remains easy?

These, then, are the conditions under which management by individual transferable quotas must be expected to fail. There was an unexpected profitable market for the fish, inducing heavy competition in a short period of time; enforcement was inadequate and it was easy to misreport; annual quotas increased, hindering long-term stability of the fishery; there was uncertainty about the management system, which was guaranteed for only a decade; the fishers overvalued their quotas, probably because they included the misreported harvest, making it difficult for all but the naive to purchase quotas; and the market was unstable—the herring fishery has been buffeted by the meal market, the roe market, the collapse of North Sea herring stocks and recent growth of East European markets.

The initial years of individual transferable quotas in the Atlantic herring fishery may be one of the least successful attempts in the world. Like the other attempts, though, it has been an interesting experiment, for experiments that fail often tell us as much as those that don't. Any fishery management system will fail if too many aspects are unstable, if cheating is extensive, if stock estimates are far too high or the total allowable catch is unreasonably inflated. Economists suggest that for individual transferable quotas to work, they must be possible to hold in perpetuity, not for just a decade, for otherwise they lose most of their value as time passes. For efficient reduction of a fleet to occur, making it possible for fishers to turn a profit over a long period of time, enforceable and enforced quotas must exist that can be freely bought and sold without restrictions. Half measures—even if their intent is to sustain wide employment—make this system of management ineffective. Environmental organizations find this position extreme and intolerable, since it ignores the human factors and abandons fishing communities to unemployment, poverty and collapse of longstanding traditions. They propose that if management by individual transferable quotas is to exist, it must be restricted with care.

Nonetheless, the Atlantic herring remains an excellent candidate for management by individual transferable quotas. It is a single-species fishery, uncomplicated by the concerns of the groundfish multispecies fisheries. There are only a small number of participating fishers, making the human management side of the issue surely less complex than in the much larger multi-user fisheries such as the Pacific salmon fishery. The costs of the enforcement that is so obviously necessary will have to be paid by the fishers themselves, but this is true of whatever management system is used. The fishery has plenty of potential.

SHARING THE PROBLEM: THE EUROPEAN UNION

What happens when different countries share fisheries? Is management by individual transferable quotas still conceivable? Enclosed or semi-enclosed seas such as the Yellow Sea, the South China Sea, the Mediterranean or the North Sea would be reasonable examples to assess. Part IX of the 1982 Law of the Sea states that countries bordering such seas must cooperate in managing their shared fisheries. Expecting agreement on fisheries issues is hardly likely, however, when the countries sharing the coastline of the sea in question are in political conflict with each other. If joint management involving individual transferable quotas is possible, then the North Sea must be the best candidate. It is surrounded by seven countries, six of which are in the European Union and presumably have some intention of acting cooperatively.

The European Union, a title that rather overstates reality, is struggling to act in all of its affairs with responsibility and unity, obviously with varying degrees of success. It does have the Common Fisheries Policy, mandated to manage the fisheries in its Exclusive Economic Zones in the North Atlantic, the South Atlantic, the Indian Ocean, the Mediterranean and, most important, the North Sea.

The North Sea is one of the world's most complex fishing grounds. It is shallow and productive, rich in fish, with a long history of exploited fisheries. Twenty species of fish are still of commercial interest, and of these, ten support major fisheries. Until 1987, these fisheries were managed as if multispecies interactions didn't exist, each species managed independently. Dominated by trawlers and seiners, these fisheries fell victim to the familiar cycle of overfishing, declines in stock and the need for subsidies, while fish were wasted, black market sales flourished, and enforcement of existing regulations was as inadequate as it has been everywhere else. Now the Common Fisheries Policy divides the total allowable catch for each species into national quotas: each member country gets a fixed percentage each year. But little else is done. Fish stocks continue to decline at an alarming rate, and the EU governments disagree on how to stop the overfishing. In October 1996, Emma Bonino, the fisheries chief of the European Union, called for a 40 per cent reduction in catches, a reduction in the size of the fleets and a multibillion-dollar program to retrain or retire fishers. As she told a news conference, "Everyone knows there is overfishing, but there is no consensus on the therapy. Unless strong action is taken, market forces will simply lead to the law of the jungle." The North Sea is a region in need of better management, and individual transferable quotas should be an intriguing option to consider. They raise some interesting questions.

Can management by individual transferable quotas succeed in a complex multispecies fishery? The experience in New Zealand indicates that it ought to be possible. Can it succeed in a multicountry, multispecies fishery? There is the challenge. The main fear is that monopolies would emerge, that gradually over time all the fishing would be concentrated in the hands or nets of a relatively few fishers or companies. The fishing fleets of whole countries could disappear from the North Sea, for quotas could be traded across the community of countries. Not only would some coastal fishing communities die, but fishing might end in a country that has fished the North Sea for many centuries.

But there are always options. Obviously joint ownership of a fishery by seven countries is a lot more difficult than ownership by one or even two countries. At least proposals for multispecies management in the North Sea that limit fishing now exist, even if they haven't been implemented. Further proposals are not much more difficult to imagine. Starting with multispecies total allowable catches, each country could receive a percentage of the total allowable catch to then administer through individual transferable quotas. To prevent one country from monopolizing the fishery, a maximum percentage any country can own could be established.

Enforcement is probably the greatest problem, and it could prove to be too great. Everyone would have to agree to police each other, for otherwise misreporting and black market sales would become too tempting. But the EU is either a cooperating community, capable of such agreements, or it isn't. It has the

growing bureaucracy that should make individual transferable quotas, cooperation and enforcement possible to propose and perhaps even to implement.

What's to lose, anyway? People remain deeply concerned about the inevitable social disruption of fishing communities that is associated with management by individual transferable quotas. But unless some alternative system—
perhaps cooperative comanagement—evolves soon in those communities, they
will be disrupted anyway. The fishers of Denmark, for instance, know that
their fish have declined, that their current management system isn't working and
that they have far more fishing capacity than they need to catch the remaining
fish, yet, staring community catastrophe in the face, they remain opposed to
individual transferable quotas for fear the quotas will be concentrated in the
hands of a few fishers and traditional fishing will slip away. Economists looking at a situation like this ask in frustration, what are we trying to preserve—
poverty?

RESTRAINING THE SYSTEM

Open-access fishing results in overfishing and overcapitalization. When it is
only controlled by increasingly restrictive regulations, it results in the so-called
race for fish, marked by increasing capitalization and, in the worst cases, in
fishing derbies where the fishers may become frantic and exhausted and the
fishing is wasteful, chaotic and unsafe. Forced by the need to fish aggressively
in order to pay the bills of crew and mortgage, the boats fish every day the season is open, no matter what the weather. The weather can be dreadful, and
smaller boats are particularly vulnerable. In the past decade 160 fishers have
died in the fishing derbies just in the Gulf of Alaska.

In contrast, management that includes individual transferable quotas ought
to eliminate the overfishing and overcapitalization, along with the insanity of
the fishing derbies. Both fish stocks and fishers ought to be safer. The fishing is
still wasteful, so the problem of the bycatch remains to be resolved. And we are
haunted by the prospect that the largest vessels or the largest corporations will
acquire all the available quotas and push the smaller vessels and companies out
of business, along with the coastal communities that support them.

Neither scenario is tolerable. If management by individual transferable quotas is going to continue to spread around the world, as is likely, it will need to
be constrained in order to limit the social disruption that will accompany it. In
the United States, environmentalist organizations such as the Sierra Club and
Greenpeace have taken the lead in proposing constraints. Their vehicle has
been the reauthorization of the Magnuson Act.

In 1976 the U.S. Congress passed the Magnuson Fisheries and Conservation

Act, a far-reaching piece of legislation that governed the management of U.S. fish stocks. It established the 200-mile U.S. EEZ, it divided the seaboard up into management regions, and it developed stock assessment procedures for all species. It provided a forum for many different perspectives on management questions. Until 1996, reauthorization of the act has been fairly automatic, involving extensions of existing laws. Reauthorization of the act in 1996 has been quite another story.

≈≈≈≈≈≈≈≈≈≈≈≈≈≈≈≈≈≈≈≈≈≈≈≈≈≈≈≈≈≈≈

If management by individual transferable quotas is going to continue to spread around the world, as is likely, it will need to be constrained in order to limit the social disruption that will accompany it.

≈≈≈≈≈≈≈≈≈≈≈≈≈≈≈≈≈≈≈≈≈≈≈≈≈≈≈≈≈≈≈

Environmentalists, fishers and politicians, concerned about overfishing, wasted fish and a need to protect fishing communities, seized on the reauthorization as an opportunity for change. The proposals moved slowly through the U.S. House and Senate and their committees and finally got Senate approval in early autumn of 1996, in time to help the legislators in their run for reelection. The new version, renamed the Sustainable Fisheries Act, works to prevent overfishing, reduce the wasteful bycatch, strengthen habitat recovery and encourage the buyback of boats and licences in order to reduce the fishing fleets. It redefines optimal yield to mean long-term sustainability in both economic and ecological terms. And it faces some of the issues raised by management by individual transferable quotas.

There is now, in the United States, a moratorium on new initiatives to manage by individual transferable quotas, allowing time for a federal study to assess the benefits and drawbacks of the system. Where individual transferable quotas currently exist, those who hold the quotas will be charged a fee to pay for enforcement. Programs that hold back some of the total quota for the use of coastal communities already exist, particularly on the Alaskan coast of the Bering Sea, where Native communities depend on fishing. These programs will continue to exist, but no new ones will be permitted in the Bering Sea.

There is a clear undercurrent of conflict in these changes to the Magnuson Act. The fishing corporations will certainly continue to lobby hard for management by individual transferable quotas, while the environmentalists will push for more restrictions. The Sierra Club has taken a clear stand out of concern for both fishery and fishers. It states that the quota a fisher buys or is given must not be considered a private right or title to what is a public resource; if the stock needs protection or if the needs of other resource management programs intrude, it is essential that the quota can be eliminated. The Sierra Club opposes ownership of a large portion of any fishery by large factory trawlers. No one should be able to accumulate a large amount of the total quota of a fishery—the club suggests that 20 per cent is a reasonable maximum. It proposes that 10 to 50 per cent of the potential harvest of a fishery should not be allocated, leaving a sizable buffer to protect the fishery from unexpected decline and to provide small-boat fishers with something to fish for. The quotas given to the small-boat fishers need not be transferable, provided they are sufficient to support the fishers and the traditions of their communities. Enforcement should involve observers on every vessel, adequate training of observers, strict recordkeeping and fees collected from quota holders not only to pay for the enforcement but also for the costs of managing the quotas—up to a maximum of 5 per cent of the value of the catch. These are not extreme measures, and they ought to be workable.

Management by individual transferable quotas is with us, if not to stay, then at least as long as it results in the more efficient harvest of fish or until better alternatives emerge. It is a system that can be made more acceptable by restricting it to prevent monopolization of the fishery and to protect small-boat fishers. One of the toughest issues that remains is how to divide the total allowable catch of a fishery in a way that is fair to inshore commercial fishers, large factory trawlers offshore and recreational fishers. It may also be reasonable to manage offshore fisheries through individual transferable quotas but manage inshore fisheries that the small-boat fishers and their communities depend on through quite a different, community-based system of management. Failure or refusal to consider both the restrictions and the alternatives to individual transferable quotas will provoke social costs that are unfortunate and unnecessary, even though the fish may be better off.

CHAPTER 9

COMANAGEMENT: BUZZWORD FOR THE MILLENNIUM

"You show me a lobster fisherman fifty miles from home, and I'll show you a poor lost son of a bitch."

Herring fisher,
quoted by James Acheson
THE LOBSTER GANGS OF MAINE

COMMUNITY-BASED MANAGEMENT

Since most fisheries of most countries are declining, are at their maximum level of exploitation or have crashed, and since most management in recent years has been by some agency of the central governments, many people have started to question the government's ability to manage. The endless challenge is to sustain fish, income, jobs and communities, and under government management of fisheries all of these have too often eroded to depressing levels. There simply must be alternatives to government control. No matter how successful and efficient management by individual transferable quotas turns out to be, wherever it is established there is a risk that it will destroy any traditional coastal fishing practices that may exist. There must be other options to think about, some other solution besides management by individual transferable quotas or the capital-intensive, fleet-intensive, high-tech methods of modern commercial fisheries, administered from afar.

Such solutions exist, but they have been mostly ignored and disparaged and are often unable to compete with the high-tech commercial operations of recent decades. Most of the people who actually fish, even now, are the inhabitants of coastal communities, fishing the inshore shallow waters with low-tech gear from small boats. Communities around the world's coasts, including Pacific islanders, Southeast Asians, Native North Americans and northern Norwegians among many others, have exploited the fishable populations close to shore for hundreds and sometimes thousands of years. They have worked out ways to reduce conflicts over access to the fish and to be relatively equitable in deciding who gets what fish. Although coastal fisheries everywhere are largely overfished, some communities have developed ways to prevent overfishing. Community-based management may be the way of the past, but it still has much to teach us.

The Pacific islands such as Kiribati and Fiji and the coasts of Asia, from India to Japan, are the best places to look for community-based control of fisheries, for western methods have been slower to intrude there. Even so, in most places we really don't know much about how the control is currently carried out. We also don't know what these communities were like before the stresses of recent decades have brought in centralizing governments and western technology and have made people more mobile and less loyal to their communities. Continuity is easily lost and traditions prove to be fragile, existing only in the memories of a dying minority. Some places, such as Kiribati and Japan, seem to be successful at managing their nearby fish populations, but with others it's hard to tell; and still others, such as Malaysia and Singapore, seem to have failed as the human population has increased. The questions are important, though. Can community-based management work? And even if it does work, can it have much relevance in most of the world? The answer, as always, is maybe, sometimes, some places, with help from the central government. How it is structured varies greatly.

KINSHIP-BASED COMMUNITIES

A community can only hope to control the waters nearby, waters that it can actually watch. The sea in front of the community is part of its territory, where it has exclusive rights to fish. The territory may extend to the reef's edge, if a reef is present, but usually not much farther; 16 kilometres (10 miles) seems to be about the maximum extent offshore a territory may reach. Those who fish this exclusive area all come from the community, working from small one- to three-person boats, returning daily or nightly to the community. The territory may extend along the coast until it hits the territory of the next community, but it has strict boundaries.

Despite the many differences in how communities organize and control fishing practices, even when they exist in the same region, they share some essential features. For example, a community authority lays down the law and resolves conflicts; that authority may be a village council, a village elder or chief, or perhaps a fisheries specialist in the community. Rarely is the fishing open access, available to all members of the community; instead, the number of fishers is strictly restricted. Who fishes usually depends on birthright, marriage

≈≈≈≈≈≈≈≈≈≈≈≈≈≈≈≈≈≈≈≈≈≈≈≈≈≈≈≈≈≈≈≈

*Fishing in most places has been a way of life,
not simply a commercial undertaking.*

≈≈≈≈≈≈≈≈≈≈≈≈≈≈≈≈≈≈≈≈≈≈≈≈≈≈≈≈≈≈≈≈

and kinship, whether the community is in Sri Lanka or the Philippines. Rules govern not just the basic right to fish but also what gear gets used, when different species are fished, what behaviour is unacceptable and how the catch will be distributed. The rules state who can fish where in the community territory and usually stipulate ways of ensuring that fishers take turns fishing the more productive sites, often by lottery. Fishing gear that others consider harmful, such as a trawl, is prohibited, but gear that others consider to be too efficient, giving its owner an unfair advantage, may also be prohibited.

Enforcement again is critical. The community is most sensitive to outsiders trying to fish in its territory. An outsider may be granted the right to fish in a community's territory under unusual conditions, and only by permission of the village authority. Anyone from outside the community fishing without permission is dealt with quickly and probably painfully. In Western Samoa when someone within the community breaks the rules, he or she is usually shamed and ridiculed—a remarkably effective way of modifying human behaviour. Repeated or more serious offences may result in ostracism, banishment, fines, destruction of gear, forced labour, even death. These days, offenders are generally fined.

Just because a human activity is longstanding doesn't mean that it is necessarily good or useful. Sometimes it is, but it usually is marginally interesting just because it has survived. The fishing traditions that have grown up in so many coastal communities are not necessarily conservationist. Sometimes they are, since breeding populations of fish are often left unfished. But for the most part the communities have been small enough, the rules restricting membership to the group of fishers strict enough and the resource abundant or unpredictable enough that the fish, jobs and community have all kept going. Fishing in most places has been a way of life, not simply a commercial undertaking. To be fair, most traditions are just local customs that change over time as circumstances change and knowledge builds or decays. The local customs of coastal communities may work, may have persisted for many years because they do work and are therefore worth assessing to see if they can be transferred to other communities and other fisheries. Or they may not be helpful in the least.

GOVERNMENT INVOLVEMENT: COMANAGEMENT

Community-based management is unlikely now to ever be completely free of government intrusion. The extent of government involvement may vary considerably, and as a result it is almost impossible to define exactly what the relationship between community and government should be. It is increasingly recognized, however, that community and government can actually cooperate in the management of coastal fisheries. The best examples of such comanagement are in the island country of Kiribati and in Japan, but others exist in western countries now as well. Comparing them, and their success, should help us assess whether comanagement is a humane and realistic alternative to privatization.

Kiribati

Kiribati, pronounced "Kiribass," is a country of coral atolls north of Fiji and the Samoan Islands, sprawling over 3300 kilometres (2000 miles) of the Pacific. Some thirty-nine low, nutrient-poor atolls of what was known in colonial days as the Gilbert, Ellice, Phoenix and Line Islands make up Kiribati, now an independent state with a history that is typical of the region. Annexed by the British around the turn of the century, the islands, especially Tarawa, the main island of the Gilbert part of the chain, were invaded and occupied by the Japanese in 1941 and then lost by the Japanese to the Americans in 1943. After the war, Christmas Island became famous as the site where the British tested their atom bomb. Thirty years later the islands became the independent state of Kiribati. Somehow, despite the prolonged and detailed attention of the Europeans, Japanese and Americans, the traditional ways did not get lost. Since the country depends on fish for protein and trade, the old traditions of community fishing have remained particularly strong. Because Kiribati has so many islands scattered over such a great distance, the new Law of the Sea gave the country possession of 13 million square kilometres (5 million square miles) of sea. Managing the fisheries of such an immense EEZ is extremely complex, but Kiribati has treated the inshore coastal fisheries independently of any arrangements it has made concerning its new offshore exclusive fisheries zone.

With the inshore fisheries, the government of Kiribati has converted local traditional practice into law. Each island has autonomous control over its coastal fisheries, and coastal communities have clear territorial rights. Local government councils, one per island, recognize the traditional ownership rights of each village, clan or family and punish any breaches of the laws. They manage the inshore fisheries, while the central government of the country manages the offshore fisheries. Each clan of relatives, living in a group of houses sharing a piece of land, has the rights to a strip of reef and lagoon. The rights are inherited by the eldest son, the territory to be shared equally with his brothers. Women inherit nothing, since they are expected to marry into another clan, with its separate rights. The village elders hold authority over the use of the fisheries. The law is clear: fishing without authority in any traditional fishing ground of any clan is illegal. The rules can be very specific—for instance, using fishing nets in the flying fish fishery is illegal, for it disturbs the fish and is unfair to those who lack such nets to fish with. On one island, Tamanan, disturbing a school of feeding tuna by dropping a paddle or releasing a fish or letting a pole touch the water has also been considered a severe offence. Anyone who breaks the rules could be banned from fishing for a season or possibly have his canoe wrecked, though these days a fine or imprisonment is more likely.

Is this community-based management? Well, mainly. Legislated into law by the central government, the management system gives fishers no option but to fish according to the community rules. The enforcement comes not only from the village; it is backed up by the island council, which in turn has the power of the central government behind it. Is Kiribati a useful example? It has a small population, a long coastline, many villages, a society largely dependent on fish and a long tradition of community-level control that somehow survived the political upheaval of the past century. It works for Kiribati, but can it work elsewhere?

Japan

Tradition, some isolation from commercial fishing vessels and legislation enforcing the tradition—is that what it takes to initiate or sustain community-based management? The rather remarkable arrangement in Japan suggests it might be. There, once again, coastal fisheries have been controlled at the village level for centuries. The concept of open access, of individuals competing greedily against one another without restraints, has always been alien, not the Japanese way. As in Kiribati, tradition has become law. In Japan community-based management was legislated by laws in 1901 and then again after World War II in 1949. Community territories that go back many centuries were mapped and registered in 1901, when formal Fisheries Association Cooperatives were established around the entire country except at the major ports.

Unlike Kiribati, Japan is a complex, crowded, industrial state, and it alone of the world's developed states manages all of its coastal fisheries at the local, community level.

Japan treats its three major fisheries sectors quite differently. The distant-water fleets fish beyond the 200 mile-limit of the EEZ; boats of 10 tonnes or more fish offshore, inside the 200-mile limit but seaward of the coastal fisheries;

≈≈≈≈≈≈≈≈≈≈≈≈≈≈≈≈≈≈≈≈≈≈≈≈≈≈≈≈≈≈

Once again, as in Kiribati, coastal community-based fisheries management is really comanagement between higher state authority and the local communities.

≈≈≈≈≈≈≈≈≈≈≈≈≈≈≈≈≈≈≈≈≈≈≈≈≈≈≈≈≈≈

and the coastal fishers fish from smaller boats, near shore, near their home ports or communities. Boats such as large trawlers and purse seiners that fish for highly mobile fish species with gear that must be moved around are licensed individually and operate under free competition. In contrast, small boats that fish for coastal, inshore species use fixed gear, and territorial rights to those fish are carefully negotiated and enforced. Rights are given for different types of gear, such as traps or beach seines, or for nets set for herring, trout and salmon.

The Fisheries Association Cooperatives are the critical units, comparable to the island councils in Kiribati, but they are more complex, in keeping with the greater size and complexity of the problems that need to be resolved in Japan. Each is the centre of activity of its community. All fishers must belong to one, which then protects its members from other fisheries. To have the right to fish, one must live in the community and already be an experienced fisher. This has the ring of Catch-22 to it, except that a fisher becomes experienced by helping someone else in the family, an apprenticeship that could last for years. Each cooperative gives out fishing rights, allocates fishing territories and distributes territories by lottery when there is reason to. Conflicts are inevitable; a greater belief in cooperative approaches doesn't mean that people somehow agree with each other more easily. The usual conflicts occur, over territorial rights, over gear use, over intrusions by outsiders. When a conflict arises, all parties involved meet, negotiating and making compromises until consensus is achieved; rule by majority vote is not the essential Japanese way either.

Five thousand cooperatives initially covered the coast. Since 1949, some have fused, sometimes because of local depopulation of that part of the coast as people have migrated to the cities, sometimes because the area was heavily fished by several cooperatives and fusion allowed for more successful sharing of sea space and resolution of conflicts. But the system remains as it was intended, loosened a little in recent years by the increasing mobility of people. Once again, as in Kiribati, coastal community-based fisheries management is really comanagement between higher state authority and the local communities. The national government sets out basic policies, such as the laws of 1901 and 1949. On behalf of the Ministry of Agriculture, Forestry and Fisheries, prefecture offices grant coastal fishing rights to the cooperatives in the prefecture, and the cooperatives then allocate those rights to the fishers within their memberships. It is quite a heavy bureaucracy, as perhaps might be expected.

Fishers have no options; if they want to fish in coastal waters, they must be members of the community cooperative. Otherwise they cannot fish. They must keep the rules of the cooperative or risk ridicule, punishment and loss of fishing rights. Nevertheless, individual fishers are still as competitive and secretive as fishers are everywhere else. Success varies among fishers, for skill varies and individuals have secret fishing spots that may be more productive than other spots. They guard their secrets well, eventually pass them on to their sons and are rewarded for their greater skill and knowledge with higher prestige within the community.

Norway

Is mandatory, nationwide community-based management of inshore fisheries really possible outside of places like Japan and Kiribati? Does the whole nation need to follow the same policy, or can different fisheries be run by different management systems? And just how important is it to base management on centuries of tradition? The solution to the problems that arose in the Norwegian fishery for Arctic cod suggests that different roads can lead to similar destinations.

Norwegians fish for Arctic cod around the Lofoten Islands, a couple of degrees north of the Arctic circle, where the fish migrate to spawn between January and April. During the nineteenth century, more and more boats worked the grounds, fishing with hand lines, gillnets, longlines and seines. Conflicts, especially over use of gear, escalated as the boats became crowded together. As a result, the government stepped in with comanagement legislation in the late 1890s, delegating much of the management responsibility to the fishers. District committees, representing the different types of gear, established the rules, determining when fishing could take place, where each type of gear could be used and how much space could be given to the different types of gear. Elected inspectors had the job of enforcing the rules, but that didn't work well, for it's tough to police the community you live in and grew up in.

Better to ignore the cheating and keep your friends, or your health, depending on the situation. In any case, the government also set up a public enforcement agency that sent in its own boats and officers to the fishing grounds to make sure that fishers fished for what they were supposed to, when and where they were supposed to and with the type of gear they were supposed to use.

So perhaps comanagement will be easier to transfer to appropriate fisheries than we might have expected. The rest of the Norwegian fisheries are not managed in this way, but to fish for Arctic cod, fishers again have no choice but to keep to the rules of the district committees or not fish. The management scheme wasn't built on tradition but on a need to eliminate chaos, suggesting that tradition in itself isn't necessary for successful comanagement. A strong central government probably is, if only to legislate decentralization. Central authority may also be necessary to enforce regulations, since in Norway the enforcement methods of Kiribati and Japan, involving personal pride and shame, are unlikely to operate.

The United Kingdom and the United States

The examples of Japan, Kiribati and Norway suggest that tradition may not be necessary, but it helps. Rules must be enforced through local or state methods. And there can be no choice: people cannot opt out and still participate in the fishery. In places in the United Kingdom, Canada and the United States, there are instances where comanagement has developed with varying degrees of optional membership and success. They should help us to understand just where and how community-based management of fisheries is likely to work.

In the United Kingdom, a kind of comanagement operates not in a coastal fishery but in an offshore fishery. Before 1984, the government issued individual fish quotas to individual fishers, a familiar example of management at the state level. Then, when a decision was made to decentralize fishery management, the government gave the authority to regulate the fishery to local producers' organizations; there were about fifteen in 1986. Instead of allocating individual quotas, the government allocated a total allowable catch to each organization. Each organization then divided that total among its members, essentially dishing out individual quotas, taking over that responsibility from the government. No territories were allocated, as in the examples of coastal comanagement. Regulations were enforced only by enforcing the individual quotas of the member fishers. This system is still in place, and apparently it is working reasonably well. Because enforcement is in the hands of the local organization or cooperative, however, the fishery has the same inherent problems as the Norwegian cod fishery. Even more of a problem, though, is that fishers do not have to belong to the cooperative; if they don't like the rules, they may drop out and negotiate their individual quotas directly with the government, as they had done before. Still, conflicts remain, for different organizations may share the same port but have different regulations, and so inequities may persist and fester. Inequities, probable cheating, voluntary membership, offshore fishing out of sight of community observers—maybe this arrangement can be sustained a while longer, but it isn't stable and will not last. It just hasn't failed yet.

A more interesting example, but one that like so many others is slipping into history, is the lobster fishery of Maine. The State of Maine sets the regulations: any lobster that is kept to sell must fall within a minimum and maximum length; no female with eggs can be kept; a female caught carrying eggs must have her tail notched, identifying her as a breeder, never to be kept when caught again; and all traps must have an escape vent to help undersized lobsters escape. For the most part, the lobstermen accept the regulations, though they resist any increase in the minimum size. It would be nice to think that lobsters have a chance to breed before they moult to a size large enough for them to be kept when trapped, but the minimum size is still too small for most to have bred even once. A small increase in the legal minimum size would mean that lobsters might have a greater chance of breeding before they are caught for the last time. It would also mean that lobstermen would suffer a one-year loss in catch rate, since the lobsters would probably need another year to grow to the new minimum size. Short-term pain is always difficult to sell. In any case, government managers and biologists regulate this fishery. Only permanent residents of Maine are licensed to trap lobsters, but otherwise there is no strict licensing nor inheritance of licenses, as on the east coast of Canada, for instance.

Until recently, the state-regulated lobster fishery of Maine was also very much a community-based fishery. In each bay, the local lobstermen fished from territories they had inherited or negotiated for, controlled membership in their group and ruthlessly prevented outsiders from sharing in the fishing. They have been described as lobster gangs, each with its own fiefdom. They represent a successful effort at comanagement, grown from tradition, neither legislated by the state nor particularly sanctioned by the state either. Each gang defended its territory, usually a bay along that remarkable coastline of bays. The lobstermen used ritualized threats to scare off intruders from adjacent bays. In *The Lobster Gangs of Maine*, James Acheson writes, "The violator is usually warned, sometimes by verbal threats and abuse, but usually by surreptitious molestation of lobstering gear. Two half-hitches of rope may be tied around the spindle of the buoy, or legal-sized lobsters may be taken out and the doors of the trap left open." If these signals were ignored, the gangs resorted to destruction of gear and occasionally to violence. Each gang had ways to restrict its membership and to control where each members set their traps. It was effective community-level action, restricting fishing and ensuring that enough lobsters remained to support them all. In recent years, however, the familiar events have occurred: lobstermen have overcapitalized and increased their efforts to catch the same number of lobsters, more are trapping the lobsters, the community gangs have not been able to persist except in more remote areas, and the fishery has lost much of its comanaged structure. Without legislation that makes the gangs in some way legal, they have little hope of survival. Whether or not they should survive is a different question.

SO WHAT DO WE HAVE?

Central, state-controlled management isn't the only option. Local, community-based management has existed in most parts of the world through long tradition. Cooperative organizations have also emerged in places that provide a vehicle for local management where long tradition may not exist. But local management without government sanction, without legislation supporting it, isn't likely to work for very long; when in conflict with central government policy and high-tech boats, small-scale fisheries lose every time. With government backing, however, community-based management has a chance to work, particularly for inshore, coastal fisheries; even then, though, it cannot be voluntary.

Comanagement comes in many forms, ranging in the extent of government involvement. Pure community-based management, without any government intrusion, might be possible to imagine, but it is too unrealistic to expect. With any comanagement, the state still has a major role; at the least it legislates the general principles of the cooperation between the communities and the central government, giving the arrangement the formal sanction it needs. Then state managers usually set the catchable quotas for the various species; the state divides the quotas among the community cooperatives or organizations; and each cooperative then allocates its quota among its members and ensures that fishers don't cheat. Enforcement is truly the stickiest issue, for no one wants the job; we still have much to learn and many methods to try in order to make it work.

Comanagement lets the community carry as much responsibility as possible. Each cooperative or organization sets its own rules and can try to provide more equitable sharing of fishing rights. At its best, it can accommodate individuals who have experienced hardships or who have many dependents. It can provide a decent way to resolve local disputes and represent the group in conflicts with other sectors. It ought to allow more rapid response to the changing conditions that are typical of every fishery, for if anyone knows what is really happening to a local stock of fish, the fisher fishing for it ought to.

But comanagement is no cure-all for the complex problems of the complex state of fisheries management. Greed and cheating; conflicts over gear, territory, licences, quotas and cooperative regulations; enforcement; uncertainty

≈≈≈≈≈≈≈≈≈≈≈≈≈≈≈≈≈≈≈≈≈≈≈≈≈≈≈≈

Community-based management of fisheries, where it works, suggests that the tragedy of the commons is not inevitable.

≈≈≈≈≈≈≈≈≈≈≈≈≈≈≈≈≈≈≈≈≈≈≈≈≈≈≈≈

about the true condition and size of the fish populations and hence what the catchable quotas ought to be; political manoeuvring that occurs almost every time more than three people get together to try to decide something—all these problems continue.

However, the objective remains to conserve jobs, fish and communities. Conserving all three will be difficult, but comanagement gives the people doing the fishing a role in the decision making and greater stakes in the conservation of the species fished, and it may reduce the cheating. Providing individuals with quotas or territories eliminates some of the competition that otherwise drives the fisheries to extinction. Controlling membership at the local level may not really be equitable, since only a few members may end up getting the jobs, but at least it is a local, community decision, not one delivered from on high.

Success at comanagement probably depends most on the ability of the local group to resolve conflicts. Village elders, group consensus or majority vote may be used to resolve conflicts, depending on the cultural traditions. Conflicts don't disappear, and anyway they are well known to stimulate compromise and change. But if the local organization is too large, embracing too many interest groups—for instance, those using different types of gear, those fishing for different species or those representing different sectors of the fisheries—then agreement can be elusive and the organization will probably fracture. If the group is small and represents only a very small constituency, agreement may come easily, but most competing interests will not be considered and the group will be parochial and ineffective.

Community-based management of fisheries, where it works, suggests that the tragedy of the commons is not inevitable. As more and more fishers participate in an open-access fishery, the resource will eventually crash. But along many of the coasts of the world, where people fish close to shore, interact with each other, watch each other and discipline each other, open access hasn't existed. Open-access competition is a western phenomenon unknown to traditional coastal fisheries. Overfishing occurs where there is no clear enforcement, where regulations and stock estimates are inadequate, and where overcapitalization of fleets and improved hunting equipment push the fishers to longer hours and greater success at finding what is still there. It occurs where community-based management, traditional or recent, cannot reach or has broken down. But humans have shown over and over again that at the community level they can regulate themselves and their resources and that the commons tragedy need not apply. It does apply where central governments have legislated open access, believing it to be more equitable or more cost effective. Then the dire predictions seem accurate: stocks crash, fisheries are closed, jobs are lost, and communities decay.

CHAPTER 10

THE EMPTY BANKS

I saw this documentary about how codfish have been gill-netted into extinction in Newfoundland in Canada, so I went out to Burger King to get a Whaler fishwich-type breaded deep-fried filet sandwich while there was still time.

Douglas Coupland
MICROSERFS

A crisis is that turning point beyond which things can never be the same again: they may change for the better or they may result in disaster, but there is no going back.

Rosemary Ommer, "One Hundred Years of Fishery Crises in Newfoundland," ACADIENSIS

Of all the stories about the world's fisheries, this is the saddest. Many catastrophes have occurred in fisheries around the planet in recent years, but none is quite as devastating as the closing of the fishing banks from Cape Cod to Newfoundland along the northeast coast of North America. This area once supported the richest of the world's groundfish fisheries. Now most fishing is banned, and coastal fishing communities are dying. We talk about hopes for some limited recovery of some of the fish in the years ahead, fearing we will never return to how things were just a few years ago.

Real change can be very difficult to accomplish when all is going relatively well—or at least seems to be. Only when no options are left but to restructure or to start over in new ways because the old ones simply did not work and when everyone agrees that the old ways have failed can true change occur. Fish are resilient, and fish populations should recover on the fishing banks. People will then certainly fish the banks again, but the renewed fisheries will have to be managed in new ways. There is no other choice.

The glaciers of the most recent ice age, the Wisconsin Ice Age, which withdrew 14 000 to 10 000 years ago, covered the land as far south as Long Island, and the land then extended to the edges of the current fishing banks. The glaciers left terminal moraines, or hills of till, as they began to withdraw. Where they paused in their withdrawal, and the till accumulated even more, the glaciers left behind what is now Cape Cod and Long Island, Martha's Vineyard and Nantucket Island. As the glaciers melted, the sea rose and flooded inland, drowning

≈≈≈≈≈≈≈≈≈≈≈≈≈≈≈≈≈≈≈≈≈≈≈≈≈≈≈≈≈≈≈

Many catastrophes have occurred in fisheries around the planet in recent years, but none is quite as devastating as the closing of the fishing banks from Cape Cod to Newfoundland along the northeast coast of North America.

≈≈≈≈≈≈≈≈≈≈≈≈≈≈≈≈≈≈≈≈≈≈≈≈≈≈≈≈≈≈≈

the lower hills of till. These hills are the famous fishing banks, dominated by Georges Bank in the south, off Cape Cod, and forming the southern side of the Gulf of Maine and the Grand Banks, off southeastern Newfoundland.

The interaction of tides, winds, currents and submerged offshore banks forces the mixing of surface and bottom waters and provides some of the most extensive nutrient-rich waters in the world. Immense blooms of phytoplankton feed immense populations of zooplankton, which have the potential to nourish huge numbers of small fish, which in turn are preyed upon by larger fish. The abundance of groundfish in this ecosystem has made the banks famous since they were discovered by the Europeans.

THE FISH OF THE BANKS

The groundfish, or demersal fish, that have dominated the fisheries on the banks are cod and codlike fish, a variety of flatfish and redfish, which are also known as ocean perch. As stocks of these species have declined, spiny dogfish shark and an assortment of skates, which are related to sharks but feed rather like flounders, have flourished. Although the groundfish have been the most valuable stocks, pelagic fish have also been heavily harvested. They include Atlantic herring, Atlantic mackerel that migrate in seasonally from warmer water, seasonal migrants of giant bluefin tuna and, in the northern part of the region, capelin, which are small, streamlined fish of the smelt family.

The Atlantic cod has always been the most abundant and most important of all the groundfish along the Atlantic coast, but haddock, pollock and silver hake have been heavily fished as well. Both haddock and pollock have the deep bodies, three distinctive dorsal fins and two anal fins that are typical of fish of the cod family. Haddock never really recovered from the intense fishing of the 1960s, whereas pollock became more valuable in the commercial harvest as the numbers of haddock declined. Silver hake is a thinner fish, and its dorsal and anal fins are less clearly divided than those of cod, but it is still quite closely related. North Americans seem not to have acquired much of a taste for it, but distant-water fleets have eagerly fished for it.

Among the flatfish, four are small species: American plaice, yellowtail flounder, witch flounder (or gray sole) and winter flounder (Figure 10). Each has its particular shape, habits and life history. Once they are filleted, however, they all look and taste alike, and all four are marketed as "sole," sold as fresh or frozen fillets. Two much larger flatfish, Atlantic halibut and turbot or Greenland halibut, are also harvested; both prefer colder water, living as far north as the coast of Greenland. Not quite as large as Pacific halibut, Atlantic halibut can still grow to over 45 kilograms (100 pounds), though of course far smaller fish were harvested as the larger ones disappeared. Halibut steaks deserve their reputation, and for some people they are even worth the high cost. Turbot, however, has not caught on in the North American supermarkets, despite its fame in 1995 as the source of the skirmish between Canada and Spain in their brief "turbot war."

THE DOMINATION OF COD

For almost five full centuries, the northeast coast of North America has been famous for its fish, and none more than the northern cod. From the time of Henry Cabot's first trip in 1497 until the 1950s, cod were thought to be almost unlimited in numbers, easily caught by jigging and in inshore traps they swam into but could not swim out of. A steady catch from the 1850s to the 1950s of about 200 000 tonnes per year, sustained by an adult population of about 1.3 million tonnes, in turn was clearly sustainable.

The Europeans began fishing for northern cod even before 1500, for word spread very quickly following Columbus's first trips. The Portuguese, French and Spanish came first, followed by the English. Britain, wanting dry-cured salt cod, established settlements along the coast of Newfoundland. By the early 1800s, the inshore catch reached about 150 000 tonnes and grew slowly to about 250 000 tonnes by 1920. The first trawlers arrived with the Spanish fleet in 1927, and others arrived with the Portuguese in 1936. But the fish stocks appeared to be able to withstand the growing pressure.

The drastic and catastrophic change in harvesting rate only occurred with the coming of the large factory trawlers in the late 1950s; it took just another

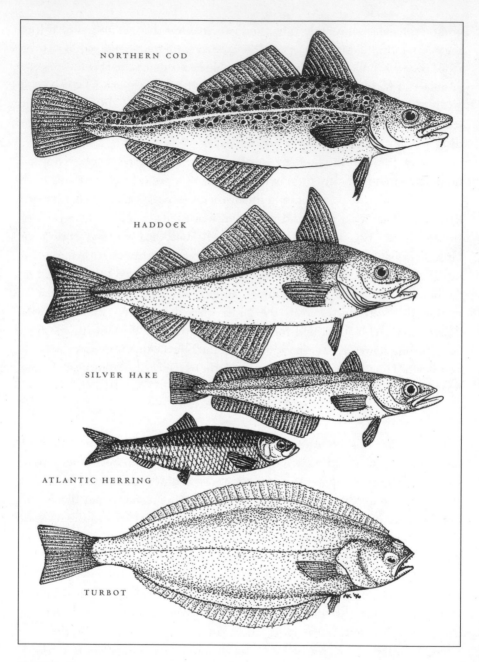

NORTHERN COD

HADDOCK

SILVER HAKE

ATLANTIC HERRING

TURBOT

FIGURE 10

Fish of the Northwest Atlantic Fishing Banks. The groundfish such as northern cod, haddock and silver hake have supported major fisheries, the turbot or Greenland halibut almost caused a fish war between Spain and Canada, and the Atlantic herring is valued primarily for its eggs or roe, which are sold to the Japanese market.

fifteen years after that to deplete one of the planet's greatest fish stocks. The former Soviet Union sent in its first freezer trawler in 1958 and was joined by East Germany, Poland, Iceland, Norway and the United Kingdom in the early 1960s. By 1968, the annual catch of cod reached 783 000 tonnes. The fish were harvested at the absurdly unsustainable rate of two-thirds of the total fishable

≈≈≈≈≈≈≈≈≈≈≈≈≈≈≈≈≈≈≈≈≈≈≈≈≈≈≈≈≈≈≈≈

Five hundred years of fishing and fifty years of research, and we still don't know enough about cod to predict its numbers and movements with accuracy.

≈≈≈≈≈≈≈≈≈≈≈≈≈≈≈≈≈≈≈≈≈≈≈≈≈≈≈≈≈≈≈≈

biomass in a single year. The small-boat, inshore fishery suffered terribly, its total catch dropping from 172 000 tonnes in 1956 to just 35 000 tonnes in 1974. Not surprisingly, total stocks, inshore and offshore, declined precipitously to 214 000 tonnes by 1976, despite intense efforts to catch a lot more.

When the fishing limit was extended to 200 miles in 1976, the foreign fleets moved elsewhere and Canada energetically invested in its own offshore fleet to replace the departing vessels. The total allowable catch grew from 160 000 tonnes in 1977 to 266 000 tonnes in 1985. While Canada fished heavily and unsustainably within its new 200-mile limits, other nations, particularly from the European Union, continued to fish heavily on the nose and tail of the Grand Banks, the bits that protruded beyond the 200-mile limit.

Five hundred years of fishing and fifty years of research, and we still don't know enough about cod to predict its numbers and movements with accuracy. Cod migrate inshore in spring along deeper, warmer trenches (all of 2° to 3° C, or 36° to 37° F) underneath colder shelf waters that are near 0° C (32° F). The large schools, hundreds of millions strong, were last detected in the spring of 1990; in 1991 and then again in 1992, before the moratorium, they were far smaller. While in their migration schools, the cod keep about eight to ten body lengths apart, about the distance they can probably see and scan for prey in the very dim light remaining at a depth of 350 metres (1150 feet) or so. A school usually stays intact until it hits prey such as capelin and shrimp, and then the cod disperse to chase them down.

At the beginning of the spring migration, the adult cod gather and spawn. They court and pair up on the bottom and then rise off the bottom in spawning pairs, shedding eggs and sperm into the water, where the fertilized eggs develop and hatch into planktonic fry. During this time the huge aggregations move very slowly, at 1 to 2 kilometres (about a mile) per day, and the fish are very dense, about one body length apart, gathered together for spawning, not for feeding. Only after several weeks, when spawning has been completed, does the migration inshore start in earnest, and the fish spread out more, seeking prey as they migrate. Why these migration schools form is an open question. If one reason is to teach the later-joining juveniles the routes to follow to get inshore, then the recent collapse of the populations could have further, unfortunate repercussions. Little is known about the smaller juveniles except that they avoid the schools of larger juveniles and adults, for besides capelin and shrimp, larger cod prey a lot on smaller cod. A meal is a meal.

The large migrating schools of feeding fish, following their prey inshore, made the harvesting easy. Yet even though the fishery really peaked as long ago as the mid-1880s—at least as far as what each fisher could expect to trade fish for—and even though life in places such as Newfoundland's outports has never been easy and should not be idealized, no one seriously thought we could actually run out of cod or other groundfish on the fishing banks.

THE GROUNDFISH CRASH

The factory trawlers that came in the 1960s trawled up immense numbers of all the groundfish species, far exceeding what had ever been caught before. The Magnuson Act in 1976 extended U.S. jurisdiction to 200 miles offshore, and Canada extended its economic control to the same extent. Evicting the foreign fleets, both countries then proceeded to replace them with large boats of their own. Both countries fished at what they considered to be maximum sustainable levels or yields, but these were well beyond what the fish stocks could actually sustain. By the end of the 1980s, the fishing fleets were far larger than necessary to catch the available fish, and the vessels were high-tech trawlers that caught far more fish far more efficiently than the old inshore fishers had ever done. The numbers of cod, flounder and haddock plummeted.

Then the end came. In 1992 Canada announced a two-year moratorium on cod fishing in Canadian waters, and thousands of fishers lost their jobs. In 1994, Canada extended the moratorium indefinitely and radically cut the quotas for haddock and flatfish. Many more thousands of people lost their jobs, and Canada put together an aid package of $1.9 billion.

In 1994, the United States and Canada also agreed to greatly reduce the Georges Bank fisheries for cod, halibut and haddock, and parts of Georges Bank were closed to groundfishing. The reduction and closure had to happen, and they had to be cooperative, since the international boundary separating the EEZs of the two countries runs through the bank. In 1995, much of Georges Bank and parts of the Gulf of Maine were again shut down. The same year the New England Fisheries Management Council decided to regulate the fishery more strictly, recommending long-term slashes in the allowable catches of cod, haddock and winter flounder until stocks had recovered. The cuts will continue for some years, depending on the growth and reproduction rates of the different species. The alternative, which would have been better for the fish but far worse for the fishers, was to close the fisheries completely for five to ten years.

≈≈≈≈≈≈≈≈≈≈≈≈≈≈≈≈≈≈≈≈≈≈≈≈≈≈≈≈≈

In 1992, Canada announced a two-year moratorium on cod fishing in Canadian waters, and thousands of fishers lost their jobs. In 1994, Canada extended the moratorium indefinitely.

≈≈≈≈≈≈≈≈≈≈≈≈≈≈≈≈≈≈≈≈≈≈≈≈≈≈≈≈≈

About 350 trawlers used to fish Georges Bank, mostly from Gloucester and New Bedford in Massachusetts; it is now unthinkable for all of them to continue fishing. Even cutting the fishing effort by half, as proposed by the New England Fisheries Management Council, may not be enough, and greater cuts may be necessary. The fishers are ever more nervous. They know that such severe cuts mean that many of them have permanently lost their jobs. Many believe that the government has overreacted, but it hasn't. It should have closed the fisheries, not cut the quotas. Recovery will be just that much slower.

To try to compensate the U.S. fishers for their lost employment, the U.S. government provided $30 million in 1994, spending another $2 million on buying boats back from their owners. In 1995, in an attempt to cut the groundfish fleet from two thousand to a thousand boats, another $25 million was invested. It is a slow business, however, for another $75 million will probably be needed to complete the buyout, and the remaining boats will still have to be controlled. The goal, no matter what the route, is to reduce the catch by reducing the size of the fleets, whether U.S. or Canadian, to limit what the remaining boats may catch and to monitor the surviving stocks carefully. Old management methods will be replaced, perhaps by individual transferable quotas. The options are very few.

HOPE FOR THE COD?

Amazingly, despite the disappearance of the cod and a universal sense that for now the last one has been caught, signs of hope keep flaring up. In 1994, Canadian fisheries scientists reported that they found juvenile codfish in all the areas they sampled. A patch of juveniles about four years old, covering 80 kilometres (50 miles), was found offshore on Hamilton Bank off Labrador, a sign that the population may no longer be shrinking. In July 1995, a slug of about 40 000 tonnes of adult codfish turned up in Trinity Bay in Newfoundland. In late 1995, the Canadian fisheries minister suggested the fishery might reopen sometime soon, in a modest way.

We can only hope that the politicians will back off. The cod stocks haven't gone extinct; they crashed. They are quite capable of recovery, along with other depleted stocks of other species. But they do have to be left alone for a few years. How long depends on how fast they grow and how quickly they reproduce, and these factors vary among species. Even limited harvesting, of the sort that still exists for some species, will slow recovery considerably. Short-term gain, or harvesting, is just not worth the price at this point, and an indefinite moratorium of all depleted species remains the best move. Nonetheless, in the autumn of 1996, because of some slim signs of recovery, the politicians reopened the inshore Newfoundland cod fishery for a few days, permitting fishing for personal use only.

For most of the fishers, hope barely exists. Unable to fish, they carry heavy mortgages on their boats. Some have turned to alternative fisheries, like crab on Fogo Island, or lobsters. Most probably just want a fair buyout now, but though the buyout is under way, it can never be adequate compensation. Most fishers will not fish again, at least not commercially. Ray Fennelly, a former fisherman in Newfoundland, quoted in the *Toronto Star*, believes a wake should be held for the cod fishery: "The fact is that something has died, something big, something serious, the most important thing of our existence. It may come back to some degree, but not the fishery as we know it. We have to get it out of our system."

WHAT CAUSED THE COD COLLAPSE?

Many wrong decisions were made at every level by both countries. Biologists overestimated sizes of stocks. Managers proposed quotas that did not allow for natural large declines in populations, and they consistently set quotas that were higher than what the biologists proposed. Fishers lobbied hard for greater access to the fish. Trawlers scooped up everything that could swim. Bycatch levels were high; as much was wasted as was kept. Politicians lacked the strength to listen to the biologists and managers who called out warnings, knowing that statements about stock sizes were really estimates and that estimates are often wrong. Fishers, with little role to play in setting the rules, fished when they were allowed to and broke what rules they could get away with in order to make ends meet. At the same time, at this worst of times, the temperature of the summer sea was lower than usual, since the Labrador Current was pushing more strongly farther south than usual. As a result, some of the fish may have moved away. When it became clear that stocks were dropping rapidly, quotas were reduced, but it was too little too late. Northern cod stocks in 1994 had dropped to less than 5 per cent of their 1990 level.

It has been tempting to level blame elsewhere. Low temperatures forced the cod to leave. Their main prey, capelin, shifted in distribution or abundance. Harp seals ate the capelin that the cod should have eaten, or ate the small cod. Although all these statements may have some truth to them, none account for the crash. The true culprits were foreign fishing, large offshore trawlers, Canadian overfishing since 1976, quotas that were set far too high, overcapitalization and probably well-intentioned but certainly unsuccessful management. In a word, overfishing has been responsible for the crash—overfishing by two of the most experienced fishing countries on the planet, with some of the most sophisticated and detailed management knowledge and with extensive investment in research, management and enforcement.

The depletion of the fish stocks of the banks took about three decades. The loss is beyond measure, not just to Canada and the United States but to all those countries and fishers around the world that in some way used the resources that now are lost. It is an embarrassment, and it should never have happened. This loss is held up to the rest of the world as an example—*the* example—of how not to manage a fishery and of what could happen elsewhere if care is not taken.

Who is to blame? Everyone. Fishers, processors, biologists, managers and politicians—no one comes out of this looking good. This is the same story told over and over and over again. Why do we learn so slowly? Everyone agrees that now there really are no choices and that management must change. Fishers' voices will be listened to, for they know the fishery best. Biologists will sound less uncertain and insist that conservative estimates be considered real. Regulators, whether the Canadian federal ministry or the New England Fisheries Management Council, will set much lower total allowable catches, reduce fleet sizes, close off fishing areas to allow the replenishment of the stocks and seek other ways to sustain the stocks. Both countries agree that they have sinned most grievously, have learned their lessons and will not let it happen again. In addition, both countries know that this situation means the end of many fishing communities along their coasts and that the communities will find ways of diversifying or they will also disappear.

BOUNDARY DISPUTES

Even countries that get along better than most can find it impossible to agree on political boundaries between them when the rich resources of the fishing banks are at stake. When Canada and the United States tried to draw a boundary between their EEZs, each claimed virtually all of Georges Bank. France, which owns the tiny fishing islands of St. Pierre and Miquelon off the south coast of Newfoundland, tried to claim 200 miles in all directions of the islands in the middle of Canada's EEZ in that region. Both disputes had to go to the international court for mediation and took years to resolve.

The dispute between France and Canada was bizarre, and the outcome looks rather silly. France has kept the two small islands over the past couple of centuries as a base for its fishing fleet on the banks. When coastal Canada extended its fishing jurisdiction to 200 miles and evicted distant-water fleets, France felt understandably vulnerable and tried to grab a share of the banks. Canada of course resisted. France wanted a significant piece of the cod action, and its demands were certainly excessive. Finally, in 1992, the court of arbitration drew its map and gave its decision. France got an odd strip of sea extending south from its two islands, 10 miles (16 kilometres) wide and 200 miles long. The dispute between the two countries still continues, despite the boundaries, for the rights of the French to fish in Canadian waters remain quite ambiguous; old treaties can be read in different ways.

Far more was at stake in the boundary dispute between Canada and the United States. Georges Bank is extremely productive. Because it is shallow, and because of the strong winds, waves and tides, there is continual upwelling of water over the bank, effectively mixing the water and its nutrients. Hundreds of species of fish and shellfish thrive there. In particular, the eastern part of Georges Bank was at stake in the dispute, for much of the inner or western part of the bank had already been overfished by 1976. Both countries continued to claim all of the more productive eastern part of the bank (Figure 11).

From 1977 to 1984 the conflict continued. Because of the uncertainty over its ownership, fishers from both countries overfished the region, competing among themselves, knowing that no enforcement would occur until the boundary was agreed upon. In 1984, the International Court of Justice drew what is now called The Hague Line, a compromise between the demands of the two countries but giving Canada a substantial portion of the eastern part of the Georges Bank.

The U.S. fishers were not pleased, to say the least. They knew the part that Canada got had the richest remaining stocks, and the boundary seemed to be an arbitrary line in the water. So they ignored it and kept fishing where they wanted to. In response, Canada stepped up its surveillance of the region and its ability to detect vessels that crossed over from the U.S. side of the line. Expensive patrols by Canadian patrol boats and aircraft, resulting in further conflicts, replaced rational transboundary management of shared resources. Stocks of all species straddling the boundary across Georges Bank were ever more at risk of crashing.

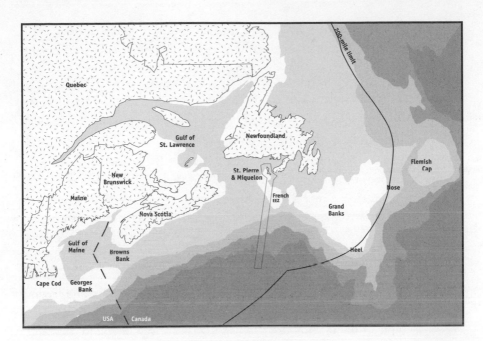

FIGURE 11

Boundaries on the Fishing Banks. *Provoking conflicts between countries, the continental shelf in the region of the Grand Banks extends beyond the Canadian 200 mile limit, the U.S.–Canadian border crosses the tip of Georges Bank, and France has a narrow EEZ embedded in the Canadian EEZ.*

Four transboundary species attracted the U.S. fishers: cod, haddock, pollock and sea scallops. The cod and haddock both migrate onto Georges Bank and spawn just about where the boundary lies. Sea scallops aren't mobile, but since most of the remaining populations were on the Canadian side of the boundary, U.S. scallop draggers frequently crossed the boundary in what they called "dine and dash" forays. Between 1991 and 1995, fifty-six of the scallop boats were arrested by the Canadian patrols, and another hundred boats were seen but not caught. How many were not even seen is anyone's guess. Depletion of scallops on the Canadian end of Georges Bank is certainly possible.

Sometimes situations evolve slowly towards solutions, and the Georges Bank disputes seem to be doing just that. Both sides have limited ground-fishing on the bank, so the remnants of the cod and haddock are safe for now. The Canadian Department of Fisheries and Oceans is starting to decentralize, at least in part because its methods have to date been outstanding failures, and it should grow to look more like the U.S. regional system. The New England Regional Council, responsible for the management of the U.S. side of Georges Bank, is likely to back away from unlimited fishing by licensed boats, which is at least a start in the direction of the Canadian approach to management. It is even likely that the two sides will eventually agree on a single cooperative management system for the species whose management they both share.

ATLANTIC HERRING AND GEORGES BANK

We might have expected Atlantic herring on Georges Bank to be another victim of overfishing since 1976, for a large population straddled the U.S.-Canada boundary region. Certainly there has been a Georges Bank stock of herring for as long as biologists have known anything about the species. A fishery for this stock began in 1961, and over the next fifteen years, 2.7 million tonnes were harvested. Atlantic herring spawn near the bottom, but their larvae spend a pelagic life in the plankton, preyed on by pelagic fish, including their own species. Juveniles school in the coastal bays, growing to sexual maturity when they are three or four years old. At that point they are recruited into the adult populations, which migrate between overwintering and spawning regions, and feeding grounds such as Georges Bank. In 1977, the fishery on Georges Bank crashed, a classic example of boom and bust. No herring could even be found there during the next few years. As a result, the herring stock was simply not an issue for fishers during the years when Canada and the United States bickered over the placement of the boundary.

In 1987, some spawning individuals turned up again on Georges Bank—not enough to get the fishers interested or the managers willing to talk about reopening the fishery, but enough to intrigue the biologists. Where did they come from? Did they migrate there from other stocks elsewhere on the coast, or did they come from survivors of the depleted Georges Bank stock? A fair amount of evidence tells us that they represent a resurgence of herring from the original Georges Bank population, providing a valuable lesson about crashing fish stocks.

A stock that crashes is one that is too small to fish for with any commercial expectations. When such a crash happens, the best thing is to stop fishing and wait for the stock to recover. In the case of the herring on Georges Bank, fishers should wait a few years, until there is once again a stock of about a million tonnes of spawning fish, which can support a fishery of about 200 000 tonnes per year. The critical point to remember, though, is that a stock that crashes is not a stock that has completely disappeared, fished to extinction. A genetically robust breeding stock remains, small but viable nonetheless. We can expect fish stocks to recover if we give them time. The fishing banks of the northeast coast may contain the saddest of overfishing stories, but the stories have not necessarily ended.

CHAPTER II

STRADDLING STOCKS

We're down now to one lost, lonely, unloved, unattractive little turbot clinging on by its fingernails to the Grand Bank of Newfoundland, saying: Someone reach out and save me at this eleventh hour.

> Brian Tobin, Canadian fisheries
> minister, at a news conference
> in New York, March 1995

We're great conservationists, eh? Tell it to the cod.

> John Speirs, TORONTO STAR,
> April 1995

Along various coasts around the world, continental shelves extend beyond 200 miles and fish stocks extend right along with them. In other places, the shelf is narrow, yet fish stocks may extend out into high seas waters. In either case, the fish are called straddling stocks, since they straddle the line between coastal EEZs and the unmanaged high seas. As a result, fish that are protected in coastal waters may still continue to be hunted by distant-water fleets fishing beyond the 200-mile limit. The entire fish stock then continues to decline, the coastal nation becomes increasingly angry with foreign distant-water fleets, and the distant-water fleets defend their own actions. We're in need of further help from the Law of the Sea.

The most famous confrontation over a straddling stock occurred between Canada and Spain in 1995, but there are other regions besides the Grand Banks where similar problems need to be resolved. The North Pacific in the middle of the Bering Sea, the southeast Pacific off the coast of Chile and the Patagonian shelf off Argentina are all variations on the same theme. The stakes in all cases are high, as the coastal countries defend their fisheries, distant-water fleets find that fewer and fewer places remain available for them to fish, and fish stocks remain vulnerable.

THE TURBOT WAR OF 1995

After managing cod stocks to oblivion in its EEZ and instituting a complete moratorium on cod fishing, Canada discovered true conservationism. In its new self-righteousness, it proclaimed itself to be the protector of fish stocks living on the shelf and banks beyond the 200 miles of its jurisdiction. Since the only species left in any numbers in 1995 on the Grand Banks was the turbot, or Greenland halibut, the turbot became the symbol for conservation. This symbol is not without its ironies, for though the fish tastes fine when cooked properly, hardly any Canadians know what it tastes like. Canada pretty well fished it out of inshore waters, devastated populations found offshore near its 200-mile limit and then realized that the fish were about to go the way of cod, for the same reasons. Unless it did something to protect what remained of the stock of turbot living out on the bits of the Grand Banks, known as the Nose and Heel, protruding beyond the 200-mile limit of the Canadian EEZ, no fish would remain to be fished.

On the other side of the conflict was Spain—Spain and Portugal, actually, but the world rapidly focussed on Spain, which fished the Nose and Heel of the Grand Banks. Spain refused to accept the reduced quota of turbot that Canada and the Northwest Atlantic Fisheries Organization (NAFO) had agreed to allocate to Spain for 1995. Why did Spain refuse?

Spain is one of the world's most active fishing nations. Only Koreans and Japanese eat more fish per person than the Spanish. A hundred thousand fishers hunt fish for Spanish markets, as people insist on their three fish meals each week. By 1993, Spain brought in 1.4 million tonnes of all kinds of fish per year, including the turbot it could catch on the Nose and Heel. Spain's fleet is the largest in Europe. With 19 000 vessels and 85 000 crew members, Spanish trawlers and longliners ply the coasts of India, Mozambique, Argentina, North Africa and Norway, searching for fish. They are not popular fishers, for more than most nations they are willing to flout the regulations of coastal states and the spirit of conservation. They feel hard done by; they are a fishing nation, and fish have become increasingly inaccessible to them as 200-mile limits have been enforced and stocks everywhere have declined. They have fought with other Europeans about their fishing practices in EU waters, and they were banned from Namibian waters along the west coast of southern Africa in 1993 for excessive tuna fishing. As journalist Juliet O'Neill has written in the *Toronto Star*, "The Spanish fishery seems to attract controversy as easily as its trawlers attract seagulls. And more often than not it's the one being accused of acting like pirates." In 1986, as part of the agreement that brought Spain into the European

Union, the Spanish gave up their rights to fish in European waters for a period of sixteen years—later reduced to ten years when Spain threatened to veto the entry of Austria, Finland and Sweden into the EU—while the EU granted it fishing rights for species such as cod and turbot off the Nose and Heel of the Grand Banks.

≈≈≈≈≈≈≈≈≈≈≈≈≈≈≈≈≈≈≈≈≈≈≈≈≈≈≈≈

After managing cod stocks to oblivion in its EEZ and instituting a complete moratorium on cod fishing, Canada discovered true conservationism.

≈≈≈≈≈≈≈≈≈≈≈≈≈≈≈≈≈≈≈≈≈≈≈≈≈≈≈≈

NAFO set the quotas that could be caught, and EU nations then simply ignored them, catching up to seven times the quota allocated them. This flouting of the quotas did not sit well with Canadians, especially in their emerging enlightened conservationism. Spain became the worst offender. With a fleet of refurbished British trawlers, quite willing to catch and sell undersized fish, ignoring and exceeding any quota it might have been given, the Spanish fleet only represents the extreme end of an attitude all fishing nations share: each wants more fish and is prepared to varying extents to be deceptive. It will be interesting watching the EU response now that Spain has joined in the fishing of European waters again.

This wasn't the first conflict between Canada and Spain or between NAFO and the European Union. In 1986, Canada and NAFO agreed on a moratorium on cod fishing outside of the 200-mile Canadian EEZ. The European Union, with Spain and Portugal, disagreed and set its own quota for cod, at far too high a level. Spanish and Portuguese vessels, displaced from Namibian waters in 1990 and not yet licensed to fish in European waters, headed for the Nose and Heel of the Grand Banks. It was quite clear that NAFO, the only organization that Canada could depend on, was ineffective. If any action were to occur, Canada would have to act alone.

Then the cod moratorium stopped all cod fishing, and Canada noticed that turbot stocks seemed to be on the same track as the cod. Turbot have also been protected by quota, set by NAFO and ignored by the EU, and by mesh size of nets intended to let small fish remain free. A turbot lives about fifteen years or more, growing to about a metre long and 14 kilograms (30 pounds). Most fish caught by legal nets are about six to eight years old, for larger ones are now largely fished out. But turbot don't mature until they are eight or nine years old. If they do get a chance to breed, they produce a fraction of the eggs that

fish twice their age would. So in 1995 Canada, again consistent with NAFO recommendations, reduced the quota of turbot that could be caught on the Nose
and Heel of the Grand Banks. Again the EU, on behalf of Spain and Portugal,
dissented.

Spain once again overfished its turbot quota. Canada passed a law giving
itself the right to arrest boats suspected of illegal fishing beyond its own 200-
mile limit, and turbot became the vehicle for pushing the Law of the Sea on to

≈≈≈≈≈≈≈≈≈≈≈≈≈≈≈≈≈≈≈≈≈≈≈≈≈≈≈≈≈≈≈≈

*Victory? Canada took unilateral action and broke international law, on the
premise that the law was wrong and that straddling stocks should be
managed by the adjacent coastal country.*

≈≈≈≈≈≈≈≈≈≈≈≈≈≈≈≈≈≈≈≈≈≈≈≈≈≈≈≈≈≈≈≈

new decisions. Canada argued that because turbot swim back and forth across
the 200-mile line drawn arbitrarily through the Grand Banks, the fish had to be
considered part of one single stock; Canada had to manage the fish beyond the
200-mile limit in order to protect the stock from irresponsible overfishing by
other countries.

In March 1995, a Canadian patrol gave chase to the Spanish trawler *Estai*,
fired some warning shots and boarded it with an armed team. The *Estai* was
seized and escorted to St. John's, Newfoundland. Undersized turbot filled its
hold, double accounting books were found, and the net, once it was dredged
up from where the *Estai* had cut it free and dumped it, had an illegally small
mesh size. Spain and the EU strenuously objected to Canada's tactics, accusing
the country of high seas piracy, an accurate description, since the only laws
Canada didn't break were Canada's. The president of Spain's National Association of Seafaring Fishing Officers was quoted in the *Toronto Star* as saying, "We
consider this to be a very, very serious act of maritime terrorism. Nobody has
the right to go outside their waters and capture another boat." Crowds gathered in ports in both countries, yelling enthusiastically in support of their
respective actions. Some national newspapers started calculating the size of
each country's naval power. Each country became united as it had not been for
years. Talks proceeded and rude things were said, as well as some inane things,
but in April Canada and the EU worked their way to an agreement that each
side claimed made it the winner. Spain got its boat back. The turbot quota
became a compromise between NAFO and EU levels, higher than Canada proposed but lower than Spain and the EU had demanded. Now independent
monitors are allowed on every boat in disputed waters to verify gear and catch.

To protect the fish further, the minimum size of the mesh of the nets has been increased to allow the turbot to grow large enough to reproduce once or even twice before final capture.

Victory? Canada took unilateral action and broke international law, on the premise that the law was wrong and that straddling stocks should be managed by the adjacent coastal country. As in previous cases where other countries unilaterally extended their offshore jurisdiction to 200 miles several decades ago, nothing serious happened. It was only a skirmish. The turbot is perhaps saved. And no one is more strident than the newly converted—Canada, the born-again conservationist.

THE DONUT HOLE IN THE BERING SEA

In the North Pacific, north of the Aleutian Islands, lies the Bering Sea, extraordinarily rich in cod, sole, flounder, perch, mackerel and pollock. Most of the Bering Sea now lies in the EEZs of the Russian Federation and the United States. In the middle of the sea, however, beyond the boundaries of the EEZss, is a region of high seas called the Donut Hole. It makes up about 10 per cent of the Bering Sea and has attracted the distant-water fishing fleets of Poland, South Korea, China and Japan.

Perhaps "attracted" isn't the right word. Distant-water fishing fleets used to fish the seas that now are within the United States EEZs along the coast of Alaska. At first, following the declaration of the 200-mile limit in 1977, the fleets still had rights to fish in the U.S. EEZs, but beginning in 1984, the United States gradually phased out the distant-water fleets. Displaced from their traditional fishing grounds, under increased surveillance, the distant-water fleets retreated into the Donut Hole (Figure 12).

The target fish in the Bering Sea are pollock, supplying the immense surimi market in Japan. Surimi, which means minced fish, makes up about a quarter of all the seafood consumed in Japan, and it is slowly becoming more popular in other countries, including the United States. It is crushed into a paste and then usually flavoured and shaped into imitation crabmeat; it is also made into quite convincing imitation shrimp and lobster.

With intense fishing pressure not only in the U.S. and Russian EEZss but now also in the Donut Hole, the pollock stocks crashed. In 1984, 100 000 tonnes of pollock were caught in the hole; by 1988, the catch had risen to 1.4 million tonnes. U.S. fishers believed the distant-water fleets also fished heavily and illegally in U.S. EEZ waters, and between 1989 and 1992, the United States seized eleven vessels from the fleets of Poland, Korea, Japan, China and Russia, charging them all with illegal fishing in U.S. waters. By 1992, few pollock were

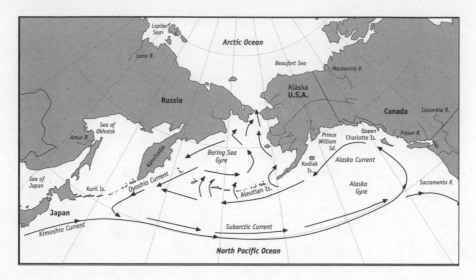

FIGURE 12

Currents of the North Pacific Ocean. *The North Pacific, dominated by the Alaska and Bering Sea Gyres, is rich in pelagic fish, crabs and groundfish, especially Alaskan pollock. The Bering Sea Donut Hole lies in the centre of the Bering Sea Gyre.*

left in the Donut Hole, and stocks had crashed in the adjacent EEZs seas as well.

The six countries, two with large adjacent EEZs, the other four restricted to the Donut Hole, met a few times beginning in 1991. They were all concerned about the stock decline, but they were certainly not in agreement on what to do about it. Then, in the first half of 1992, only 11 000 tonnes of pollock were caught, as steep a crash as one could hope to see, and the distant-water countries agreed to stop fishing for at least the next two years. The United States and Russia agreed to stop all pollock fishing in their EEZs as well.

Will the pollock stocks of the central Bering Sea have a chance to recover? The agreement protecting them is precarious. The countries with distant-water fleets believe that they have been unfairly pushed out of yet another productive fishing region. Poland stated in 1993 that it would resume fishing in the Donut Hole in 1995; if it could not return, it would probably have to cease its distant-water fishing altogether. Japan wishes to return as well, for it is having a hard time in the North Pacific; under pressure from the UN and the United States during the early 1990s, it agreed to cease using all large-scale driftnets and to stop fishing for Pacific salmon. The shrinking of Japan's high seas fisheries continues to have political fallout and economic repercussions as fishers lose their employment, fish imports increase, and it is forced to invest in, and perhaps own, the processing plants for the fish it can no longer catch.

It is hard to find good news in this story. Political agreement to cease, or at least restrict, fishing is only encouraging when it precedes the collapse of a fishery. A moratorium is the inevitable last resort, an admission of failure. Russia and the United States may propose that the Bering Sea be managed as if it were a semi-enclosed sea, giving them much stronger authority over access to the Donut Hole by the distant-water fleets waiting to return.

There are other places where restricted regions of high seas lie enclosed by the EEZs of surrounding coastal countries and contain straddling stocks of great commercial value. In the Sea of Okhotsk, which is north of Japan and which is contested by Japan and the Russian Federation, pollock again are vulnerable. In the Barents Sea, north of Norway and in between Iceland, Greenland and Norway, straddling stocks of herring and redfish are hunted. The management of the stocks in these holes of high seas will probably all become the responsibility of the adjacent coastal countries and will be considered similar to the management of other semi-enclosed seas that are too small to have any high seas remaining in them.

CHILE'S GAMBIT

The east and west coasts of South America present quite different problems in the management of straddling fish stocks, though the distant-water players remain the same. Along the coasts of Chile and Peru in the southeast Pacific, a pelagic finfish known as jack mackerel or horse mackerel schools in large numbers and supports the largest fishery of the region. It is especially abundant along the coast of Chile, where it is fished heavily by Chilean fishers within about 160 kilometres (100 miles) of shore, and by distant-water fleets beyond the Chilean EEZ. Jack mackerel breed within the offshore regions of the EEZs of Chile and Peru, but they then migrate over a vast region, covering 2400 to 3200 kilometres (1500 to 2000 miles), most of the way to New Zealand. Left uncaught, they may live for more than fifteen years and grow to about 70 centimetres (28 inches) or more. Few make it to that size or age, though. Distant-water fleets from the former Soviet Union, Bulgaria, Japan, Cuba, Korea, Spain and Poland all fished the high seas for them during the 1980s, catching the larger mature individuals. The pressure on the inshore fishery continued to grow, and the Chileans realized the total stock could be in jeopardy.

Jack mackerel are fully exploited in Chilean waters, meaning that a crash is imminent unless fishing is somehow reduced. Chile, along with Peru and

Ecuador, extended its jurisdiction over coastal waters to 200 miles in 1952, twenty-five years before most of the rest of the world did the same. Now it is proposing to take further unilateral action to protect its fisheries. In 1991, it introduced the idea of the Presential Sea, an expanded area beyond the EEZ where the coastal state would have the ability or presence to protect its EEZ and have increased authority over the adjacent high seas. Chile proposed for itself an impressive piece of the Southeast Pacific, extending almost 3200 kilometres (2000 miles) to include Easter Island. Not surprisingly, the idea of such extended jurisdiction makes every distant-water fishing nation extremely nervous, and any sort of global approval will never happen. But those countries fishing the Southeast Pacific, such as Japan, Korea, Bulgaria, Poland and the Russian Federation, have agreed to work together to conserve high seas populations of fish, including those straddling the EEZ of Chile. The threat of unilateral action by a country known to be willing to take that kind of action is clearly a useful weapon in this continuing struggle.

THE PATAGONIAN SHELF

The west coast of South America is quite unlike the east coast. In contrast to the narrow continental shelf of Chile, a very broad shelf extends 160 to 320 kilometres (100 to 200 miles) offshore under shallow seas for the full length of Argentina. At the southeast end it extends several hundred kilometres farther, and the Falkland Islands (or the Malvinas, depending on whose map you use) protrude above sea level. This is another of the world's richest fishing regions, and with such a broad shelf, many species, including a dozen that are commercially valuable, straddle international waters. The usual foreign fleets arrived there in the 1980s; fleets from Japan, South Korea, Poland, Spain, Bulgaria, the Russian Federation, China and Taiwan fish in the high seas adjacent to Argentina's EEZ for the same stocks Argentina is trying to protect within its EEZ.

Argentina is, of course, very frustrated. Without any satisfactory international laws to help, Argentina has attempted to set up bilateral agreements with some of the distant-water fishing nations. It has an immense EEZ to patrol to start with, making it difficult to restrict foreign vessels from coastal waters. Restricting high seas fishing of straddling stocks over an equally large area is just not possible.

Yet once again, surprises do occur. Argentina and the United Kingdom have agreed on how to manage stocks in the Falklands/Malvinas region that would otherwise be vulnerable to distant-water fleets. The agreement is surely an unexpected result of the absurd little war they had.

The exploited species in the area are hake, southern blue whiting, shortfin squid and common squid. In the past, the region was not a popular place to fish, for facilities to service ships or process fish really didn't exist; only a few people and a bunch of sheep stuck it out on the islands. Then Argentina and the United Kingdom fought over the islands in 1982, and everything changed.

Oddly enough, the large increase in fishing in the region has occurred since the war and despite the tensions. The squid were found after the war, the U.K. military presence made fishing a bit less risky, the lack of an agreed-upon EEZ made the area one of the last unregulated regions in the world, and the distant-water fleets squeezed out of other regions needed a place to fish and so they moved in.

The United Kingdom had not tried to institute an EEZ around the Falklands before the war, saying that it was too complicated and it would be impossible to police. So Argentina did. Then, in April 1982, Argentina invaded, only to lose the islands back to the United Kingdom a month later, helping to keep Margaret Thatcher in power for a few more years. There were renewed calls for the United Kingdom to establish a 200-mile limit around the islands. There were also concerns that Argentina would still not accept such limits, that other countries wouldn't accept them either, and that policing the region would be impossibly expensive. In 1986, the United Kingdom decided on a 150-mile (240-kilometre) EEZ, reserving the right to extend it to 200 miles sometime later. In 1987, 243 vessels were licensed to fish in the 150-mile zone, for a fee. This was a unilateral proclamation by the United Kingdom, not a multilateral agreement of the sort encouraged by the UN Law of the Sea, but it was made partly to stop the escalating overfishing that had developed in the preceding several years. Argentina was vociferously opposed but in order to maintain peace agreed not to send its fishery protection vessels into the zone.

In 1989–90 Argentina and the United Kingdom reestablished diplomatic relations and began to face the very real problems of overexploitation of the fisheries. Too many vessels had been licensed to fish, so the two countries agreed to reduce the number of vessels granted licences. They also agreed on a 150-mile EEZ around the islands, with Argentina responsible for the shelf out to the islands, and the United Kingdom and Argentina jointly responsible for an additional zone beyond the islands. Again, the solution came from negotiations between the two nations, not from application of UN laws or agreements. The agreement still needs policing, abuse of the agreement remains possible, and the Falkland Islanders want more licences sold, for they have come to enjoy their recent wealth. But at least the agreement is working, more or less, and quite in spite of the shortcomings of the Law of the Sea in dealing with the questions of straddling stocks.

THE UN CONFERENCE ON STRADDLING STOCKS
AND HIGHLY MIGRATORY FISH SPECIES

Even though many nations signed the UN Convention of the Law of the Sea in 1982, countries such as Argentina, Chile and Canada believed that the articles relating to straddling stocks were vague and ineffectual. The Conference on Straddling Stocks and Highly Migratory Fish Species, which included representatives from a hundred nations, began to meet to discuss and attempt to resolve the problems. With now typical patience and persistence, the conference met a few times and then, after a couple more years of work, met again in the summer of 1995, trying to work out policies to deal with the problems posed by high seas migrants such as tuna, swordfish and marlin and straddling stocks such as turbot, pollock and jack mackerel.

Canada and Norway had already signed an unusual mutual agreement in 1995, allowing each to arrest the other's trawlers if they were found fishing illegally outside their 200-mile zone. The two countries also agreed to bar any foreign trawlers from their ports if they broke the other country's rules. This agreement was pure politics, for the fishing fleets of Norway and Canada are unlikely to approach each other's EEZs. But the agreement is the kind that both countries want to have with all other fishing nations, under the sanction of a new UN agreement. Meanwhile, countries fishing in distant water, beyond the 200-mile EEZs of other countries, are hardly enthusiastic; Spain, Portugal, Russia and Japan oppose any new restrictions on their ability to find the fish they believe they need. But coastal countries, including Argentina, Chile, New Zealand and Canada, pushed hard to negotiate a new treaty on straddling stocks.

When the conference reconvened in the summer of 1995, the turbot war between Spain, backed by the EU, and Canada remained fresh in the minds of all parties. Most were critical of Canada for acting unilaterally and with force, though Iceland had acted in this way two decades before, helping to achieve universal recognition of 200-mile EEZs. Chile's threat to institute its Presential Sea, the bilateral agreements between the United States and the Russian Federation and between the United Kingdom and Argentina, the widespread concern that the high seas fisheries needed management—all these issues helped push the conference to a new agreement to amend the Law of the Sea. Some countries argued that aggressive steps should be taken to regulate the catch on the high seas, while others disagreed.

It really isn't that other countries don't see the need to regulate high seas fishing. They do. But they distrust a proposal that would allow a coastal state to do anything it wanted to within its 200-mile fishing zone and have increased control over the seas beyond the 200-mile limit. It just isn't clear that the tough and enforced standards that coastal countries such as Canada and Norway want to have beyond 200 miles would exist, and be enforced, within the 200-mile limit. The coastal countries simply reply: trust us.

Delegates from the one hundred nations adopted a new global treaty, concluding the work of the conference. The agreement would lead to restrictions on high seas fishing and would permit boarding of vessels that violated the proposed new regulations. Inspectors would be able to search vessels to determine

≈≈≈≈≈≈≈≈≈≈≈≈≈≈≈≈≈≈≈≈≈≈≈≈≈≈≈≈≈≈≈≈≈

We are an ever shrinking planet supporting a human population
that continues to explode and to need protein for nourishment.

≈≈≈≈≈≈≈≈≈≈≈≈≈≈≈≈≈≈≈≈≈≈≈≈≈≈≈≈≈≈≈≈≈

whether they were using illegal gear or had exceeded their fish quotas, and if so, the vessels could be detained in port. Because boarding by inspectors is not exactly a friendly act, the inspectors would be armed. The treaty would require fishers to report the size of their catches to regional organizations that would set the quotas. The treaty would require nations to reduce the appalling waste or bycatch. And the treaty would be enforced by the nations that ratified it.

A major success? Not yet. Environmentalist groups, such as Greenpeace, criticized the treaty for being far too weak. It left untouched the clear global problem of too many high-tech boats competing for the dwindling stocks. It left without comment the subsidies that support the fleets of too many countries. And yet the conference agreed on the treaty, and the remaining problems, to be fair, were not part of the mandate of the conference. The treaty would force countries to cooperate as they chase fish in international waters. There should no longer be any open, free-for-all fishing on the high seas, and no fishing by stealth.

As with the original Law of the Sea, this was only the beginning. The formal signing of the treaty at the UN began in December 1995, when twenty-five nations signed, including not only the coastal ones, which signed in obvious self-interest, but also some countries that had mixed feelings about the treaty, such as Russia and the United States. By the end of 1996, thirty more countries and the European Union had signed, but, not surprisingly, Japan and Spain remained unwilling to sign. The signing by the United States was of great significance. The United States is, of course, greatly concerned about its own straddling stocks, but greater restrictions on tuna fishing will not be popular. In addition, the United States has been resistant to recognizing any restrictions on its activities on the high seas, not out of concern about the fisheries, but for strategic reasons: it insists on being able to send its naval fleets wherever it pleases and worries about any action that could restrict it. Yet the United States signed the treaty, giving it the initial strength it needs.

Signing the treaty is just the first step. In order for the treaty to become international law, thirty nations must ratify this treaty through whatever legislative mechanisms they have in place. In June 1996, the U.S. Senate Committee on Foreign Relations approved the agreement and ratification by Congress occurred two months later. Other countries will ratify it quickly, and they in turn will probably have to press hard to get the total up to thirty in reasonable time. Before it finally becomes law, many parts of it will no doubt be in force. It surely will not take the twelve years the 1982 Law of the Sea took to be ratified by the sixty nations it needed before it became enforceable law in 1994.

The signing of the treaty is a major event. We now have an emerging law that overturns five hundred years of high seas freedom. The loss of freedom to hunt without restriction on the high seas is the only way to protect ourselves from ourselves. It is necessary because otherwise we will find ways to deplete the remaining stocks of fish that migrate immense distances or straddle the boundary between the 200-mile EEZs and the high seas. We are an ever shrinking planet supporting a human population that continues to explode and to need protein for nourishment. "Conservation," "management," "regulation" and "enforcement" are the words we associate with loss of freedom, but they are also increasingly associated with any hopes we have of sustaining fish stocks.

CHAPTER 12

HIGHLY MIGRATORY TUNA: WHO OWNS THEM?

The most valuable wild animal in the world is not the white rhino, which is killed for its horn, nor the leopard, which is killed for its hide, nor the brown bear, which is killed for its gallbladder. It is the giant bluefin tuna.

John Seabrook

DEATH OF A GIANT

The hardest fish to manage are those that migrate over extensive regions of the high seas, beyond the EEZs of coastal nations, swimming from one EEZ to another as their life histories unfold. Who has the rights to fish them? Does each country whose EEZ they pass through own all of them? When they migrate across the high seas, which nobody owns, what can protect them from being overfished? The 1982 Law of the Sea failed to answer these questions, proposing only that countries cooperate in managing the tuna. Long before the Law of the Sea finally came into force, everyone knew from painful experience how unlikely that kind of cooperation was and how vulnerable the fish could be. The best example to look at—because they are so migratory and because their fisheries are so valuable—is tuna.

TUNA

Tuna are most unusual fish. They are top predators, they can cruise at high rates of speed for a long time, they migrate immense distances during their life spans, they grow large, and they are warm-blooded, which fish aren't supposed to be.

They also taste good to most of us, either as canned tuna, broiled fresh or raw, as sashimi. Some species, such as the giant bluefin, are overfished; others, such as yellowfin and skipjack, can't be fished any more than they already are.

Tuna, especially the bluefin, are extraordinarily valuable to the Japanese, and most of the rest of the world has developed a taste for canned tuna. The economies of some of the island countries in the Pacific have come to rely on their tuna fisheries, a gift of their new 200-mile EEZs—if only they can enforce their rights to the fish. Tuna have been the basis of major conflicts between countries since territorial waters were extended in the 1940s.

They have also proven to be dangerous company. Spotted and spinner dolphins accompany schools of yellowfin tuna in particular, preying on the same schools of smaller fish. The association is a mysterious one, for the tuna school beneath the dolphins and seem to use the dolphins to detect the schools of fish they both feed on. Dolphins, as marine mammals, are supposed to be the intelligent members of this association, yet they appear to be the ones being manipulated. Literally millions of dolphins have been killed over the years by purse seiners in search of yellowfin, and this destruction, once it became well known, provoked a strong reaction from those concerned about the survival of marine mammals. Because they are so highly valued and they migrate through the EEZs of a number of developing nations, and because they associate with dolphins, which we especially treasure, tuna have forced us to try to resolve questions that are considerably more complicated than those concerning smaller, less migratory and less valuable species.

How are we to manage species that migrate through the waters of a number of countries? This is a jurisdictional question, but what is at stake is the survival of the fisheries and the economies they support.

THE FISH THEMSELVES

Tuna track their schools of prey over large stretches of the ocean, cruising at speeds other fish cannot maintain, and they can keep it up for days and weeks. They stay warmer than the water around them—in the case of the giant bluefin tuna, by as much as 20° C (36° F). In tropical latitudes, they are likely to overheat, and they tend to cruise in cooler water well below the surface, making foraging forays into the shallower, warmer water above them. They get their extra warmth from a high metabolic rate and a specialized heat-exchanging circulation system, called the retia, that prevents them from losing heat to the surrounding water. By staying warmer, they can hunt down slower, colder fish.

Tuna are marathon runners, not sprinters. They can probably swim at a few body lengths per second or faster for hours at a time. Schools of skipjack have been lost, even when tagged, because they swam away at up to 8 knots, faster than the boat trying to track them. One large bluefin tuna that had been tagged swam at least 6760 kilometres (4200 miles) from the Gulf of Mexico to Norway in nineteen days, and if we assume it swam in a straight line and didn't stop, it swam at almost 2 metres (6 to 7 feet), or one body length, per second for the whole time. Not only do tuna have higher metabolic rates than other fish—almost as high as those of most mammals—they also have larger gill surfaces for oxygen intake and more blood vessels to their muscles, adaptations that help them sustain their endless activity.

Most of the muscle tuna use in long-distance swimming is red, rich in myoglobin. Tuna do have some white muscle, useful for very rapid bursts of speed, but white muscle fatigues quickly, and it has little myoglobin. Myoglobin is a blood pigment that makes the muscle look dark or red. Like haemoglobin, myoglobin carries oxygen in the blood. It has a higher affinity for oxygen than haemoglobin and is able to carry more per molecule, and that is what makes it so valuable for migrating birds, diving mammals and migrating fish. Tuna carry unusually high amounts of myoglobin; only diving mammals have more.

THE SPECIES HUNTED

Although a variety of tuna species are caught around the world, most of the hunt is focussed on the largest and most abundant species. Albacore and bigeye, yellowfin and skipjack—these are the species filling our cans of tuna and sold fresh in our restaurants, while southern and northern giant bluefin are sent deep-frozen to the Japanese sashimi markets (Figure 13).

Northern Bluefin Tuna

The giant northern bluefin tuna migrate immense distances, following their migrating prey. They live a long time—perhaps thirty to forty years. Like all fish, they continue to grow throughout their lives, and if left uncaught, they grow very large indeed—about 700 kilograms (1500 pounds) and 2 to 3 metres (6½ to 10 feet) long. The northern bluefin used to be primarily sport fish, but they have now become the most valuable of tuna as a source of sashimi. In fact, bluefin tuna is the most valuable wild animal of all, for a single giant bluefin sells for $30 000 on the Tokyo market if it is reasonably fat. The most valuable individuals are caught off New England and Canada, where they migrate from the Gulf of Mexico, June to November, feeding on the herring, mackerel and pogies feeding around Georges Bank. The combination of cold water and lots of food lays on the fat. The prime muscle prepared for sashimi is the belly muscle from such a fish; it is surrounded by a rind of fat and contains delicate

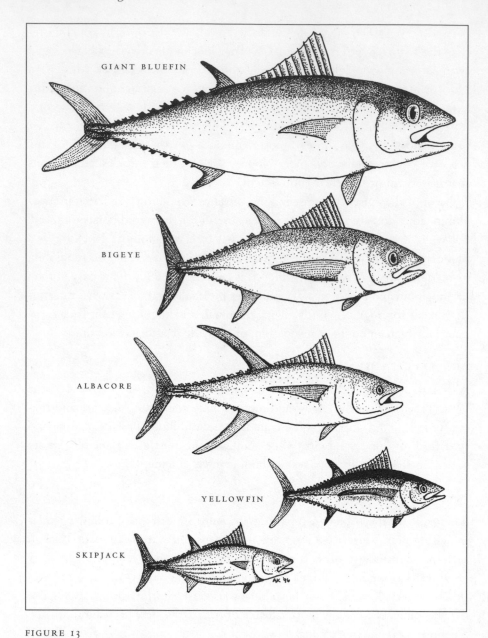

FIGURE 13

Tuna. *Five species of tuna dominate the fishery. From largest to smallest, they are the giant bluefin, bigeye, albacore, yellowfin and skipjack.*

strings of fat throughout the muscle. Two bite-size pieces sell for $75 in a Tokyo restaurant, and it is said that the best bits of the best fish never get to the restaurants at all but go to private parties of the very rich.

In the Atlantic, bluefin tuna are in serious decline. A small percentage of the east Atlantic population appears to cross the ocean and join the west Atlantic population, and the species appears not to be threatened with extinction. Yet they are so valuable that it pays to hunt the giants one at a time, just as whales were once hunted. Sometimes the tuna are trapped instead of harpooned or

≈≈≈≈≈≈≈≈≈≈≈≈≈≈≈≈≈≈≈≈≈≈≈≈≈≈≈≈≈≈≈≈≈

Bluefin tuna is the most valuable wild animal of all, for a single giant bluefin sells for $30 000 on the Tokyo market if it is reasonably fat.

≈≈≈≈≈≈≈≈≈≈≈≈≈≈≈≈≈≈≈≈≈≈≈≈≈≈≈≈≈≈≈≈≈

hooked and are then fed mackerel until they grow another few hundred valuable pounds. In either case, they are then raced to the Japanese markets. The mercury content of a giant bluefin is too high for the fish to be sold in the United States, and it is far too expensive for all but the Japanese market.

An obvious ethical issue is at stake here, for a top predator is being hunted to be sold at prices that really are absurd to satisfy the gourmet palate of a small number of people. A species of such value that it is worth hunting down individual by individual has little long-term hope of survival. This expenditure of resources is incredibly wasteful and makes no sense at all.

The bluefin really is astonishingly valuable. The following story of a Nova Scotia fisher may not be typical, but it makes the case. This fisher had suffered from poor catches of herring and mackerel in recent years and hadn't caught tuna for over a decade. In 1993 he spent $100 000 on a new boat, only to find almost no groundfish out there to be caught. In the summer of 1994, to his amazement, forty-seven bluefin tuna swam into his mackerel trap. He rented some pens and he fed the tuna there, where they gained up to another 100 kilograms (220 pounds) as he waited for an expected price jump in sashimi in Japan. Because the fish were too valuable to leave unguarded in the pens, he and his crew sat out the nights, shotguns in hand, protecting their million-dollar windfall. "I spent $109 000 on a new boat last year and the groundfishery went right to hell," he was quoted as saying in the *Toronto Star*. "This'll set me up, I'll tell you." And it did.

The current total allowable catch of northern bluefin tuna in the western Atlantic is 1250 tonnes. This amount is allocated to harpooners, hand liners, recreational rod and reelers, and five purse seiners. Each day during summer and early autumn, harpoon fishers head out from New England ports such as Boothbay Harbor. The giant bluefin are hard to catch and usually wreck gear that fishers traditionally use. Harpoons work, however. Each boat has a tuna tower, about 9 metres (30 feet) high, a skipper, a couple of crew members (including harpooner) and a spotter plane, scanning for signs of tuna. It also has colour sonar and a depth finder to help locate the tuna, as well as access to COMSAT satellite infrared photographs of sea surface temperatures, and uses loran coordinates to navigate. The harpoon itself lies at the end of an electric cable; the object is to stick the fish, jolt it, haul it on board and kill it. Harpooning and stunning avoids fighting the fish in, exhausting both humans and fish,

≈≈≈≈≈≈≈≈≈≈≈≈≈≈≈≈≈≈≈≈≈≈≈≈≈≈≈≈≈≈≈

A species of such value that it is worth hunting down individual by individual has little long-term hope of survival.

≈≈≈≈≈≈≈≈≈≈≈≈≈≈≈≈≈≈≈≈≈≈≈≈≈≈≈≈≈≈≈

and this isn't, after all, sportfishing. A good harpoonist can stick a fish 6 metres (20 feet) under water, allowing for refraction and aiming for the brain to avoid muscle damage. For a harpoon tuna boat, sticking forty bluefin in a season is about average. A tuna fisher, quoted by John Seabrook in *Death of a Giant*, suggested that there is more to it than just paying the bills: "I love these fish. But I love to catch them. God I love to catch them. And I know you need some kind of catch limits because I'd catch all of them if I could. Most guys I know don't do this for the money. They tell you they do it for the money, but it's not true." The tuna have little chance.

Not surprisingly, a drastic decline in numbers of giant northern bluefin tuna has occurred since the mid-1970s, since the Japanese market opened. In the western Atlantic, it looks like another boom-and-bust graph, with an estimated population of 220 000 in 1970 declining to 25 000 in 1990. Some of the fishers maintain that the tuna aren't really declining but instead have learned to avoid the predator boats. Fishers never like to acknowledge they may have overfished their prey.

Southern Bluefin

Like the northern bluefin, the southern bluefin is slow growing and lives for about twenty years, breeding for the first time at the age of eight. There is but a single stock, meaning that migration is extensive enough to keep different populations mixing together and interbreeding. The migrations take the fish through the South Atlantic, the Indian Ocean and the Tasman Sea. They spawn south of Java, in the high seas near Indonesia, and the young migrate from there into the Southern Ocean. Although the Japanese again want the biggest possible fish for their sashimi trade, southern bluefin are caught starting when they are two to three years old, long before they are old enough to breed. Once again, the conditions that make a species vulnerable to overfishing and fishery collapse are present; the fish have a high value and are heavily fished, often at ages that shouldn't be fished.

The Japanese care deeply about the southern bluefin fishery. As soon as the last of the post–World War II MacArthur Lines was lifted in 1952, the Japanese fleet moved into the west Pacific and then into the Southern Ocean. The peak catch occurred soon after, in 1961. Since then, increased fishing by Japan and other Pacific fishing nations has kept the stocks declining. The ability of Japanese tuna boats to deep-freeze tuna at −50° C (−58° F) gave them quite an edge in the competition, letting the fleets range further, for longer periods of time, without having to airship the tuna immediately back to Japan. Raw fish thawed from −50°C is supposedly as good as if it had just been caught.

Over this period Australia extended its fishery zone to 200 miles, along with everyone else in the world, and discovered that southern bluefin spent most of their time in the extensive Australian EEZ. Since Australia has most of the fish, and Japan most of the market and fishing expertise, Japan has negotiated to keep the tuna coming in. A rare trilateral agreement between Japan, Australia and New Zealand (a very minor player) was reached in 1993, and it was ratified in 1994. Formally called the Convention for the Conservation of Southern Bluefin Tuna, it should help limit the catch. The agreement would not have been reached if the stocks of northern bluefin hadn't collapsed, leading to a proposal to designate the northern bluefin an endangered species and therefore protected from fishing. The Japanese worried that if the proposal went through (it didn't), the same thing might happen to the southern species as well, and so they pushed the agreement though. It remains an agreement of three countries, however, and other countries, such as Taiwan, Korea and Indonesia, have increased their fishing for bluefin. They will need to sign the convention as well if the species is to be protected from further decline.

Despite the agreement, all has not been peaceful. The Australians have been warning of imminent collapse of the fishery for more than a decade, whereas the Japanese have been critical of the Australians for fishing for juveniles. In 1990 the Australians even arrested two Japanese ships for under-reporting their catch while fishing in the Australian EEZ.

Nevertheless, the overall situation has improved. Now fewer juveniles are hunted, and most of the fishing is by longline, the least damaging method for catching tuna for the sashimi market. No purse seining of southern bluefin tuna occurs in Australian waters. Australia receives access fees from the Japanese, and the Japanese are rather reluctantly training Australians how to

hook and treat a tuna to maintain its value as potential sashimi. The two countries have even begun a joint attempt to farm the species.

Skipjack, Yellowfin Tuna and Porpoise Kills

Yellowfin tuna and skipjack are fished for canning. They are far smaller than the
giant bluefin species, but they are still large fish, and there are lots of them. They
are the primary fisheries of the island nations of the South Pacific. Yellowfin are
also fished by the countries of Central America when they migrate into their
EEZs. As the global market for canned tuna continues to expand, the tuna boats
of many countries hunt both yellowfin and skipjack on the high seas and in the
EEZs of other countries.

Both species grow quickly, and biologists are arguing about whether they
migrate fast enough to swim out of the immense EEZs of some of the Pacific
countries before they are large enough to catch. Do they really need international management? Do they really migrate from one EEZ to another in a lifetime? The answer seems to be that some do and some don't. Even if most don't,
international cooperation remains essential, for they still inhabit the EEZs of
countries that haven't got the resources to fish for them themselves.

In the inshore waters of an undeveloped and remote island country, they can
still be fished with low-tech methods. The Maldive Islands are an extreme
example. The Maldives consist of twenty-six dispersed atolls in the middle of
the Indian Ocean. They have never been colonized and remain one of the poor-
est nations in the world. Fishers catch surface tuna, mainly skipjack, fishing
offshore of the reefs in boats up to 10 metres (33 feet) long, made mainly from
coconut trees, with crews of about ten to twelve. In 1974, the fleet got outboard
motors and now range up to 25 kilometres (15 miles) seaward of the reefs. Each
morning the fishers catch bait fish near the reef and keep them alive in a well in
the boat. Then each boat heads off to find a tuna school. If it finds one, one of
the crew, the chummer, tosses the bait fish into the water, keeping the tuna
school tight in around the boat. The rest fish for the tuna with poles and
hooked lines. They carry no ice and must return to shore each day.

In dramatic contrast, tuna are also fished by high-tech purse seiners. The
modern purse seiner has become the most efficient of fishing boats—probably
too efficient, as it tracks schools with sonar and with its ship-based helicopter.
And in the hunt for yellowfin, many dolphins and porpoises are destroyed as
the fishers seine in the fish, outraging many people and environmental groups,
particularly in the United States, the primary market for the captured tuna. We
don't get especially upset about the slaughter of fish, but we do get upset over
the slaughter of dolphins and porpoises.

A helicopter from one of these super tuna boats searches for a pod of dolphins, knowing that beneath it swims a school of yellowfin. When a dolphin pod is located, the tuna boat approaches and sends speedboats out to encircle the pod with a purse seine, herding dolphins into the seine, even though the intent is to catch the school of tuna below them. In the early years, before the American public heard the details, the number of dolphins drowned in the nets set for tuna was staggering. In 1961, at least half a million died in the nets in the eastern tropical Pacific. Monitoring the kill began in 1971, and in 1979, observers were placed on both U.S. and foreign purse seiners, to the predictably intense displeasure of the captains and their sponsoring companies. In the United States, the Marine Mammal Protection Act of 1972 eventually led to the greatly reduced mortality quota of 20 500 for the U.S. fleet; a lot still died, but catching yellowfin with purse seines without some dolphin deaths so far is apparently unavoidable.

The tuna fishers don't wish to kill the dolphins. Even if the fishers think that concerned conservationists are just a bunch of meddling bleeding hearts, they know it is bad business to kill dolphins, for boycotts can be effective. A number of safety features to help free the porpoises were introduced in the U.S. fleet and adopted by others. Captured dolphins were encouraged to escape over the lowered end of the purse in the "backdown manoeuvre," and a skin diver monitored their escape. Some still got entangled and drowned, however. Nets were set in the daytime so that dolphins could be seen, but sometimes they could not be pulled in until after dark, and more drowned then. The nets could also collapse or canopy, or get into unexpected currents or storms, and still more dolphins drowned. During the 1980s, the U.S. tuna boats were careful, and about 60 per cent of nets that were set didn't kill any dolphins. In another 30 per cent, however, as many as ten dolphins were killed, and occasionally the kill was disastrous. Observers remained unwelcome; not only was it impossible to put an observer on every U.S. tuna boat, it was even difficult to put observers anywhere in other fleets.

During the early 1990s, protests against dolphin kills in the purse seines grew once again. People were concerned not just about those killed but also about the damage to the social relationships and individual health of the captured dolphins. Pressed by public sentiment, U.S. tuna canners announced in 1990 that they wouldn't accept tuna caught by dolphin encirclement. First the United States and then the European Union countries, in 1994, stopped importing tuna caught that way by the tuna boats of Mexico and other nations. Cans of tuna were clearly labelled "dolphin-safe" so that consumers would know how the tuna had been caught. Most of the U.S. fleet gave up and left the eastern tropical Pacific, while the Mexicans continued to protest what they considered to be unfair restrictions. In 1995, Mexican and U.S. representatives met to reconsider the dolphin-tuna situation. They proposed that the embargo on tuna caught by dolphin encirclement be lifted, provided that no dolphins actually got killed in the process and that an honest observer be placed on every boat to ensure the dolphins' survival. The bill before Congress would have allowed imports of tuna caught by purse seiners provided that no more than five thousand dolphin are killed each year in the process. This would have let the U.S., Mexican and Venezuelan tuna fleets fish for yellowfin in the eastern Pacific and sell their tuna to the U.S. and European markets once again. The bill was passed by the U.S. House, but the Senate failed to act before Congress adjourned prior to the presidential election, and so the bill died.

The proposed bill has split the U.S. environmental groups. It is supported by Greenpeace and the Environmental Defense Fund, which find it an acceptable compromise. A spokeswoman for the Center for Marine Conservation said, "The legally binding agreement that is envisioned—including monitoring, enforcement and incentive measures—makes it far more likely to have fewer and fewer dolphin deaths in coming years." The opponents of the proposed bill include the Humane Society, the Sierra Club, the World Wildlife Federation, and Friends of the Earth, and they are concerned that the dolphins are being sacrificed because of pressure from international trade agreements. They emphasize that unobserved and unrecorded dolphin mortality would occur because of the harassment and stress of the encircled dolphins. The director of Earth Island Institute, David Phillips, said, "If this bill passes, the only winners will be the Mexican dolphin-killers, who will be able to dump their dolphin-lethal tuna onto U.S. supermarket shelves." Since Republican representatives in the U.S. Congress tend to support the proposed bill, along with the Clinton administration, some version of the bill is likely to become law.

Purse seiners searching for yellowfin and skipjack started working the east Pacific in the early 1960s. They then spread to the Atlantic, the west Pacific, Indonesia, and finally, in the mid-1980s, to the Indian Ocean. No virgin grounds, no new stocks remain to be discovered. The fishery for both species expanded threefold during the two decades since 1970, to a total of about 2.5 million tonnes per year; it won't expand much further.

Albacore

Albacore really got the commercial tuna fishery going. It's a mid-sized species, bigger than yellowfin, but still considerably smaller than the giant bluefin. It migrates in close to the California shore, where in the late 1800s and early 1900s the Portuguese immigrants developed a taste for it. The first hunters were Portuguese whalers originally from the Azores, and when they ran out of whales, they shifted to albacore. The immigrant population enjoyed the strong taste of the cured, not canned fish. Fishers of Portuguese ancestry still dominate the American tuna fishery, and in fact a grandson of a nineteenth-century Portuguese whaler became president of the powerful American Tunafishermens Association after World War II.

Still, the fishery didn't spread until a Japanese fishery biologist arrived with his knowledge of tuna fishing. He caught sardines for baitfish, chummed up albacore next to his boat with the bait and then hooked the tuna with barbless bamboo poles. The technique spread, but a market developed only when someone else tried baking the meat in steam before canning it, resulting in more or less the same product we know now.

This was still early in the century. By 1917 and 1918, higher summer temperatures and intensive fishing made the fish harder to find. They began to occur erratically in coastal waters, and the California inshore fishery staggered on only to finally collapse between 1926 and 1930—the familiar story unfolding again.

Other species, such as bluefin, yellowfin and skipjack, had a stronger taste and at first weren't canned. But with the decline of albacore in the years between the world wars, tuna boats began to venture farther offshore for yellowfin and skipjack. Japanese fishers, arriving in California via Hawaii, did most of the tuna fishing. A global fishery for tuna began to emerge.

THE GLOBAL FISHERY

A global fishery depends on boats that can travel far from their home ports, remain at sea and bring back fish still fit to eat. In the years between the wars, new tuna boats, 30 to 36 metres (100 to 120 feet) long, with diesel engines, could cruise up to 8000 kilometres (5000 miles) without refuelling, and could stay at sea for about thirty days at a time. Each boat carried live bait tanks in the stern, with circulating seawater, and each could carry 150 tonnes of tuna back in its refrigerated holds. The boats were independently owned but were under contract to specific California canneries. By 1928, thirty-one canneries operated. Like whaling a century earlier, the fishery expanded over the Pacific and into the Atlantic, gradually becoming global in scale, dominated by the U.S. tuna boats, canneries and market.

With the outbreak of World War II, the fleet ceased to operate as tuna boats. The U.S. navy commandeered the fleet for military work in the South Pacific and incarcerated the Japanese in internment camps. Tuna had a few years of relative peace while the war raged. Even albacore returned to Californian coastal waters, which were coincidentally cooler during those years.

When the war ended, the fishery truly took off. The old commandeered fleet returned, and new and larger boats were built. Consumer demand mushroomed. The United States took possession of the Trust Territory of the Pacific Islands, gaining unfettered access to their tuna resources in the process. When the United States extended voluntary jurisdiction over its coastal waters, U.S. tuna fishers became nervous that other countries would do so as well. As Latin American countries extended their territorial limits to 200 miles offshore, conflicts between the United States and the Latin American countries grew. The tuna boats had to collect their baitfish from inshore waters, within the 200-mile limits, and they expected to fish for tuna there as well. By 1954, twenty U.S. tuna boats had been seized by Latin American nations for fishing, they said, illegally in their territorial waters. Even so, the Americans prospered.

Then, with U.S. aid, postwar Japan emerged with a competitive fishing fleet and fishers who had not forgotten their fishing methods. They sold canned tuna on the U.S. market, underselling the California canneries, which began to fold. By 1960, the American Tunafishermens Association was bankrupt.

Things improved during the next decade, however. The combination of a strong new fibre for seine nets and powerful blocks for hoisting the heavy nets allowed for baitless tuna fishing for the first time. The United States built a new fleet of even larger boats, now all purse seiners. Free of dependence on inshore water for baitfish, able to compete efficiently with the Japanese, the United States regained its dominance in the fishery. The main target was yellowfin, and the large incidental dolphin kills began. By the mid-1960s, yellowfin stocks showed the familiar signs of overfishing.

TUNA PIRATES

With the signing of the UN Convention of the Law of the Sea, every state that hadn't already done so rushed to establish 200-mile EEZs, including the scattered island states of the Pacific. Huge amounts of ocean suddenly lay in their jurisdiction, providing access to valuable tuna. Although these countries needed the funds the tuna could bring in to support their relatively weak economies, they lacked the technical expertise, the boats and the canneries to take advantage of their new tuna resources.

Article 63 of the Law of the Sea Convention calls for cooperation among neighbouring coastal states over shared stocks of highly mobile or migratory species such as tuna. The island states of the Pacific interpreted this provision as indicating that the fish were theirs to manage when they migrated through

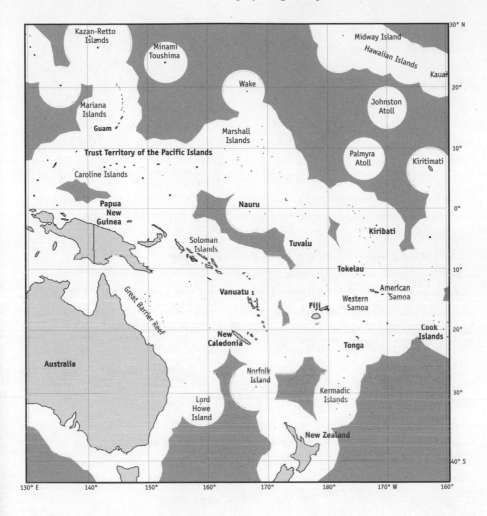

FIGURE 14

EEZs in the South Pacific. The South Pacific was once almost entirely high seas, dotted with islands. Now that the island countries and the island possessions of distant countries all have 200-mile EEZs, very little high seas space is left.

their EEZs (Figure 14). Japan accepted the interpretation and negotiated with the island countries. The United States, however, influenced by the powerful lobbying of the American Tunafishermens Association, interpreted Article 63 to mean that highly mobile species belonged to no one. Thus, the United States refused to acknowledge the rights of island nations to manage their own tuna resources in their EEZs and sent in their own tuna boats. The large purse seiners fished where they wished, ignored the opinions of international critics and became known as tuna pirates.

Too much was at stake. The United States didn't want to accept any restrictions; the island countries needed the income and detested the intrusions. To strengthen their hand, the island countries formed the South Pacific Fisheries Association, and they all joined: the Cook Islands, Fiji, Kiribati, Nauru, Niue, Papua New Guinea, Solomon Islands, Tonga, Western Samoa and Vanuatu, as well as New Zealand and Australia. They agreed to cooperate on fisheries management relations with distant-water fishing nations such as the United States and Japan and to use surveillance and enforcement, if necessary. They also agreed that an offence against one of them was an offence against all. Only when Papua New Guinea and the Solomon Islands took unilateral action and the island nations agreed to act in unison did the United States back off and change its policy.

The first act occurred in 1982, when Papua New Guinea arrested a U.S. purse seiner, the *Danica*, for fishing in its EEZ without a licence. The captain was convicted and fined. In retaliation, the United States invoked its dreaded Magnuson Act, planting an embargo on fish products from Papua New Guinea. Papua New Guinea released the *Danica* to its owners for a fine of $200 000, even though the value of the catch and the vessel was closer to $13 million. Papua New Guinea entered into an agreement with the American Tunafishermens Association, giving U.S. boats unlimited access to its waters under better terms than the Japanese had. It wasn't a clear victory for either side.

The second act occurred in 1984. This time the Solomon Islands arrested the U.S. purse seiner *Jeanette Diana* for illegal fishing. The captain and owner were charged and fined about $100 000, and they had to forfeit their vessel, gear, catch and helicopter. The Solomons tried to sell the forfeited vessel and gear to anyone in the world, but the United States threatened potential buyers with recriminations. Once again the United States invoked the Magnuson Act and established a U.S. embargo of fisheries products from the Solomons. To convince the Americans to lift the embargo, the Solomons raised the stakes: no new licences would be issued to U.S. vessels, all U.S. vessels would be banned from the Solomons' EEZ, and the Soviet Union would be allowed in to fish in the Solomons. Seven months later, following a change in government in the Solomons, the two countries reached an agreement and the United States lifted the embargo. The Solomons sold the vessel back to its owners for about one million dollars.

The United States hadn't changed its opinion about access to highly migratory species, but it needed to concede something. It was just about to meet with the South Pacific states to negotiate access, and if the standoff with the

Solomons persisted, the negotiations would fall apart. The fact that Kiribati signed a one-year treaty with the Soviet Union just after the arrest of the *Jeanette Diana* certainly helped increase the sense of urgency to reduce the conflicts through diplomacy.

The agreements between the Pacific countries and the distant-water fishing countries mostly held together. Japanese compliance is probably greatest, since Japan relies so heavily on fish. Countries such as Taiwan and South Korea, with expanding distant-water fleets, tread less cooperatively. And the old problems remain. Everyone is greedy, everyone cheats if they can, enforcement is difficult, and surveillance is prohibitively expensive. But it could be worse.

Although it may be several years before the treaty that came out of the UN Conference on Straddling Stocks and Highly Migratory Fish Species in 1995 actually becomes international law, the high seas fishing nations such as the United States, China, South Korea, Taiwan, Japan and the countries of the European Union will have to try to implement it anyway. The treaty proposes a number of changes that should help to protect the stocks of high seas migratory fish such as tuna. It also expects that nontarget species of fish, seabirds and marine mammals will be conserved. It insists on cooperative management of fisheries by the countries involved, and it bans from the fishery any country that does not comply. There will be binding arbitration of disputes, making it impossible for countries simply to opt out the agreement. This is not an impossible dream, for this time the United States pushed hard for a strong treaty; indicating that there is a shred of rationality in politics, the United States ratified it promptly, and others will soon follow. Tuna stocks should have the protection they need to prevent collapse.

CONCLUSIONS

Tuna have changed the politics of the Pacific. Tuna are forcing continued development of international access to resources beyond the 200-mile limits of FEZs. Tuna are nearly fully exploited, and international agreements on their conservation now await ratification. Problems remain unsolved, and even unconsidered, however. Any use of driftnets is an ugly and wasteful method of capturing fish, including tuna, and driftnets are still used. The death of dolphins is unavoidable in the purse-seining of yellowfin, but the death of any is disturbing. And for a small tuna boat to hunt giant bluefin one at a time, in the manner of whale hunters, is an absurd waste of resources; in a global economy under the stress that ours is and will continue to be for a long time, such waste is unacceptable.

The amazingly swift and warm-blooded tuna will survive, though bluefin could be hunted to extinction. Pacific island economies will survive with the support of income from the tuna fishers, though some will be luckier than others. The taste for sashimi and canned tuna certainly won't lessen. At the same time, the high seas will have lost much of the freedom we have long associated with them.

CHAPTER 13

SALMON: THE GREATEST CHALLENGE

The most luxurious [Atlantic salmon] anglers are the Americans. . . .
Their rods, their reels, their flies are works of art; expensive ones too, as
they take care to inform you. They are always self-satisfied, always droll,
always hospitable. They never go anywhere without pistols and champagne.

John Rowan, 1876,
quoted by Farley Mowat
SEA OF SLAUGHTER

The Atlantic salmon fishery has all but closed down. Pacific salmon have almost disappeared from the Sacramento–San Joachin river system in California and from the Columbia River in Washington, and many streams that used to have annual breeding runs in British Columbia no longer have them. In the early 1990s, vast numbers of salmon that were expected in British Columbia didn't show up, though some showed up when they weren't expected in the summer of 1996. From Japan to California, those that do return to their streams to breed are smaller than they used to be. At the same time, the breeding migrations in Alaska have never been greater, and the Alaskan fishery is thriving. What in the world is going on here, where the fishery ranges from collapse to apparently sustained success?

EVERYBODY'S FAVOURITE

Salmon must be the perfect fish, from a human, fish-eating point of view. It is relatively large, it is agile and strong, its flesh is a beautiful red-orange, and its taste, whether the fish is smoked, raw or carefully cooked, can be to die for. As adults, the size we want most to catch, salmon concentrate in large numbers in predictable places as they migrate near shore and up rivers to breed. Recreational fishers, commercial fishers and Native fishers compete for the rights to catch them. If there ever were a fish destined for extermination by humans, it must be salmon, for it tastes too good, it looks too good, and it swims right into the hands, or nets, of inshore and upriver fishers.

In the Pacific, seven species are fished, five on both sides of the ocean, two on the Asian side only. They breed, or used to breed, in coastal rivers extending north from San Francisco Bay along the west coast of North America to Alaska, in the rivers draining the Arctic Ocean and in the Asian coastal rivers of Russia, Japan and Korea. In the Atlantic, only one species exists, breeding in coastal rivers from Maine to Newfoundland and Labrador, in Iceland and in Europe from Norway south to Great Britain. They have been harvested by every country they approach, and probably in every river and stream they breed in. They have been hunted on the high seas in both oceans and are still hunted by the Japanese in the western Pacific and the central Bering Sea.

≈≈≈≈≈≈≈≈≈≈≈≈≈≈≈≈≈≈≈≈≈≈≈≈≈≈≈≈≈≈

If there ever were a fish destined for extermination by humans, it must be salmon, for it tastes too good, it looks too good, and it swims right into the hands, or nets, of inshore and upriver fishers.

≈≈≈≈≈≈≈≈≈≈≈≈≈≈≈≈≈≈≈≈≈≈≈≈≈≈≈≈≈≈

The fishery for Atlantic salmon is in dreadful shape, much of it closed down. In the Pacific, south of Alaska, despite the fishery's growing reputation over the decades before the 1990s as a well-managed fishery, everything that could go wrong has recently gone wrong. Biologists have made the wrong predictions, managers and politicians the wrong decisions. Fish wars—in reality small skirmishes—between countries that ought to know better have erupted, and fishers have argued with each other about gear use and with regulators about regulations. The spawning habitats have been destroyed by pollution from logging, mining and urbanization. A lack of enforcement has made poaching easy and a source of considerable resentment. Meanwhile, changing water temperatures and currents have played a role in changing migration patterns and reproductive success, confusing everyone in the process. No better example exists of how complex the issues are and how unlikely we are to understand them and ourselves enough to protect the species as well as the jobs of the fishers. Salmon fisheries present a picture of failure, for all too familiar reasons, and a picture of success. Yet where there is failure, there is optimism about long-term recovery. Where there is success, there is nervousness and concern about how fragile that success is.

A VULNERABLE LIFE CYCLE

Salmon are born in the headwaters of cold, clear streams from eggs laid in gravel beds. In most species, the juveniles spend a year or more gradually moving downstream, in the process creating a permanent memory of the flavour of the unique chemistry of the stream. Then they move on out of the estuary into the open ocean or along the adjacent coast. Over the next year or more, they may migrate large distances to feed in cold, food-rich, more northern waters. In the Atlantic they may migrate to the coasts of Greenland and Iceland. In the Pacific they may migrate north into the Alaskan Gyre. Then they migrate back to the rivers and streams they were born in, homing in on their own specific stream by searching for the water with the flavour they must remember from as many as three years before. In the Atlantic, some may return to the sea after they breed to feed and then return to breed another year; in the Pacific they undergo more profound physical changes as they migrate to breed, and they all die after they spawn for their one and only time (Figure 15).

Everywhere they are hunted—on their migrations in the high seas, on their inshore migrations, as they congregate to begin their upriver migrations to their spawning pools and throughout their upriver migrations. Seiners, trollers and gillnetters fish their quotas, and the quotas are further divided among commercial, recreational and aboriginal fishers. These quotas are all too easily filled.

LOST RIVERS, LOST FISH

Sockeye, pink, chum, chinook and coho—each species of Pacific salmon has its own unique life history. The species differ in how far upstream they go to breed, how far offshore they migrate to feed and how old and how large they are when they return to their rivers to breed. Even within species, life histories may vary. For instance, sockeye usually migrate across the North Pacific, north of 40 degrees, but some populations never leave fresh water at all; these are known as kokanee salmon. Among coho, males return after different lengths of time feeding at sea. Some return after just six months, as jacks, whereas others wait another year to return as much larger, bright red hooknose males. Jacks are too small to be able to compete directly with hooknose males for the chance to fertilize the eggs that females lay at their nest sites, but a jack will sneak in on a spawning hooknose male and female and fertilize what eggs he can get near. The hooknose doesn't chase the jack away, though he ought to; jacks probably just don't look like real competitors to a hooknose.

For breeding to be successful, all salmon need clear water, clean gravel beds for nest sites and a river system free of dams. But logging sends eroded soils downstream, suffocating eggs and alevins, or newly hatched fish. Road and rail

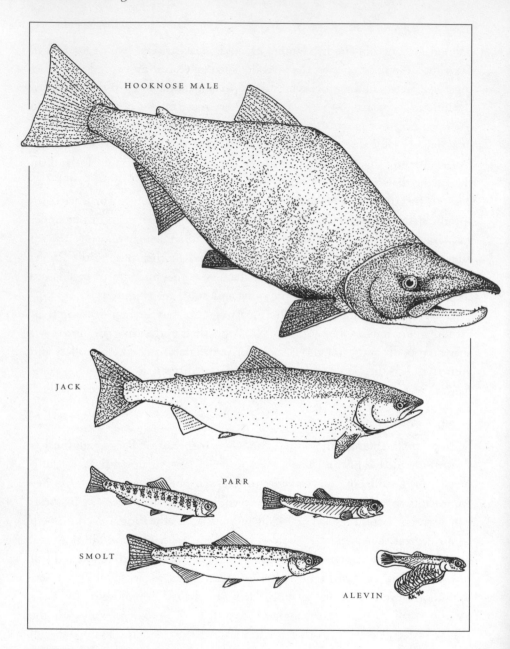

FIGURE 15

Life History of the Sockeye. *Developing from newly hatched alevins into parr and then smolt in fresh water, sockeye then migrate to the sea, where they grow to sexual maturity. Young adult males return to fresh water as jacks, while older, larger males develop the distinctive hooknose and humpback before they return to breed.*

construction has produced landslides that block rivers. Power dams have made migration by salmon an almost impossible challenge. Mining operations have destroyed gravel beds in highland streams, and smelting by-products have polluted the water. The coexistence of logging, mining, hydroelectric power and salmon fishing remains exceedingly difficult and may not really be possible. Nonetheless, attempts to protect the salmon while they are in the rivers go back centuries, and renewed efforts are occurring now.

Atlantic salmon first gained some protection in England in 1215 from the Magna Carta, which gave them the right of free passage up English rivers and streams. Perhaps the first written management scheme, it suffered from the same poor enforcement that has plagued recent management systems. Salmon have disappeared from most of the streams of northern Europe. Many of those that remain still migrate across the high seas to the eastern side of Greenland, where they feed for a year or more before returning to breed. On the other side of the Atlantic, Atlantic salmon used to breed in the rivers of New England even south of Cape Cod, almost as far as Long Island, and they once migrated down the St. Lawrence River, breeding in the rivers draining into all sides of Lake Ontario. The first commercial fishing stations in North America were built by the French in the St. Lawrence region in the 1650s, near breeding runs in the adjacent rivers. All those rivers are lost as breeding rivers for the salmon, a result of dams and pollution from logging, sawmills and other sources, leaving the rivers of Nova Scotia, New Brunswick, and Newfoundland and Labrador, as well as a few in Maine. It is difficult to determine how much of their original freshwater habitat has been lost as a result of habitat destruction, but estimates range from 30 to 40 per cent. Among the rivers they still return to, those in New Brunswick are the least attractive, since they continue to be polluted by the lumber industry, which so totally dominates the province. Even without the intense fishing they have experienced, Atlantic salmon stocks would surely have declined in response to the loss or pollution of so many of their great breeding rivers.

In the Pacific, rivers have been lost to the salmon in the same way. In the rivers of California, chinook salmon had been fished heavily but sustainably by indigenous people, probably for four thousand years before the arrival of the Europeans. They were well recognized as a limited resource, and the indigenous people appear to have managed them by controlling who had access to fish them.

With the arrival of the Spanish in California in the 1770s and the Mexicans in the 1830s, followed by settlers from elsewhere in the United States, the

discovery of gold in 1848 and the subsequent gold rush, the indigenous population was mostly obliterated, and the salmon streams became clogged with mining debris. In the 1850s, New England salmon fishers arrived, having abandoned
their fished-out and polluted streams and rivers back east. They developed the
California chinook fishery, setting seine nets in the Sacramento–San Joachin
River systems of central California. Greek and Italian harvesters followed.

≈≈≈≈≈≈≈≈≈≈≈≈≈≈≈≈≈≈≈≈≈≈≈≈≈≈≈≈≈≈

*The coexistence of logging, mining, hydroelectric power and salmon fishing
remains exceedingly difficult and may not really be possible.*

≈≈≈≈≈≈≈≈≈≈≈≈≈≈≈≈≈≈≈≈≈≈≈≈≈≈≈≈≈≈

Canning spread salmon across the globe, just as it later did for tuna.
Beginning slowly after 1850, by 1880–85 twenty-one canneries competed on the
Sacramento for the salmon brought in by 1500 boats. The heavy fishing pressure, partly a result of the more efficient bottom trawling that began in the
mid-1870s, along with loss of suitable breeding habitat, resulted in the familiar
crash of the salmon populations in 1886, and the last of the Sacramento canneries closed in 1919. The familiar response by the canners and the fishers was to
move north, on to the larger run of the great Columbia River in Washington.
As Atlantic salmon disappeared from the rivers of Norway, Norwegian salmon
fishers also left their own river towns and immigrated to southern British
Columbia and the Fraser River in the 1920s. Like the New Englanders before
them farther south along the Pacific coast, they started over, fishing as they had
fished before, doing to the new streams and rivers what they had done to the
ones they had abandoned in Norway.

As the decades and centuries pass, we have pushed salmon from the streams
and rivers in the lands we occupy in our own increasing numbers. On the two
North American coasts we have pushed them north, or rather we have largely
eliminated them from the more southern parts of their ranges, as we use their
rivers for other purposes. Although they are gone from the rivers of most of
New England and from California, and they are disappearing from the rivers
of British Columbia, nowhere in our recent memory is their decline more dramatic than in the Columbia River in Washington State.

The Columbia River is the largest river flowing into the Pacific Ocean from
North America. It wanders more than 1900 kilometres (1200 miles) from its
source on the crest of the Rocky Mountains in southern British Columbia,
eventually flowing westward, marking the boundary between Oregon and
Washington, en route to Portland and the Pacific. A century ago it was perhaps

the greatest of the salmon rivers. Now the run is small, maybe 15 per cent of what it once was, a victim of all the other uses the river has come to have.

Of greatest impact on the Columbia River and other rivers of the Pacific Northwest such as the Snake River are the enormous dams that were built during the middle decades of this century. What's good for power production is dreadful for salmon. With the building of the dams and their turbines, a run of millions declined to a run of thousands. Despite the ladders built to help the salmon drive upriver and the efforts to help juveniles swim downstream, probably 95 per cent of fry and smolt in the Columbia River died in the turbines en route down the river. Finally, after decades of such destruction, under pressure from environmental groups, including the Sierra Club, the government agreed in the summer of 1996 to help the migrating juveniles get past the lethal turbines by arranging for spills over the dams during the migration period. The spills carried many juveniles down the river, and the experiment seems to have been a success. Less power is produced during spills, however, for then all the water doesn't go through the turbines; short-term power shortages are likely and will be the necessary cost of assisting the salmon. It is not yet clear that the cost will prove to be acceptable.

ENHANCEMENT PROJECTS

To compensate for the loss of wild salmon stocks, biologists, managers and fish breeders in both northern Europe and North America have tried a number of different approaches. These include stream rehabilitation and salmon hatcheries. Stream rehabilitation is certainly worthwhile, for part of the decline of wild salmon populations is due to the destruction and pollution of their spawning beds. Rehabilitation is slow work, for it involves rebuilding stream banks, building fences and cleaning out sediment and other debris. Loggers will soon be forced to leave wider buffers along streams in the watersheds they cut, and that will help to protect the spawning beds from the runoff of eroded sediments. In some rivers, such as the Elwha River in Olympic National Park in Washington, even the dams are being removed to restore the salmon runs. Restoration of the salmon runs of both the Atlantic and Pacific coasts of North America will proceed slowly, much destruction will have to be reversed, and competing interests in the streams and rivers will have to accept the new restrictions, but a start has been made.

Fish hatcheries are also a source of controversy. In a salmon hatchery, the eggs are hatched and the fry are raised to smolts and then released. Salmon hatcheries should and often do work well. The young fish grow well and return as adults to the rivers they were released in, and so the hatcheries have helped to sustain some of the declining wild stocks. Probably the best example is coho, the preferred species of recreational fishers. On the coast of British Columbia, where one hundred streams used to account for 90 per cent of spawning coho, coho now spawn in only twenty streams; the rest spawn in hatcheries, sustaining the stocks.

A serious genetic problem has emerged, however. Selection in hatcheries is quite different from selection under wild or natural conditions. The traits eggs and fry need to survive and grow in hatchery environments are associated with hatchery conditions, not natural ones. The hatchery-reared fish appear to be swamping the wild population with their hatchery-related traits. Genetic diversity will certainly decrease, and the decline in size and strength observed in returning adults may be a result of hatchery rearing.

In Alaska, hatcheries also started up to help sustain the salmon stocks of the Gulf of Alaska. In the early 1990s, they still seemed to be a good idea, and the state government invested heavily in them, owning half of the thirty-four hatcheries and subsidizing all of them with hefty loans. Now, though, because there are too many salmon coming in from the Alaskan commercial fishers and from the world's salmon farms, the hatcheries are less valuable. The fishers propose that they be closed down, or at least lose their subsidies; others suggest the answer is to develop more diversified markets for salmon. The politicians are attempting to settle the question.

The most recent issue to emerge in the Alaskan salmon fishery is the practice of stripping eggs from the females, or roe stripping, so that the eggs can be used in the hatcheries. The catch of chum salmon in southeast Alaska in 1996 was about double the expected 10 million fish, in part because of the success of the hatchery program for chum. The price of chum dropped so low that excess salmon couldn't be given away. Because of the low value of the fish, seven hatcheries began to roe-strip their salmon, discarding 2½ million salmon carcasses in the process. It took a serious hunger strike by an activist from an emergency food assistance group for the state governor to suspend all permits for stripping roe and dumping carcasses and to seek new ways to use the excess fish.

The wild populations of salmon need protection, and so do their natural spawning sites. The efforts to supplement the salmon fisheries by means of hatcheries may be of value where the wild stocks are in decline, but hatcheries also create unexpected problems and pose disturbing threats to the wild stocks.

SALMON FARMS

Salmon are also raised in large pens, or farms, in protected coastal inlets. The farming of salmon has quite suddenly become competitive with the commercial fishing of wild stocks, and it has resulted in a glut of salmon on the world markets. Farming began in Norway in the mid-1970s as a way to compensate for the declining wild stocks of Atlantic salmon. Norway still produces about half of the world's farmed salmon, but salmon farming has spread to British Columbia, Chile, the United Kingdom, the United States, Japan and even the Faroe Islands. Along the B.C. coast there were ten salmon farms in 1976, forty in 1984 and another seven hundred in 1988. In 1976, 100 tonnes of B.C. farmed salmon reached the world markets; in 1996, the farms produced a total of over 500 000 tonnes—for the first time, more than the Alaskan commercial fishery landed. The glut of salmon has resulted in rock-bottom prices. Commercial fishers would like to see the farms banned, as they have been in Alaska, for the success of the farms is a serious threat to the commercial fishery.

Environmental groups, which have quite different concerns, also seek restrictions on salmon farming. The farms take up valuable space in coastal inlets, and because the fish consume a great deal of food and are confined in a small area, the farms may pollute the inlets. Also because of their close confinement and unnatural conditions, diseases and infections frequently develop and have to be controlled by antibiotics and other drugs. In addition, the salmon stocks in the farms are genetically different from wild stocks and are probably not able to grow and survive as successfully in wild conditions. As a result, there is a real fear that diseased or genetically inferior fish that have escaped will mix and interbreed with the wild populations. And yet, as journalist Larry Pynn has written, "Despite the use of vaccines, antibiotics and synthetic caretenoids to turn the flesh pink, farmed salmon has gained wide acceptance with restaurants and customers." The conflict between fish farmers and both commercial fishers and environmentalists can only grow, although at present some humour remains, at least on the bumper stickers. One reads, "Real fish don't eat pellets."

COLLAPSE OF THE ATLANTIC FISHERY

Atlantic salmon have fed the coastal communities of the North Atlantic peoples since human settlement began. In North America, the French began fishing for salmon on a commercial scale around 1650. Fishing pressure grew gradually, enough that attempts to protect salmon began in 1860. By the 1950s, with driftnets offshore, and gillnets and trapnets inshore, they were clearly being overfished. Also in the 1950s they were discovered in very large numbers in Davis Strait off the west coast of Greenland, and the Greenland fishery opened, dominated by the Danes.

Salmon from Canada and the remnants of the salmon populations from the United States, the United Kingdom and Ireland congregate in Davis Strait off southwest Greenland (Figure 16). Salmon that breed in Iceland's rivers migrate only to the east coast of Greenland, where they grow to sexual maturity. The Danes began to use driftnets to catch salmon in Davis Strait in 1965, provoking an angry response from Canada, since about 40 per cent of the fish they caught came from Canadian rivers. The Danes ceased to use driftnets, but Canadian fishers had their own long driftnets out. By 1971, so few salmon returned to the rivers in Quebec and New Brunswick that the fishery appeared in danger of collapse, and the driftnets were banned. To protect the remaining fish, Canada banned commercial salmon fishing in 1972 in New Brunswick, Quebec and parts of Newfoundland, but the ban had little effect. Fish bound for the protected rivers were intercepted, caught at sea long before they reached the coast. Illegal fishing continued as fishers poached where they could. Many salmon came in as bycatch of other fisheries. Recreational and Native fishers kept on fishing, since the ban did not effect them. The fishery really remained uncontrolled, the ban unenforceable. As a result, during the 1970s, poaching along with the Native catch in the Canadian rivers drove the remaining stocks even lower. In 1978, Maine ended its rod-and-reel fishery in the few sites the salmon still returned to. In New Brunswick, the government offered to buy back licences, and the major rivers of the province—the Restigouche, the Miramichi, the St. John—were all closed to salmon fishing.

With such a reduction in fishing, the stocks appeared to recover, and so the Canadian fishery reopened in 1981 with a total allowable catch of fifty thousand fish. Catches quickly fell once again, and a total collapse of the New Brunswick and Quebec fishery again appeared likely. In 1985 the fishery in New Brunswick closed permanently, and the fishery in Newfoundland came under further restrictions, though it was not completely closed. The government again bought back all remaining licenses. The catch in Davis Strait continued to drop, reaching its lowest level in eighteen years in 1990. Finally, in Greenland, in 1994, the United States funded a buyout of the fishing rights held by the Greenland hunters and fishers' organizations, and the Davis Strait fishery ended, forty years after it was discovered.

On the coasts of North America a recreational fishery persists; Newfoundland didn't close its rivers despite low returns of the fish; interception of adults at sea continues; and an aquaculture effort struggles along—the fishery is not quite dead. Meanwhile, in Europe, net fisheries in Scotland and Ireland continue, and Norway continues to support an active rod-and-reel fishery. The species remains in sufficient numbers to support some level of harvesting, but the underlying questions remain unsolved. A change in management strategy is overdue, and comanagement is clearly the way to go, but it isn't happening.

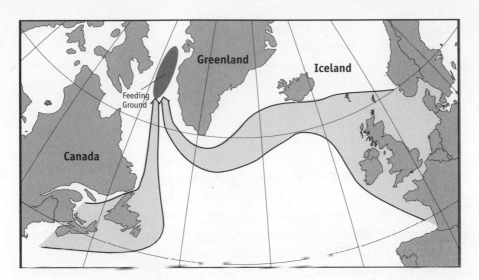

FIGURE 16

Migration of the Atlantic Salmon. *Atlantic salmon migrate from both sides of the Atlantic to feed along the west coast of Greenland.*

PACIFIC SALMON: TOO MANY CONFLICTS

The conflicts on the Pacific coast seem to be almost unlimited. Processors are fighting to keep their jobs in light of the U.S.–Canada trade agreement. Fishers are angry with the forestry operation, which is so important to the West Coast economy, for pollution from pulp mills and loss of breeding habitats due to logging reduce the number of rivers available to the salmon ever more each year. Additional breeding sites are lost as rivers are made unsuitable by ever more valuable hydroelectric projects. Native fishers feel constrained by the limitations imposed on what they can do with what they catch and want to sell salmon in competition with the commercial fishers, who believe such competition would be unfair to them. Recreational fishers want a larger slice of the harvest, pointing out how important they are to the local economy, while commercial fishers think the recreational fishers have already been allocated too much, favoured unfairly once again at their expense.

Gear wars then rage on, as each group argues for more fish to be allocated to it at the expense of the others. The trollers point out that the fish they catch are more valuable, for they have not yet begun the decay that entering fresh water induces. Seiners point out that they are the most efficient fishers, able to search out and capture schools at the least expense per fish. Finally, gillnet fishers point out that they can target specific runs and can develop close ties with coastal communities to develop a comanagement solution, which would involve their self-interest, survival of a culture of fishing communities and conservation of the salmon stock.

The Pacific salmon are carefully counted or estimated by fisheries biologists, who allow a certain number to migrate upstream to spawn, monitor the numbers migrating during the migration seasons and then reassess how many can be fished by the various constituents as the season progresses. This approach should reduce the possibility that a gross error in estimating numbers of fish will occur and thus cause catastrophic overfishing. But it comes at a price. Monitoring must occur frequently, a lot of data need to be analyzed quickly in order to determine what management action to take and the regulations have to be well enforced, another extraordinary expense. Probably no deliberate overfishing occurs, but the various species are fished at the heaviest rate that the managers think they can sustain. With coho and sockeye, this approaches 70 per cent of the adult population; with chinook and pink, it is more like 30 to 40 per cent; with chum, the least productive of the five species, it is around 15 to 20 per cent.

In British Columbia, the trollers, fishing up to 50 kilometres (30 miles) offshore, are allocated 20 per cent of the harvest, and catch the migrating fish first, at their healthiest, before they begin to suffer the stress of adapting to fresh water. Fishers close to shore, the purse seiners and inside trollers, get another 50 to 60 per cent of the harvest. Up the rivers, any narrow space along the migration route may be fished by gillnetters, mostly Native fishers, allocated another 20 per cent. Recreational fishers get the rest, about 5 per cent.

This is very tight management, and it is smothered in regulations. Regulations focus on types of gear, quota size, the size and location of the fishable area, the number of days a week that fishing must be restricted in order to let enough fish through to spawn. The fish need more refuges, but the fishers are increasingly mobile and can track them efficiently and rapidly. With such tight management, so many regulations, such a great need for enforcement and diminishing funds to support that level of management, the temptation to cheat is difficult to resist. Creeks and streams can be easily robbed, catches can be misreported, B.C. fish can be landed in the United States, boats can claim that different gear was used, and fish can be sold in underground markets.

Population crashes inevitably occur. The high harvest rates don't prepare us for them, but the close monitoring is supposed to recognize a decline in time and allow adaptive adjustment of catch rates. When any crash occurs, recovery is possible, and can even be rapid, if all harvesting stops for a while; if harvesting persists, even at a low level, recovery is much slower. In 1913, during the building of the railway across the mountains in British Columbia, the builders caused a massive landslide at Hell's Gate on the Fraser River. The sockeye population crashed, harvesting persisted at a reduced rate, and it took another fifty years for the stocks to recover to their pre-landslide levels.

FRAGILE TREATIES

When fish are abundant in one part of their range but not in another, when changes in the environmental conditions induce fish to move from one part of their range to another, and when the extent of management authority varies along the range the fish inhabit, then management gets ever trickier, and conflicts are inevitable. Canadian trollers off Vancouver Island can intercept

≈≈≈≈≈≈≈≈≈≈≈≈≈≈≈≈≈≈≈≈≈≈≈≈≈≈≈≈≈≈≈≈≈≈

The salmon fishery in the Pacific Northwest essentially ended in 1994.

≈≈≈≈≈≈≈≈≈≈≈≈≈≈≈≈≈≈≈≈≈≈≈≈≈≈≈≈≈≈≈≈≈≈

chinook bound for Washington and Oregon. U.S. trollers can intercept fish migrating to the Fraser River in the Juan de Fuca Strait. Alaskan boats can intercept chinook and sockeye migrating to B.C. rivers. U.S. federal authority over fisheries is much weaker than Canadian authority, so conflicts between U.S. states are quite possible. Alaska is able to ignore not only Canadian complaints but those of Washington and Oregon as well.

It can sound rather petty. The United States and Canada have had a reasonably workable agreement about who gets how much of the salmon stocks. But these agreements depend on the salmon's return in consistent numbers along consistent routes. If they return along a route that avoids U.S. waters in northern Washington, or if they shift north in any general fashion following the cooler waters, U.S. fishers miss them and Canadians get them. The U.S. and Canadian fishers used to split the Fraser River fish about 50/50. But warmer water that pushed north along Oregon and Washington pushed the salmon north as well, changing the split to 90/10 in favour of the Canadian fishers.

The salmon fishery in the Pacific Northwest essentially ended in 1994. The area was declared a fisheries disaster area in order to be able to compensate the fishers with unemployment assistance. Some former fishers have taken jobs restoring breeding habitats. In Washington, the state government has bought back fishing permits. The hydroelectric dams, the destruction of breeding habitats and the prolonged warming of the sea have given Washington, Oregon and Northern California a long-term bust in a fishery whose history is one of boom and bust. For now, an era is over.

THE MISSING FISH

Predictable though returning times and places are, there are limits to the predictability. With sockeye, for instance, the time they return to shore to breed is related to the open ocean temperature in winter. Populations that breed at different sites along the coast may one year arrive at discretely different times and another year may arrive all at the same time, making counting them very difficult for biologists. Counting the returning fish is essential to successful salmon management, for then quotas for the next year's harvest can be set with some hope of accuracy. Migrating routes should also be predictable, but they may vary from one year to the next. Again sockeye make a good example. There are two routes around Vancouver Island to get to the Fraser River. One way takes the fish through U.S. waters, where U.S. seiners hope to catch them. The other goes north around Vancouver Island and avoids U.S. waters. The fish went north from 1978 to 1984, perhaps following colder water pushed north by the El Niño warming of Pacific waters, for they avoid water warmer than about 9° c (48° F). Many returned along the more southern route in the later 1980s, but the recent higher temperatures may have pushed them north once more out of U.S. waters. Or perhaps instead they are following prey; perhaps there are changes in circulation patterns, in Fraser River discharge odours or in salinity that affect them. In any case, they may change their route, and that makes counting them difficult or inaccurate.

Probably the most famous fisheries farce of the decade is the case of the missing sockeye, most famously from the Fraser River but also from other major rivers in southern British Columbia, such as the Adams. In 1913, an estimated 30 million sockeye ran the Fraser River. In 1980 the total B.C. run of sockeye was about 14 million. In 1994, the runs were almost obliterated. Expecting relatively high numbers of fish to return, government biologists set the quotas at the usual rate of 80 per cent of returning fish. There is an incredibly high risk in setting a quota that high, for if the estimate of returning numbers is for some reason off by 20 or 30 per cent, the entire population of returning fish could be taken before they have had a chance to breed. This almost happened.

After three years at sea, three million fish were expected to return to the Adams River. For reasons that people are still arguing over, more than two million didn't show up. As a result, the government closed down the fishing. Since it is hard to count and estimate fish numbers and it is difficult to react in time when numbers are dropping precipitously, most fisheries are closed when it's too late to be of much help. But closing the sockeye fishing did let a small proportion of the run get through and breed; if the fishing had remained open for another few days in August 1994, there might have been none left to breed. In the Fraser River, another 1.3 million fish also seem to have arrived and then got lost somewhere, phantom fish. The stock will be a long time recovering, and the salmon fishers aren't doing so well either: "I raised a family and put my kids through school by fishing, and now I can hardly feed myself, let alone my kids," lamented a fisher quoted by journalist Darcy Henton in the *Toronto Star*. "There are some guys who have hardly got their nets wet this season."

Losing a few million fish is embarrassing, particularly when so many people are interested and watching. What happened here? Did they die at sea from starvation related to warmer waters? Was there great mortality on the migration rivers? Everyone blamed everyone else. The commercial fishers blamed the aboriginal bands—who were given the rights to fish commercially for the first time in 1994—charging them with overfishing and asking the courts to impose a ban on their fishing. The recreational fishers were accused of taking far more than their share. Rivers have badly deteriorated, and loggers were blamed. Government biologists may have made faulty estimates, based on overly optimistic projections. Temperatures in the Fraser were perhaps too high, and the fish may have swum around in the mouth, getting themselves counted and recounted and badly skewing the estimate. Perhaps there really were that many fish in the river, but they lacked the energy in the warmer water to swim upstream and were particularly vulnerable at places such as Hell's Gate, and so they died, stressed and blown out. Unfortunately as well, the funding for enforcement dropped in 1992–93, making it almost impossible to enforce regulations, for there are limits to what a few fisheries officers can do. When enforcement breaks down and fishers do not share in owning the resources, everyone overfishes and poaches. The fish never really had a chance.

Whatever the reason, what once appeared to have been a reasonably well managed salmon fishery in British Columbia, held up as an example of successful central management by a government agency, is now in deep trouble, caused by too many regulations, too little ability to enforce them, no sense among fishers that they should cooperate in reducing fishing pressure, too many user groups, too many boats, fish that are too easy to find, destruction of breeding habitats, uncertain effects of hatchery fish on wild stocks—all superimposed on changes in distribution of the fish related to changing temperatures at sea. The result is anger, conflict, declining fish numbers and a fragile fishery on the edge of collapse.

In 1995 the salmon again returned to their breeding rivers in far lower numbers than expected, and the fishery continued to suffer. Biologists predicted that too few sockeye would return in 1996 for the fishery to open at all, and salmon fishers prepared themselves for a season without sockeye. Then, to everyone's surprise, sockeye returned in greater numbers than expected to the Fraser River and the fisheries biologists allowed a brief commercial harvest after all. The same thing happened in the Skeena River, farther north on the B.C. coast, where three to four million fish were expected, and an extra two million showed up. Why was this a better year? It suggests that food supplies at sea have a great influence on the numbers of fish that return to the coast to breed, but in reality we know very little about the biology of salmon during their years at sea. Accurate predictions of the numbers of returning fish seem almost impossible. There is still so much to learn.

What should be done that hasn't been done to protect the salmon and sustain the fishery? Because of the difficulty of enforcing regulations and because of the poaching that occurs, community-based comanagement of the fishery is the best route to go, for it would involve all the fishers—commercial, recreational and Native—in protecting the stocks. It would also allow almost stream-by-stream management, essential in such a complex five-species fishery. The mouth of the Fraser River, polluted and urban, is not a place where community-based comanagement is easy to imagine working, but the many communities north along the coast of British Columbia should be far more suitable.

An alternative is management by individual transferable quotas. The commercial fishing fleet is certainly larger than it should be, and in recognition of the strain on the fishery, the government is buying back salmon fishing licences. It seems determined to cut the fleet size in half, however, without establishing fishing quotas for the vessels. The danger remains that fishing will continue to be just as intense, only fewer boats will be involved, and many fishers will lose employment. Introducing individual transferable quotas would protect the fish; limits to the size of those quotas as well as their transferability could keep reasonable numbers of fishers employed, and a percentage of the quota could continue to be allocated to recreational and Native fishers.

What is certain is that the current form of management is not working. In his controversial report on the B.C. salmon fisheries, "Fish on the Line," Carl Walters—an outspoken fisheries biologist at the University of British Columbia—goes further in his recommendations. Besides favouring community-based comanagement and reduction of the gillnet, seine, troll and trawler fleets, he proposes that all government subsidies for hatcheries and fishers be eliminated and that gillnets be banned from the rivers and streams, replaced by traps, which are much more selective. The fishery will probably stagger on, but the prospects are poor unless relatively radical changes such as these occur.

As it stands, sustainability is probably not possible in the B.C. salmon fishery. The stocks were steady until about 1990, but because the fleet is so huge and powerful and competitive—even if it is now cut back—and because the season is open for only a brief period, an error in the wrong direction in estimating the size of the stock will mean too much intense fishing in the time offered, and another stock collapse will occur. The fishery was just lucky that no disasters occurred earlier. The current low numbers of sockeye will take many years to recover unless there is the will to close the fishery for several years at least. Such will, with all the political baggage it carries, is hard to come by.

The unpopular solution remains easily stated: the fleet needs to be reduced, the huge management bureaucracy must largely disappear, enforcement must be substantially improved, the growing demands of the aboriginal fishers and recreational fishers must be constrained, far fewer people should be doing the fishing, and fishing communities need to sustained. A tough agenda, in need of that elusive will to make the changes happen.

ALASKA SUCCESS

Paradoxically, there are plenty of salmon, especially sockeye and pink, in Alaskan waters. The Canadian fishers and those of Washington and Oregon consider some of these to be their fish, intercepted by the Alaskan fishers before they return to their more southerly breeding rivers. The Alaskan fishers of course disagree. In the salmon conflict that broke out in 1994, the Canadian government encouraged its fishers to fish beyond their quotas on the west coast of Vancouver Island, intercepting the fish that the U.S. seiners would normally have had a shot at. In fact, the fishers were told to "fish aggressively," the loveliest words an over-regulated fisher could ever hope to hear. U.S. ships travelling north to fish in Alaska were charged a tariff for using the sheltered Inside Passage along the B.C. coast to get there. All these events occurred between countries considered to be good neighbours and two of the world's most experienced fishing nations. With the breakdown of a treaty intended to protect a species from overfishing, people become understandably angry; unfortunately, the fish get overfished.

In 1995, Alaska didn't wish to restrict its salmon fishing, even though the Pacific Northwest states joined with Canada in trying to negotiate a reduced harvest in order to keep the fish returning to the B.C. rivers in sufficient numbers to sustain the B.C. and Washington fishers—not to mention the breeding runs. Alaska has hardly cooperated, quite immune to pressure even from other U.S. states. Fifty-two million fish were caught in Alaska in 1993, and 1995 was another excellent year. The salmon war continues, though less stridently, as each side has made some concessions, but the situation remains unstable. While the salmon fisheries to its south flounder, Alaska continues to fish with success.

The North Pacific in fact is now producing record numbers of salmon, particularly pink, sockeye and chum, for the Subarctic Current, driving east across the Pacific, has, in recent years, deflected more to the north when it reaches North America (see Figure 12 in Chapter 10). The result is greater nutrient upwelling and marine production in the Gulf of Alaska and thus more food for the salmon. The catch by Alaskan fishers has swollen from the 13.6 million kilograms (30 million pounds) of the early 1970s to almost 90 million kilograms (200 million pounds) now. Quite an astonishing success story in a world of few comparable successes. Why has it happened in Alaska, while disaster hit the Northwest states and seems to be hovering over British Columbia?

Certainly a different kind of management is part of the answer, though so also is some good luck. The Alaskan fishery has been built somewhat on the Japanese model. The coastline has been divided into seven independent regions by state legislation. Each region has a formal association, representing the various interested groups of users. The associations are young yet, still creating the culture and traditions that will determine their long-term success and survival. Despite their youth, five of the seven associations appear to be profitable.

What has emerged is another experiment in comanagement, with communities cooperating with state government. The state enabled the regional associations to exist, and the state sets the quota of salmon for each region. In turn, the associations are partners with the state in planning how to use the resource, in conducting programs to enhance the fishery (mostly through egg hatcheries), in assessing stocks, planning the harvest, and allocating the stock to the various users. Licences are limited, with about 150 to 200 purse seiners fishing in each region.

The hatcheries are important to the fisheries, or at least they were until the current glut of farmed fish arrived on the world's markets. Originally set up with money from oil revenues provided by the state, the hatcheries enhance the stocks of each of the gulf species. Each region has its own strategy for how much enhancement each species gets. To finance the hatcheries, the sale of a certain percentage of the catch now goes back into their operation. Because of the concern that the hatchery fish may be harming the wild stock, the smolts are released at a time when they will not overlap with the wild stocks. Their ear bones, or otoliths, are marked by a one-day marker that is absorbed into that day's growth ring when the fish are still in their hatcheries, and the fish are then examined on their migration back as adults; hatchery fish can always be distinguished from wild ones by removing their otoliths, cutting a slice through the spherical stone and peering down a microscope at the slice in search of a single marked ring near the centre of the slice. Thus, growth rates, return rates and fecundity of wild and hatchery stocks can be assessed and compared. The regional associations fund the research they consider important to their operations.

Even where the management system seems to be working and local communities are deeply involved in the management and the success of the fishery, unexpected, unpredictable events intrude—not just environmental changes but political changes across the planet. With the collapse of the Soviet Union, Russia suddenly entered the pink salmon market of Japan and Europe. In addition, Japan could get pink salmon cheaply in Russia's economic zone in exchange for technical and market assistance. Dealing with a glut of cheaper fish, both wild and farmed, has been hard on the Alaskan fisheries since the early 1990s. The market value of many fishery products can fluctuate wildly, and salmon are not immune.

THE CONTINUING CHALLENGE

Much is known about salmon when they are not out at sea. This knowledge is good for managers, for their predictions are likely to be more accurate, but everybody else shares that knowledge. It is no wonder that the fisheries have declined and crashed or persist only under very detailed and close management.

Salmon have, however, taught us a great deal about the complexities of management. Can a comanagement system, comparable to Alaska's, be set up in British Columbia, or are the problems there simply too great? Giving the province greater autonomy over its fisheries seems to be reasonable, provided that the new provincial authority would also have the will to reduce the fishing fleet and the quotas and to seek alternative ways of management.

Perhaps in places crowded with humans, such as southern British Columbia, there are too many different interests that need to be satisfied to think that comanagement is even a possibility. Perhaps the salmon are just too accessible, too vulnerable to legal and illegal fishing, and we should instead redirect our concerns to other species that can be managed more easily by individual transferable quotas or by comanagement. Perhaps as well the pollution at the mouth of the Fraser River has ruined the river for salmon. Perhaps hydroelectric needs are more economically important uses of rivers such as the Columbia and the Fraser than to make them safe for migrating salmon.

Political will becomes increasingly important. If salmon fisheries are to survive south of Alaska, and even recover where they have collapsed, the number of fishers will have to be restricted and the number of fish they catch will have to be reduced. These restrictions must apply to commercial fishers, recreational fishers and Native fishers, no matter what they contribute to the local economies, and no matter what their traditions may be. Stream rehabilitation will continue to be essential if the wild salmon stocks are to persist. Because of the environmental and health risks associated with excessive farming, salmon farming is not a single long-term solution. If comanagement is impossible, then enforced management by individual transferable quotas should look tempting; certainly we should abandon the over-regulated, derby-style fishing of recent years.

True recovery of salmon along the coast of the Pacific Northwest states, and perhaps southern British Columbia, may have to wait until the eastward-flowing Subarctic Current once again is deflected more to the south and delivers more of its colder water and nutrients to these coastlines. Such a shift in the current will happen sooner or later, as it has in the past. Even politicians can't change ocean currents when they want to, however, and we are left with trying to repair what we are stuck with. The effort is worthwhile, for the stakes are high. Success in managing the hardest of all species to manage would give us more confidence that in the decades ahead, as the human population continues to grow, we can still maintain a level of self-control. If we can manage the salmon, we should be able to manage any species of fish. We have the knowledge and the ability. Only the political will seems to be in question, and there are growing signs that we have some of that as well—if it isn't already too late.

CHAPTER 14

POLITICS AND THE PACIFIC COAST OF ASIA

Both Japan and South Korea claim two islets in the sea of Japan. Military analysts say such islands are the reason for a growing naval race in Asia as nations in the region seek to claim rich fishing grounds, oil, possible underwater mineral deposits and even vacation spots.

REUTERS, TORONTO STAR

Men and nations behave wisely when they have exhausted all other alternatives.

Attributed to Abba Eban

Politics intrudes at every level of human affairs, and certainly the management and preservation of the world's fisheries is no exception. From the moment a biologist estimates a total allowable catch of a particular species, political interests essentially take over. As soon as a fish stock is shared by more than one nation, political complexity escalates. The ratification of the UN Convention of the Law of the Sea has helped resolve and prevent many potential disagreements, but disagreements still continue. Even nations such as the United States and Canada, or Canada and the EU countries, which more or less get along quite well with each other, still argue over fishing rights.

The management of fisheries along the Pacific coast of Asia is even more complex. The coast is really five major semi-enclosed seas, extending from the winter-frozen Okhotsk Sea in the north to the tropical South China Sea in the south. The extensive continental shelf and productive seas have provided essential protein for the increasingly dense human population for many centuries. But all of these seas have recently experienced overfishing of their coastal waters, habitat destruction and pollution. Here, perhaps more than ever, the political issues dominate and make cooperative fisheries management particularly difficult.

≈≈≈≈≈≈≈≈≈≈≈≈≈≈≈≈≈≈≈≈≈≈≈≈≈≈≈≈≈≈

*From the moment a biologist estimates a total allowable catch of
a particular species, political interests essentially take over.*

≈≈≈≈≈≈≈≈≈≈≈≈≈≈≈≈≈≈≈≈≈≈≈≈≈≈≈≈≈≈

The players along the Pacific coast of Asia are the Russian Federation and Japan, North and South Korea, China and Taiwan, and to the south, Vietnam, the Philippines and Indonesia. They include developing, developed and largely undeveloped economies, as well as remarkably diverse political systems. Conflicts range in seriousness as well, but some of them are potentially very volatile. Russia and Japan argue over ownership of the Kuril Islands north of Hokkaido; North and South Korea stare menacingly at each other across the Demilitarized Zone; China puts on military displays close to the coast of Taiwan, which it considers to be a province of China, not an emerging independent country; Vietnam and China fight over atolls in the South China Sea. At the same time, the collapse of the Soviet Union has undermined the stability of fisheries management by the surviving Russian Federation; Japan has had to pull its distant-water fleets back into Japanese waters and to rely more and more on imported fish; China, South Korea and Taiwan, in contrast, have all expanded their distant-water fleets; and Vietnam is metamorphosing itself into a market economy. North Korea remains hidden from the world; it is not a member of the UN and is not governed by the UN Law of the Sea, and it is unwilling to form fisheries partnerships or to share any fisheries data. Meanwhile, China is becoming an ever stronger regional military power as the U.S. presence in the region continues to shrink.

THE SEA OF OKHOTSK

The Sea of Okhotsk is far to the north on the Pacific coast of Asia, and because it is on the west side of the Pacific, unwarmed by mitigating currents flowing north, it is a cold sea (Figure 17). Most of it lies between 50 and 60

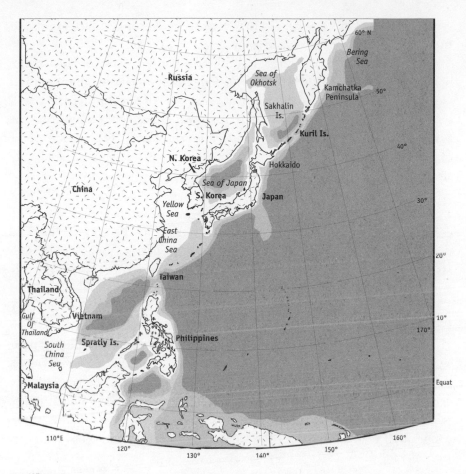

FIGURE 17

The Seas of the Pacific Coast of Asia. Five semi-enclosed and very productive seas lie on the continental shelf along the Pacific coast of Asia: the Sea of Okhotsk, the Sea of Japan, the Yellow Sea, the East China Sea and the South China Sea. Lighter shades in the ocean indicate more shallow water.

degrees north latitude, similar to the latitude of the frozen coast of Labrador on the west side of the Atlantic, and it is far colder than the southern coast of British Columbia or the North Sea, which also lie between the same latitudes. The sea is enclosed by Siberian Russia, with the Kamchatka Peninsula extending south along its east side.

It is not, however, a completely Russian Sea. The Kuril Islands extend from the southern tip of Kamchatka to northeastern Hokkaido, the most northern island of Japan. Sakhalin Island extends down the west side of the Sea to the northwestern end of Hokkaido. Together the Kuril Islands and Sakhalin Island almost fully enclose the sea, and in fact in glacial times, fifteen thousand years ago, the Sea of Okhotsk was fully enclosed and people walked into Japan from the north along both island routes.

Japan has a major stake in the sea's fisheries, partly because of its own EEZ north of Hokkaido, partly because of its long history of fishing in the sea and partly because it disputes the Russian ownership of the Kuril Islands and Sakhalin Island. It has, in the past, at least shared in owning the islands and has never accepted losing them at the end of World War II. The islands are of obvious strategic value, but when the EEZ lines of Japan and Russia are finally clearly drawn, the islands will be far more valuable to whoever owns them.

Much of the Sea of Okhotsk is shallow, lying on the continental shelf, with a cold current circulating around it. It is large enough to have high seas in its central region, an area known as the peanut hole. It lies beyond the limits of the Russian EEZ and has attracted the distant-water fleets of Japan and Poland, after they had been squeezed out of the nearby Bering Sea because of the collapse of the pollock fishery there. Sea ice covers most of the Okhotsk Sea in winter. In summer, inshore waters often warm only to 5° or 6°C (41° to 43°F). Pink salmon still migrate up some of the coastal rivers, and the smaller Asian salmon known as masu is still fished. Whelks, crabs, sardines, squid, scallops and Pacific halibut all support regional fisheries. Like the Bering Sea, however, the most valuable fishery is pollock, and it is hunted by the Russian, Japanese and Polish fleets. The current pressure on the pollock is likely to push it to the same low level that it is in the Bering Sea, despite growing Russian-Japanese cooperation to try to preserve the stocks and to exclude other fishing fleets from sharing it.

Of the coastal seas along the Pacific coast, the Sea of Okhotsk is the least politically controversial. Yet even there, because of the uncertainty over ownership, the dwindling ability of Russia to manage its fisheries, Japan's need to sustain its fisheries and the Polish fleet's desire to hang on to a place to fish, fish stocks are overfished.

Some predictions are certainly possible. It is likely that the sea will become a Russian sea, or one shared with Japan, and that it will be managed by UN mandate as a semi-enclosed sea, its high seas centre no longer available to the fishing fleets of other nations. A start was made in the summer of 1996, when the United States and Russia signed a bilateral agreement that all fishing in the peanut hole should be in line with Russian regulations. But the fish stocks may not be much better off, for the political resolve to conserve and to enforce protective measures may be difficult to find. Comanagement or management by individual transferable quotas may be similarly elusive, for Russia's economic and political instability is a continuing worry.

THE SEA OF JAPAN

To the south of the Sea of Okhotsk, the Sea of Japan presents further complications. Japan shares this Sea with Russia, North Korea and South Korea. Japan and South Korea are arguing over ownership of a couple of islands in the sea, Japanese fishers are lobbying to have Japan declare its 200-mile EEZ to protect them as inshore fishers, and at the same time Japan is worrying that South Korea will proclaim its EEZ and force Japanese fishers from its coastal waters. The two little islands between them are likely to become ever more important.

≈≈≈≈≈≈≈≈≈≈≈≈≈≈≈≈≈≈≈≈≈≈≈≈≈≈≈≈≈≈

The squid of the Sea of Japan carry the highest PCB load of any species known in the world.

≈≈≈≈≈≈≈≈≈≈≈≈≈≈≈≈≈≈≈≈≈≈≈≈≈≈≈≈≈≈

There is as well a growing concern about contamination. The Sea of Japan is deep in the middle; it lacks a broad underlying shelf except along the southern half of Japan. Because of its depth, both Russia and Japan have used it as a dump for radioactive waste, and Russian safeguards are notoriously weak at present. Coastal pollution is also great and will certainly increase as development proceeds. Already the squid of the Sea of Japan carry the highest PCB load of any species known in the world. People involved in aquaculture or fish farming, particularly along the southern coast of Japan, know that their products must be untainted if they are going to sell them. They have to get the politicians to listen to their protests—and to then act—the world's toughest assignment.

This sea has also been overfished in recent decades, and as the stocks of various species have dwindled, the ecosystem has changed. Snow crabs have declined despite regulations to protect them. Heavy trawling for shrimp has caused far too much discard waste of flounders, and the sea bottom has been scoured in the process. Since the mid-1980s, stocks of sardine, anchovy, sand eel and shellfish have all decreased, partly because of intensive fishing, partly because of changes in the temperature of the sea.

The countries of the region are quite aware of and concerned about the problems. Japan has for years dealt with its fishing problems by negotiating with other countries individually and has tried to avoid multilateral agreements. It has assumed that it can get the best deal for itself when it doesn't have to consider the competing needs of several other countries at a time. But times have changed. In other parts of the world many of its bilateral agreements have collapsed as coastal nations have become more capable of fishing for their own stocks without Japanese assistance. Now, with the UN Law of the Sea in force, Japan can no longer afford to attempt bilateral agreements. As South Korea and China have moved towards declaring their 200-mile EEZs, Japan has become particularly worried about losing access to fish stocks it has long hunted and agreed in 1994 to participate in setting up a committee to protect the fisheries of the Sea of Japan. Joining it are Russia, South Korea and China, and North Korea has been invited as well. And this is news. Out of such agreements to try to achieve something emerge the mechanisms to draw territorial lines in the water, reduce overfishing and perhaps preserve the fish stocks before they are too low to fish for any longer. Pressed by a growing sense of catastrophe in the sea's fisheries, uncooperative countries can be forced into cooperation. Success rests on the political will to do so.

THE YELLOW SEA AND THE EAST CHINA SEA

The Yellow Sea lies on the other, western side of the Korean peninsula, opening on the south into the East China Sea. China clearly dominates the coast, while its reluctant province of Taiwan marks the southern limits of the East China Sea. The continental shelf underlies both seas, and the region is certainly a productive one. The two seas are rich in shrimp, which are trawled; filefish, whose separate stocks need protection; hairtail, which are overfished; and anchovies and sardines, whose frequent declines cause squid populations to decline as well. Yellow croakers were once abundant but were trawled to oblivion in the 1970s. Because of the heavy fishing, the ecosystems of the two seas are unstable. Russian fleets don't fish this far south, but Japan definitely considers both seas to be part of its fishing region. The existence of rich fishing, shallow seas, coastal pollution and competing fleets is leading to a growing awareness that the arrangements are going to have to change. Now China, Taiwan, Japan and South Korea should be involved, and somehow North Korea must be convinced to join them.

China's role in the management of the fisheries of the Yellow and East China Seas, as well as the South China Sea, is understandably great. China is now the world's third largest fishing nation, if the catch from marine and freshwater culture is included on top of the 5 million to 6 million tonnes of marine wild fish captured annually by its fishing fleet. The shelf beside China is also one of the world's broadest, making up 27 per cent of the world's total. The main fishing grounds on the shelf are all semi-enclosed seas: the Yellow Sea in the north, the East China Sea and, south of Taiwan, the South China Sea. Nourished by the nutrients of the great rivers of China, which mix with the coastal waters, about two hundred species have had high enough economic value to be worth fishing.

Most of the Chinese fishing has been done by collectively owned fishing enterprises, which now employ about 1.8 million fishers, involving over 150 000 vessels. For years the fisheries have been growing at about 10 per cent per year and are showing the usual signs. Fewer and smaller fish of the target species are being captured, and boats are bringing in less and less each year. The fisheries are overcapitalized, with too many boats fishing for too few fish. The regulations are inadequate and poorly enforced. Fisheries biologists determine the size of an allowable catch and estimate a maximum sustainable yield, which is at least partially ignored in order to keep the fishers employed. This model of management hasn't worked elsewhere and does not work here either. Meanwhile, as the favoured yellow croaker and hairtail species disappear, they are replaced by smaller, less valuable species (Figure 18). Traditions run deep; not only have generations fished for their living, but families often live on their boats. The end of the fishing will mean extraordinary loss for these people, and other jobs will be hard to find. This is the same story told in Newfoundland and Oregon, but the scale is radically greater.

Confounding the situation is the question of political jurisdiction, of who actually owns what part of the two seas. Because the seas are semi-enclosed and shared with other countries, China has fishery agreements with each country. But the countries are hardly any kind of economic union. Despite their differences, the countries of the European Union struggle towards common goals, including fishery controls. But the Asian countries could hardly differ more in politics, economics and world view, and their mutual distrust is great. If UN agreements such as the Law of Sea are not going to be applied to resolve their differences, then multilateral agreements between them are essential.

Part of the problem is that China has an unusual perspective on the UN Law of the Sea. It is only now starting to make formal claims to territorial waters and EEZ or continental shelf ownership. It has declared a 12-mile (19-kilometre) territorial sea. It has considered the continental shelf to be the logical extension of its territory and, where it is in conflict with other countries over ownership of the shelf, rejects the principle of an equidistant median line in favour of consultation and negotiation between the countries concerned. At stake, for example, is ownership of much of the East China Sea, where Japan has a narrow shelf and China a broad one. Nonetheless, China signed the 1982 UN Law of the Sea and finally ratified it in 1996. Ratification doesn't mean approval of the whole convention, however, for parts of it remain unacceptable to China. Instead it sees the Law of the Sea as an evolving arrangement and a tolerable beginning to what will continue to be modified under negotiation. All things considered, this is really quite an enlightened attitude.

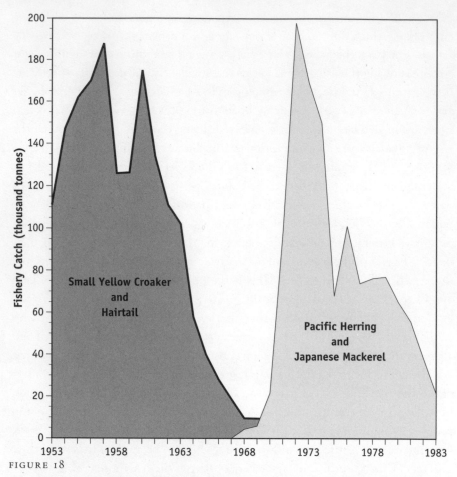

FIGURE 18

Boom and Bust in the Yellow and East China Seas. Small yellow croaker and hairtail were harvested heavily for less than two decades before their collapse in the mid-1960s. Fishers then shifted to Pacific herring and Japanese mackerel, which in turn collapsed by the late 1970s.

Multilateral negotiations in fact are under way. The Japanese don't want to lose fishing access to the Yellow Sea, which could become completely the jurisdiction of China, South Korea and North Korea. Japan really ought to be the leader in developing regional agreements, for it has so much at stake, so much economic power and such a long history of fishing in the region. The meetings that are starting seem to be at South Korea's initiative, however, perhaps symbolic of how economic power is gradually shifting in the region, and they may last for years.

It probably doesn't much matter who initiates the meetings. What's critical is that proposals for management of the region's fisheries emerge soon, establishing EEZs and international boundaries, replacing bilateral agreements between the various countries and settling conflicts over ownership of islands. In the process, plans to sustain the fisheries will develop, involving better monitoring to reduce cheating and proposing more discriminating gear and fishing methods to reduce the great wasted bycatch. The process is slow, the mistrust great, the memories of past hatreds perhaps too vivid for agreements to emerge quickly.

A recent conflict over a string of rocky uninhabitable islands in the East China Sea illustrates some of the tensions that exist between these countries. Known by the Chinese as the Diaoyu chain and by the Japanese as the Senkakus, they lie east of China's southeastern coast and west of Japan's Okinawa, within the potential EEZs of both countries. In July of 1996 a few nationalistic Japanese built a small lighthouse on one of the islands and provoked an uproar from China and Taiwan, for whoever owns the islands will be able to claim large areas of the surrounding sea for fishing rights and oil exploration. Japanese coast guard vessels have since protected the islands from Chinese nationalists wanting to tear down the lighthouse. Taiwan has found itself backing China, urging the use of military force if necessary. China and Taiwan agree that the islands have belonged to China for centuries, while Japan claims it took over the islands when it defeated China and occupied Taiwan in 1895. The occupation of Taiwan lasted until 1945, leaving bitter memories that have now resurfaced. Despite the tensions, nothing violent will probably happen over these islands, although one Taiwanese activist drowned while protesting the Japanese protection of the little lighthouse. Neither China nor Taiwan can afford to offend an economic power such as Japan.

THE SOUTH CHINA SEA

The South China Sea is the largest of the semi-enclosed seas of the Asia coast, extending from the Tropic of Cancer to the equator. Nutrient-rich rivers dump their turbid loads into the sea along the edge of the shelf, making the region productive in fish and shellfish. The South China Sea is a tropical sea, with all the complexity of tropical systems. Many species are fished, and management by either single-species or multispecies models looks difficult. The sea is not yet heavily polluted, but ten rapidly developing countries almost fully enclose it, and increasing amounts of industrial waste and untreated sewage are being dumped into the sea. Hong Kong, China, Taiwan and Vietnam are attempting to draw up a plan to map and study the sea in order to protect it from the pollution, but it is heavy going. As Chen Jay-Chung of the Hong Kong University of Science and Technology was quoted in *Nature*, "Vietnam doesn't want anything to do with China, they will only deal with us." But it is a start.

Unfortunately, political interests are likely to continue to override biological concerns, and the political concerns are considerable. The collapse of the Soviet Union still has ripple effects. The withdrawal of the United States from the Philippines has changed the power base in the region, while China continues to emerge as a maritime power (for defensive purposes only, it says). South Korea, Taiwan and Singapore are all new and significant economic powers in the region. Vietnam and Malaysia continue in their efforts to strengthen their own economies and develop their own fisheries. Little cooperation exists at present, and as these various coastal nations attempt to establish the limits of their EEZs, the likelihood of cooperation lessens.

THE SPRATLY ISLANDS

The underlying continental shelf slopes gradually to about 200 metres (650 feet) in the South China Sea. The central part of the sea then gets deeper and contains deep valleys and steep plateaus. Some of these break the surface as islands, such as the Paracels and Spratlys, that sit exposed right in the middle of the sea.

The Spratly Islands in particular bear watching, for they are the most contested bits of land on the planet. They consist of one hundred reefs, atolls and mostly uninhabited islets, scattered over the sea about halfway between Vietnam and Malaysia, 1100 kilometres (700 miles) south of the most southerly coast of China, and about 800 kilometres (500 miles) south of the Paracel Islands, which belong to China. The largest island, Itu Aba, is nevertheless tiny, with an area of less than a square kilometre. The Spratly area is a breeding ground for sea turtles, seabirds, marine mammals and tuna. Fish that live in the area as juveniles are recruited to the regional fisheries. The area is fragile and exceedingly beautiful and ought to be a marine park. Instead, it is a territory fought over by six nations.

The Spratly Islands also lie in the middle of the major international sea lanes in the region. Because of the strategic position of the islands, a very vague promise of oil deposits nearby and the potential of 200 miles of EEZs in all directions, whoever controls the Spratly Islands controls a huge part of the central South China Sea. Not surprisingly, six adjacent nations claim one or more of these essentially uninhabitable islands and have placed troops there to defend their claims.

China, Taiwan and Vietnam claim all of the islands, and each cites historical interests dating back one or two thousand years. The Philippines claim several islands by right of discovery, and Malaysia claims several others, arguing that they are on the edge of its continental shelf. Brunei claims a single reef, using the same argument as Malaysia.

There are literally hundreds of troops from Vietnam, Taiwan and China stationed on various of the islets and threatening each other. In 1988, China and Vietnam even had a brief naval battle over possession of the Spratly Islands, and three Vietnamese vessels were sunk. Other violent confrontations are likely to occur, and the islands are clearly under stress—about as distant from being a marine preserve as possible.

The best bet is that they will end up in China's hands, simply because China has the largest navy. Taiwan's historical interests in the islands may be the same as China's, and Taiwan has its own formidable navy, but the islands are over a thousand miles south of Taiwan. Despite their provocative war games close to each other's coasts, Taiwan is unlikely to make too large an issue out of ownership of the islands. If geographical position were the only consideration, then Vietnam and Malaysia ought to share the islands, but this conflict is about power, not geography. In any case, China has more rights to the Spratlys than the United States, France or New Zealand have to any of their Pacific island territories.

The issue, though, is control of a large part of the South China Sea. China is reaching out to take as much as it can, while at the same time it begins to draw its territorial lines elsewhere along its coasts. In part it must feel it has no choice, for Taiwan, a province of China that continues to seek ways of creating the impression it is really an independent country, is attempting to establish its own EEZ. Until the EEZ lines are drawn and agreed upon, cooperative fisheries management is impossible, no regulations will exist in contested waters, and even if some existed, none would be enforced. Resolving this one is going to challenge the most adroit of negotiators.

UNCERTAINTY

Fish are a main source of protein for more than a billion people living along the Pacific rim of Asia. As the population continues to grow for the next few decades, the demand will not be possible to meet. Aquaculture will be challenged to meet the difference, but that will be asking the impossible as well. The fisheries need to be controlled or they will all crash, and the route is comanagement or management by individual transferable quotas or both. Unfortunately, we have to expect that years and even decades may pass before all of the EEZs will be established and true cooperative management can begin. In the meantime, the political instability of the region may prove to be disastrous to many of the shared fisheries.

Fisheries management is a business of politics at every level. Within a community, and among communities, political decisions determine who fishes for what. Politicians decide how seriously to take biologists' recommendations, just as they decide where finally to draw the lines in the water between adjacent countries. Politicians have worked out agreements between the United States and Canada, Namibia and South Africa, between clusters of countries with a common point of view, such as the EU, the island countries of the South Pacific or of the Caribbean, or the countries of Latin America. But what are the possibilities where the coast is productive and where the same problems of overfishing, overcapitalization and coastal pollution exist but where the political boundaries are uncertain and political relationships are strained? There is hope as multilateral talks slowly expand and the Law of the Sea is gradually applied in the region. There will also have to be considerable patience.

CHAPTER 15

TAKING STOCK

They say you can't do it, but sometimes it doesn't always work.

Casey Stengel,
quoted by Leonard Koppet
A THINKING MAN'S GUIDE
TO BASEBALL

There is no they, only us.

Bumper sticker

Sometime in the next century the global human population should level off at about twice the size it is now. Feeding so many people adequately will be difficult—some think impossible. Fish already supply as much as 30 per cent of the protein for the people of many coastal countries. As the need for protein increases, the need for fish will also increase, and not just in coastal countries. Now is the time to ensure that fish stocks are large enough to sustain harvesting and to protect their habitats from destruction.

To conserve the fish stocks, fish quotas must be cut and the number of licensed vessels must be reduced, for far too many are fishing in almost every fishery. Understandably, the greatest fear in coastal communities around the planet is that the fishers and processors will lose their jobs. This fear is justified. In order for the fish stock to persist—never mind recover—jobs and boats will be lost from the fishery. The alternative is worse, and unthinkable: let fishers catch more than the stock can sustain so that they can keep their jobs a little longer, making less and less money until the stock collapses, all jobs are gone, and no vessels fish. We have gone this route often enough already, and the outcome is the most miserable one. Reducing the fleet and the quotas now may still carry misery for many, but at least the resource will survive and some people will still be able to fish. No matter what the short-term cost in jobs and communities, we cannot afford to lose the protein source that fishing provides us. Where possible, the ideal will be to sustain jobs, communities and fish stocks. Where protecting all three is not possible in the short-term, then the fish must have priority; we are going to need them. The fish stocks must be protected at all costs.

RECOGNIZING THE PROBLEMS

Three major problems dominate the world's fisheries—overfishing, overcapitalization and a wasteful bycatch. Fish at present are harvested at dangerously high levels, the global fishing fleet is far larger than it should be, and probably more than 50 million tonnes of fish are discarded each year, unsold and dead. Coastal pollution and degradation of fish habitats also remain serious threats, and political conflicts over fish run on chaotically in many parts of the world. In combination, these conditions lead to the collapse of fish stocks and the demise of fishing communities.

≈≈≈≈≈≈≈≈≈≈≈≈≈≈≈≈≈≈≈≈≈≈≈≈≈≈≈

Fish at present are harvested at dangerously high levels, the global fishing fleet is far larger than it should be, and probably more than 50 million tonnes of fish are discarded every year, unsold and dead.

≈≈≈≈≈≈≈≈≈≈≈≈≈≈≈≈≈≈≈≈≈≈≈≈≈≈≈

At least we now recognize that these problems exist. Several decades ago we were generally unaware—and certainly unwilling to recognize—that we were overfishing the world's fisheries, even though plenty of fish stocks were collapsing. Now we may not know exactly what to do about overfishing, overcapitalization and wasted fish, but by recognizing these problems we can seek solutions. We recognize that fish populations need to be conserved, that people need jobs and that coastal communities ought to have a chance to survive. This recognition is no minor achievement.

Because the problems have become so clearly identified, possible solutions emerge. Fishers, fisheries biologists, economists and politicians debate the new approaches to managing the fisheries, the new perceptions about conservation and avoiding the risk of stock collapse, and the new national and international laws and agreements. The issues are often very basic. How should access to a fishery be limited? Should the fishery be run by a central governmental authority, or are more local levels of management still possible in our modern world? Is comanagement by government and community truly a possible compromise? How should regulations be enforced and who should do the enforcing? How can small-scale and large-scale commercial fishing coexist without the demise of the small-scale operations and the communities they represent? Should gear types such as driftnets and bottom trawls be restricted or banned? How should other user groups be accommodated—for instance, aquaculturists wanting to use the same space, recreational fishers wanting to have something left to fish for or Native fishers wanting to have their rights to fish recognized?

CHANGING THE MODELS

The emerging science of fisheries management has had a rough ride during these past several decades. Its failures are famous, its successes too few to compensate. During the 1950s and 1960s, fisheries management evolved around a powerful concept for harvesting fish stocks at maximum sustainable levels that has turned out to be inadequate, driving stocks to collapse instead of protecting them. This failure occurred because the size of fish stocks can be unpredictable, regulations are difficult to enforce, and the cultural divide between politicians and scientists is great. Management by maximum sustainable yield still occurs in many of the world's fisheries, but the shortcomings of the approach are now well known. Fisheries biologists, managers and economists have replaced the concept of maximum sustainable yield with concepts that take into account the unpredictable nature of most fish stocks and that reduce the total allowable catch. They continue to develop new models to manage fisheries, while fishers and environmental groups watch carefully and criticize their proposals.

The biologists' dream of management at a larger scale—at the level of marine ecosystems—is likely to develop only slowly because of the size and complexity of the systems that we know so little about. Multispecies management is possible at a less ambitious scale, however, where competitive and prey-predator interactions are included in the models. Iceland and Norway are applying it to some of their fisheries, and if it can work anywhere, it ought to work there in the relatively simple ecosystems of cold temperate regions. For multispecies management even at that scale to be possible, there will need to be a strong government authority to set and enforce the regulations. For management at the level of the ecosystem to even be thinkable, there will also need to be a high degree of cooperation among countries sharing the ecosystem. The best places to start are in those ecosystems that are controlled by single countries and that are in northern temperate regions, which are ecologically less complex than those in the tropics. The potential for managing at this scale is exciting, though it may sound like a manager's nightmare; any attempts to manage on a large scale will take more time and patience and provoke more resistance from the affected constituents than managing fish one species at a time. The attempts are nevertheless worthwhile.

CONTROLLING ACCESS TO THE FISH

Whether management is based on single species of fish, on groups of interacting species or on whole ecosystems, much more than setting a total allowable
catch for each fishery is necessary. Access to the fish must also be limited. The
era of free and open access, where fishers compete with each other to accumulate as much as possible of the total allowable catch, may not quite be over, but
it soon will be. The derby-style race for fish, a result of too many vessels forced
to fish in seasons sometimes reduced to just a few weeks or days, is dangerous
to both fishers and fish stocks and is obviously absurd. Ways to limit access
have taken a variety of forms. The two major approaches that are in use in various parts of the world—community-based management and individual transferable quotas—provide both hope and options. They also pose quite different
challenges.

≈≈≈≈≈≈≈≈≈≈≈≈≈≈≈≈≈≈≈≈≈≈≈≈≈≈≈≈≈≈

*Comanagement works best where the central government is not
overbearing and where coastal communities have some
tradition of controlling their local fisheries.*

≈≈≈≈≈≈≈≈≈≈≈≈≈≈≈≈≈≈≈≈≈≈≈≈≈≈≈≈≈≈

Community-based management, in which coastal communities and the government comanage the fisheries, is attractive because it should ensure the survival of fishing communities. Management by individual transferable quotas,
where fishers own a percentage of the total catch and can buy or sell the quotas
they have been allocated, is attractive because it is the most clearly efficient, at
least economically. Both should be considered possible routes to explore.
Comanagement works best where the central government is not overbearing
and where coastal communities have some tradition of controlling their local
fisheries. Then, while government managers establish the total allowable catch
for the community, community members determine who fishes and help to set
and enforce the regulations. Comanagement has a long history in the coastal
waters of countries such as Japan and Kiribati, but it has also emerged in more
recent times with variable success—for example, in the lobster fishery of Maine
and the salmon fishery of Alaska.

Where the fishing traditions have been completely lost or new ones are not
possible to develop, and where populations have grown too large and coastal
communities have lost their identities, comanagement may be difficult to resur-
rect. Where the fisheries are offshore and distant from coastal communities,
community-based management is difficult and probably unworkable. Then

management by individual transferable quotas is an alternative worth considering. Wherever too many vessels compete with each other in a fishery, management by individual transferable quotas should result in fewer vessels fishing more efficiently, but it remains a target of intense criticism. The right to fish is likely to end up in the hands of a few corporations that may have no association with the adjacent coasts, forcing coastal fishing fleets into idleness and destroying what might be left of coastal fishing communities. Because of such concerns, when the United States reauthorized the Magnuson Act in 1996—and renamed it the Sustainable Fisheries Act—it stipulated that there be no new initiatives involving individual transferable quotas for the next three years while studies were done on those fisheries managed that way in U.S. waters and elsewhere. Iceland and New Zealand will continue to be watched with great interest, as will the Pacific halibut fishery off the coast of British Columbia and the wreckfish fishery off the coast of South Carolina. With care, however, management by individual transferable quotas should work—provided there is a limit to the percentage of the total catch that any one fisher or fishing firm can accumulate, and provided that a percentage of the total catch is allotted to any coastal fishing community that may be able to exploit it.

Neither system of management is the single answer. Different countries may find one or the other to work better, depending on their kind of government, culture and degree of economic development. The coexistence of both management systems in one country is also possible, perhaps distinguishing coastal from offshore fisheries. Each system may also vary in how it is organized from one country or fishery to another, accommodating the different fisheries and different human cultures. It is possible that the lines between the two systems can become blurred, for a community could decide to make use of individual transferable quotas in order to meet its objectives. In any case, the tools are there to replace open-access fishing with rational alternatives that prevent both overfishing and overcapitalization.

ACCEPTING NEW LAWS

The UN has been quite magnificent over the past several decades in establishing international agreements on how fisheries should be managed, a victory for the strategy of persistence. The 1982 Law of the Sea was finally ratified by enough countries to become international law in late 1994. Also in 1994, a section of the Law of the Sea on seabed mining was amended, making it possible for the developed nations to begin the process of ratification and thus giving the law the broad support it needed to work. Then, in 1995, another proposed addition to the Law of the Sea, with more detailed rules for managing straddling stocks and the highly migratory species of the high seas, was put forward. These are all surprising and remarkable achievements, bringing order and reason to the ways countries deal with each other and inducing cooperation in managing fisheries where cooperation never before existed. There is nothing more reassuring in modern politics—perhaps in the long history of international politics—than the evolving Law of the Sea. There remains the outstanding embarrassment that some important developed nations haven't ratified the Law of the Sea, even though they uphold the details of the agreement. Inevitably, though, the United Kingdom, Canada and the United States will have signed, and their unreasonable and prolonged hesitation will be forgotten.

In 1995, the Food and Agriculture Organization of the UN published *A Code of Conduct for Responsible Fisheries*. It lacks the authority of law and reads more like a wish list, but it promotes conservation, trade and cooperation, and it provides guidance on international agreements and on standards of conduct. It states that "the right to fish carries with it the obligation to do so in a responsible manner so as to ensure effective conservation and management of the living aquatic resources." Among its two hundred proposals of what countries should do, it recommends that the precautionary approach should be used, that coastal habitats should be rehabilitated, that the bycatch should be minimized and that the ecosystem should be managed, not just the species that is the target of a fisheries. Even though the proposals may lack legal status, they can be useful to fisheries biologists as they advise the managers and politicians. What is proposed as voluntary today can become law in the future. The Law of the Sea will continue to evolve.

CULTIVATING THE UNITED STATES

Because of the power of the United States in the world, the decisions it makes carry disproportionate weight. Things happen more quickly with U.S. support and may never happen when the United States opposes them. Agreements that banned the use of large-scale, high seas driftnets and that reduced and then eliminated most of the killing of dolphins in the tuna fishery depended on U.S. support. One of the reasons the new UN agreement on highly migratory species is likely to move successfully into international law is that the United States was one of the first to ratify it in 1996. Even the Magnuson Act, designed to resolve management questions within U.S. waters, has influenced the policies of other countries. What the United States does affects everyone else. The more active the United States becomes in conserving and managing its fish stocks, the more likely it is to pressure others to do the same, and the stronger the international agreements will become. Its influence is worth cultivating, whether the rest of us like the idea or not.

LOWERING THE QUOTAS

There is growing commitment to ensure that enough of a fish stock is left unharvested as a cushion against unexpected changes in sea temperature, available food or breeding habitat. The precautionary principle is a new guiding light, forcing a practice of conservation and responsibility that should help to sustain fish stocks wherever it can be applied. The intent is to lower the total allowable catch of each fishery to a level as low as 60 per cent of its maximum sustainable yield. Fish stocks then should not collapse, and long-term well-managed fisheries should be the result.

REDUCING THE FLEET

The UN has estimated that there are two to three times as many vessels fishing in the seas of the world than are needed to catch the fish at the current rate. In some fisheries this competition has resulted not only in the presence of too many vessels but also in too much investment in each vessel in order to make it competitive. For fishers to be able to make a living, the sizes of the fleets have to be reduced and the need to invest in ever larger vessels, better engines and more gear should be eliminated. Governments must be able to step in and reduce the fleets and, where possible, buy back the vessels or the fishing licenses from those fishers willing to sell. The buyback has begun in North America in the east coast fisheries for groundfish and in the west coast salmon fisheries; the EU has stated it needs to cut its fleets in half, acknowledging that it too must initiate a buyback program. Fleet reduction should occur naturally where management is by individual transferable quotas, but it must also occur in all coastal fisheries no matter how they are managed, enforced by local community authorities or by the central government.

ELIMINATING THE SUBSIDIES

Not only must fleets be downsized, but government subsidies of fisheries must also cease. When the cost of catching the fish is 30 per cent more than the price for which they are sold, "sustainability" is hardly the word that comes to mind. In fact, 30 per cent is a global average, so for every fishery that may be approaching the break-even point, another must be about to fall through the bottom. Thirty per cent is also a conservative estimate, for it does not include the depreciation of the fishing vessels and their gear. As a global business, marine fisheries are a disaster. Since subsidies come from governments, political will is again needed to eliminate them. It must come.

REDUCING THE BYCATCH

The most glaring inefficiency and waste of global fisheries is the bycatch, consisting of millions of tonnes of fish that are caught only to be discarded dead, and the marine mammals, marine turtles and seabirds that are caught accidentally and die in the nets. The worst offenders are the shrimp trawls, but all trawls, seine nets and gillnets catch unwanted fish. Further, where fishers are fishing to strict quotas, they may feel they have to discard valuable fish so as not to exceed their quotas, or they may discard fish already caught when they find and catch fish that are more valuable.

The bycatch can certainly be reduced. Trawls can be fitted with devices to exclude marine turtles, seabirds and different sized fish, nets of greater mesh sizes can let smaller fish escape, and observers on vessels can ensure that marine mammals are not killed or that high-grading doesn't occur. All of these things are happening, particularly in North American fisheries. Where fishers have individual quotas and fish for more than one species, quota trading lets the fishers make adjustments among themselves so as to not have to discard extra fish they may have caught.

Although it will be reduced, bycatch won't be completely eliminated. Therefore, there should be ways to keep and use the fish that otherwise would be discarded simply because they are the wrong size or species. They have value at least as potential fish meal to feed to pigs and poultry. Fish species that are considered unmarketable—perhaps because they are too ugly or are just not popular in local markets—might be sold elsewhere on the global market where consumer tastes differ, or it may be possible to disguise these species and sell them as fish sticks. Best of all would be to find a way to make fish meal acceptable as a human food—and that too should be possible. If pollock paste can be made to taste like crab or shrimp, it should be possible to make less suitable fish more enticing and palatable.

RESTRICTING RECREATIONAL FISHING

Recreational fisheries, no matter how much money they may bring into a community, do not help much to feed a protein-deficient world. If they are to continue to exist even on the coasts of North America, they will need to be restricted to a small part of the total fish quota. Fish that are caught by recreational fishers are caught at great expense, no matter how much pleasure catching them provides. In some fisheries—for example, the striped bass, bluefin tuna and salmon fisheries and the fisheries for billfish such as marlin and swordfish—recreational fishers in the United States have unusual power and influence, fighting commercial fishers through the political system in order to have a greater share of the fishery. In the case of striped bass, they wish to have all of it. Recreational fishers may be good for local economies, but they do not help in any global sense. In fact, they make things much worse, for most of the

≈≈≈≈≈≈≈≈≈≈≈≈≈≈≈≈≈≈≈≈≈≈≈≈≈≈≈≈≈≈≈≈

The worst offenders are the shrimp trawls, but all trawls, seine nets and gillnets catch unwanted fish.

≈≈≈≈≈≈≈≈≈≈≈≈≈≈≈≈≈≈≈≈≈≈≈≈≈≈≈≈≈≈≈≈

fish they catch do not feed many people, and even those that are hooked and released are often badly damaged. The sport is expensive and wasteful, but at the same time it can only thrive where people are still affluent enough to use their own resources in such a way; recreational fishing is uncommon along the coasts of the less developed nations.

RECOVERING COASTAL HABITATS

Around the world, coastal estuaries and wetlands that are breeding habitats and nursery habitats for juvenile stages of fish have been damaged or destroyed by pollution from industrial, agricultural, logging and mining operations and by the inevitable development associated with the growth of coastal cities. Wherever possible, they must be rehabilitated. It has begun on many coasts with the identification of marine reserves; some of the breeding streams and rivers used by salmon are being restored; and in tropical regions, mangroves are being protected and their value as nursery habitats finally recognized. Many fish species depend on estuaries that remain polluted, however—the rivers and estuaries of Southeast and East Asia are vivid examples. Entire marine ecosystems are still at risk.

ENFORCING REGULATIONS

For fish stocks to persist, the regulations that protect them have to be clear, reasonable and enforceable, for otherwise cheating continues to be irresistible. In inshore, coastal fisheries where community-based management occurs, fishers help to set the regulations and, if possible, regulate themselves. In offshore fisheries, observers are being placed on as many vessels as possible. Tensions and cheating are still unavoidable, but both systems can be effective. Penalties must be severe, involving loss of gear, the vessel or fishing rights for a year or more, and the likelihood of getting caught must be great. The costs of enforcement no longer need to be considered another government expense but can be paid for by the fishers themselves through licence fees or by setting aside a small percentage of the value of what they catch.

PULLING OUT THE WORST NETS

The worst of the fishing gear should be eliminated. Large-scale driftnets have been banned globally. The same should happen to the factory trawlers—they do too much damage to fish stocks and bottom habitats in too short a time. They are currently under attack by environmental groups such as Greenpeace and are likely to become increasingly constrained. They are only the most obvious target, however. Smaller bottom trawlers everywhere do indiscriminate damage and, though large-scale driftnets have been banned, smaller gillnets continue to be set in enormous numbers. Eliminating them is not the answer, but regulating where and when they are used and reducing their numbers will help.

CLOSING AND REOPENING FISHERIES

A moratorium is usually the tool of last resort in managing a fishery, but it is an effective one that should be used more often. When a stock plunges to a critical level, a moratorium should be instituted at once, ruthlessly, without waiting for another year or two of data. Recovery of the stock should then reach a considerably higher level before fishing starts up again. When fishing is resumed after a moratorium, the precautionary principle should be applied, access to the fishery should be limited and a reduced total allowable catch established.

MANAGING CONFLICTS

Because so many people, with different interests, are involved in global fisheries, conflicts are inevitable and abundant at every level. Fishers, processors, and marketers, biologists and conservationists, managers and politicians—each group has a different perspective and different needs or agendas. For example, fishers argue with each other over territorial rights and gear use; they argue with processors and distributors over prices; they argue with managers over regulations and with politicians over policies.

The hope is not to eliminate all conflict, for conflict can lead to creative solutions. But it can also easily get out of control; gear wars can erupt and fishers can kill each other, as they did in the conflict between small-scale fishers and trawlers in Indonesia, or poachers and enforcement officers can go after each other or each other's boats and equipment, or countries can impound each other's boats and fine each other for territorial infractions and then restrict trade with each other. The new Law of the Sea should resolve most international conflicts, but most countries still need groups and organizations to represent the different constituencies in internal disputes. Some places, such as Japan and Kiribati, have regional levels of government that resolve most internal conflicts. The United States attempts to resolve conflicts through the Magnuson Act, though it often fails. Other countries continue to experiment with different bureaucratic alternatives.

As if that isn't enough, conflicts or potential conflicts may occur between fisheries and completely different interests, such as seabed mining, oil exploration, the military, tourism and even forestry. The challenge then becomes even greater, often requiring that all parties agree to national and international priorities that may exclude some users. Could the need to fish for protein to feed people lose out to another use? It shouldn't. But fishing for fish meal to feed pigs or poultry or fishing for the gourmet market may be much harder to defend. Confounding the problem is the intrusion of politics and power. The conflicts that occur are rarely creative.

RECOVERING STOCKS

All the new rules, laws and ideas about management are valuable because it looks as if a fish stock that collapses is capable of recovering, that fish may return to a rehabilitated habitat and that the damage that has been done to fish stocks is therefore not necessarily irreversible. When fishers stopped fishing on the North Sea during World War II and the fisheries subsequently recovered, fisheries biologists knew that recovery could occur. When cod stocks off Norway plummeted in the 1980s because of overfishing and Norway put strict limits on the catch, the fish recovered sufficiently to support a reduced level of harvest, giving biologists greater confidence in their methods of management. When fishing for striped bass on the U.S. east coast was banned and the stripers, with a great deal of help, recovered, it became clear that a fishing moratorium was an effective tool to use when necessary.

A place to watch is Newfoundland. The cod stocks along the northern coast of Newfoundland and near Labrador show no sign of recovery, and the fishery will remain closed indefinitely. The situation along the south coast of Newfoundland is different, however. The cod stock there is in a little better shape and the coastal fishers are agitating to be allowed to fish again, for they know there are at least some schools in the inshore bays. What Canada does now will be most interesting. In the four years of the moratorium, the number of licensed fishers on the south coast has not diminished and remains around fourteen thousand. There has been no successful buyback of vessels or restriction of licenses—the same number of fishers and vessels are lined up waiting for the opportunity to fish again. The old open-access management system has not been replaced by one of the available alternatives. Nonetheless, the inshore cod fishery is likely to be reopened to allow a limited harvest. If it does so without deep changes in management, the current limited recovery of the cod will be short-lived and the fisheries biologists and politicians will be embarrassed once again. A failure of political will to keep the fishery closed and to change the management system will show the rest of the world that such changes are essential for a collapsed fish stock to recover.

PRACTISING ADAPTIVE MANAGEMENT

We tend to think of a policy as either a success or a failure. For example, comanagement appears to be succeeding in Kiribati, Norway and Japan, but it has both succeeded and failed in Canada, is failing in Maine and will soon fail in the United Kingdom. We can instead also think of each situation as an experiment from which we can learn. We can try a new form of management, or a new way of helping an old form survive, and if it doesn't work, we can try to figure out why it failed. Instead of abandoning the attempt, we can try again with our new knowledge. We can repeat a management experiment a few times to be sure that it does or doesn't work, and we can modify it to try to improve it if it shows some promise. People are calling this adaptive management. It requires patience, but it means that we don't accuse each other of failure and then demand that we or others start over again in an endless cycle of attempt and failure. Adaptive management is a rational and decent approach, even if we don't yet practise it all that much. Managers everywhere are talking about it, often in association with experiments in comanagement, whether they are trying to manage forests, cropland, urban renewal, traffic flow or fisheries. In this newly networked world, details of attempts to manage fish stocks that work or don't work travel quickly, and reinventing the wheel, or the Edsel, should be less and less common.

ACCEPTING INEVITABLE CHANGE

It might help to lower our expectations of our abilities to solve problems and to control events that may not be possible to control. For instance, we can expect the size of fish populations to oscillate widely even when we don't hunt for them. We can expect humans to cheat and to scramble for whatever wealth a fishery may provide. We can expect fish populations and even species to decline and crash. We can seek a variety of ways to prevent such declines and the resulting economic hardship for the fishing communities.

But let's not expect perfection of ourselves. We have no history of it and no reason to think we will find it now. Let's do what we can to protect both fish and fishers, but let's recognize the reality of unexpected, unpredictable change. Stability and sustainability may be illusions. What seems most predictable, whether we are fishers, biologists, economists, sociologists or politicians, is that however things are today, tomorrow they will be different.

We are ourselves too numerous as a species for the planet to return to what it was even a century ago, and there is little profit in regrets. Unpredictability, instability, chance events, complexity of systems of both fish and humans— these are our heritage. We can try to stabilize and sustain our resources and to slow down the rate of change in hopes of keeping up with it. We can try to prevent the extinction of our own species and those we cohabit the planet with, particularly, perhaps, those that we eat. But changes will continue to occur, and we will muddle through them or we won't. Mostly we'll ride them out.

≈≈≈≈≈≈≈≈≈≈≈≈≈≈≈≈≈≈≈≈≈≈≈≈≈≈≈≈≈≈

Let's do what we can to protect both fish and fishers, but let's recognize the reality of unexpected, unpredictable change.

≈≈≈≈≈≈≈≈≈≈≈≈≈≈≈≈≈≈≈≈≈≈≈≈≈≈≈≈≈≈

Nonetheless, this is an extraordinarily critical time in the history of this planet as we deal with overpopulation, overutilization of our resources and overpollution of our biosphere. With marine fisheries we have the tools, the knowledge and the growing will to manage fish stocks without destroying them. If we can pull it off, we can prove to ourselves that even under these difficult conditions we can avoid the loss of a critical resource. If we can succeed here, we can succeed elsewhere. The stakes are high.

ACCEPTING RESPONSIBILITY

A new ethic in fisheries management—and in the management of our other resources—is emerging. There could be no greater sign of hope. It is symbolized by the precautionary approach that has grabbed the imaginations of people around the world, including both environmentalists and resource managers. In fisheries management, biologists see it as a way of influencing managers and politicians when other laws or guidelines are lacking. It is incorporated in the wording of new UN agreements and proposals, and it is supported with enthusiasm by the environmental organizations.

A related aspect of this new ethic is that like it or not, we are responsible for sustaining life on this planet. We can look nowhere but to ourselves for the solutions, and our solutions must look far into the future. In the management of fisheries there is growing evidence that where fishers are involved in making decisions about a fishery, the regulations that protect the fishery become real and enforceable—everyone involved directly in the fishery has a stake in its long-term survival.

The crises in global fisheries that have developed over the past several decades have not yet been resolved. For the first time, however, we appear to have the management tools and the management ethic that we need. If all of us who use the fisheries have a sense of ownership or stewardship, and are intent on protecting and sustaining our fish resources into the distant future, then we should succeed. There is no doubt that we have much to learn as biologists and managers, fishers and politicians, consumers and environmentalists. Nonetheless, the objective of sustaining fish populations as well as the jobs and communities of fishers can be met—provided that we accept change and responsibility and keep our gaze fixed firmly on the horizon.

NOTES

Notes refer to direct quotations in the text.

CHAPTER 1

PAGE 3. Canadian Press, "Outport way of life fading fast," *Toronto Star*, February 13, 1994.

PAGE 6. Jack London, *Tales of the Fish Patrol* (London: Macmillan, 1905), 177.

PAGE 8. John Steinbeck, *Cannery Row* (New York: Viking Press, 1945), 1.

PAGE 8. John Steinbeck, *Sweet Thursday* (New York: Heinemann, 1954), 7.

PAGE 10. Timothy Egan, "Hook, Line and Sunk," *New York Times Magazine*, December 11, 1994, 75.

CHAPTER 3

PAGE 32. Sir Andrew Gilchrist, *Cod Wars and How to Lose Them* (Edinburgh: Q Press, 1978), 83 and 102.

CHAPTER 4

PAGE 42. John Finlayson, *Fishing for Truth* (St. John's: Institute of Social and Economic Research, Memorial University of Newfoundland, 1994), 133.

PAGE 49. Peter Larkin, "An Epitaph for the Concept of Maximum Sustained Yield," *Transactions of the American Fisheries Society*, vol. 106, 1977, 9.

CHAPTER 5

PAGE 68. Brad Matson, "Gaining Ground," *National Fisherman*, August 1996, 24.

CHAPTER 6

PAGE 78. Kirk Moore, "Look But Don't Touch," *National Fisherman*, August 1996, 15.

CHAPTER 8

PAGE 86. Russell Cleary, letter to the editor, *National Fisherman*, April 1996, 4.

PAGE 97. Associated Press, "Europeans urged to curb overfishing," *Toronto Star*, October 11, 1996.

CHAPTER 9

PAGE 109. James Acheson, *Lobster Gangs of Maine* (Hanover, N.H.: University Press of New England, 1988), 74.

CHAPTER 10

PAGE 120. Lynda Hurst, "And no fish swam," *Toronto Star*, February 13, 1994.

CHAPTER 11

PAGE 126. Juliet O'Neill, "Spanish fleet the bad boy of the fishery," *Toronto Star*, March 11, 1996.

PAGE 128. Bill Schiller, "Worried wives fear the worst for ship's crew," *Toronto Star*, March 13, 1995.

CHAPTER 12

PAGE 141. Canadian Press, "Fisherman hits jackpot, nets $500,000 bluefin tuna," *Toronto Star*, September 23, 1994.

PAGE 142. John Seabrook, "Death of a Giant," *Harper's*, June 1994, 50.

PAGE 146. Vicki Allen, "U.S. House panel OKs bill on dolphin protection," Reuters News Service, April 19, 1996.

CHAPTER 13

PAGE 161. Jerry Vovcsko, "Trouble on the Farm," *National Fisherman*, November 1996, 29.

PAGE 163. Darcy Henton, "Mysterious loss of B.C. salmon raises spectre of fishery's end," *Toronto Star*, August 19, 1995.

CHAPTER 14

PAGE 182. Alison Abbott, "Coordinated Plan to Protect South China Sea," *Nature* 382 (August 29, 1996).

CHAPTER 15

PAGE 190. *Code of Conduct for Responsible Fisheries* (Rome: FAO, 1995), 4.

FURTHER READING

BOOKS

Acheson, James. 1988. *The Lobster Gangs of Maine.* Hanover, N.H., and London: University Press of New England.

Berkes, Fikret, ed. 1989. *Common Property Resources: Ecology and Community Based Sustainable Development.* London: Belhaven Press.

Brown, Lester, ed. 1994, 1995, 1996. *The State of the World.* New York: Norton.

Cushing, D. H. 1988. *The Provident Sea.* New York: Cambridge University Press.

Gilchrist, Sir Andrew. 1978. *Cod Wars and How to Lose Them.* Edinburgh: Q Press.

Glavin, Terry. 1996. *Dead Reckoning.* Vancouver, B.C.: The David Suzuki Foundation/ Greystone Books.

Jentoft, Svein. 1995. *Dangling Lines—The Fisheries Crisis and the Future of Coastal Communities: The Norwegian Experience.* Social and Economic Studies No. 50. St. John's: Institute of Social and Economic Research, Memorial University of Newfoundland.

London, Jack. 1905. *Tales of the Fish Patrol.* London: MacMillan.

McEvoy, Arthur. 1986. *The Fisherman's Problem: Ecology and the Law in the California Fisheries.* New York: Cambridge University Press.

McGoodwin, James. 1990. *Crisis in the World Fisheries: People, Problems and Policies.* Palo Alto, Calif.: Stanford University Press.

Mowat, Farley. 1984. *Sea of Slaughter.* Toronto: McClelland and Stewart.

Parsons, L. S. 1994. *Management of Marine Fisheries in Canada.* Canadian Bulletin of Fisheries and Aquatic Sciences No. 285.

Pinkerton, Evelyn, ed. 1989. *Cooperative Management of Local Fisheries.* Vancouver: University of British Columbia Press.

Pinkerton, Evelyn, and Martin Weinstein. 1995. *Fisheries That Work—Sustainability through Community-Based Management.* Vancouver: The David Suzuki Foundation.

Walters, Carl. 1995. *Fish on the Line—The Future of Pacific Fisheries.* Vancouver: The David Suzuki Foundation.

SOME CLASSIC JOURNAL ARTICLES

Berkes, Fikret. 1985. "Fishermen and the Tragedy of the Commons." *Environmental Conservation* 12:199–206.

Hardin, Garret. 1968. "The Tragedy of the Commons." *Science* 162:1243–48.

Larkin, Peter. 1977. "An Epitaph for the Concept of Maximum Sustained Yield." *Transactions of the American Fisheries Society* 106:1–11.

Ludwig, D., R. Hilborn and C. Walters. 1993. "Uncertainty, Resource Exploitation and Conservation: Lessons from History." *Science* 260:17, 36.

Safina, Carl. 1995. "The World's Imperiled Fish." *Scientific American* 273 (November): 46–53.

JOURNALS

The following journals include many articles on fisheries, policies and conservation and are available in university libraries.

Ambio
Canadian Journal of Fisheries and Aquatic Sciences
Fisheries—A Bulletin of the American Fisheries Society
Marine Policy
Marine Resource Economics
Ocean Development and International Law
Transactions of the American Fisheries Society

FAO REPORTS

Ruddle, K. 1994. "Guide to the Literature of Traditional Community Based Fishery Management in the Asia Pacific Tropics." *FAO Fisheries Circular No. 869.*

FAO. 1994. "Marine Fisheries and the Law of the Sea: A Decade of Change." *FAO Fisheries Circular No. 853.*

FAO. 1994. "Review of the state of world marine fishery resources." *FAO Fisheries Technical Paper 335.*

FAO. 1995. *Code of Conduct for Responsible Fisheries.* Rome: FAO.

POPULAR MAGAZINES

National Fisherman (Journal Publications, Portland, Maine)

Although there are many magazines that focus on or include topics that concern fishers, *National Fisherman*, which is published monthly, is the best and most comprehensive.

INDEX